State Sacrifices and Music in Ming China

SUNY Series in Chinese Local Studies
Harry J. Lamley, editor

STATE SACRIFICES AND MUSIC IN MING CHINA

Orthodoxy, Creativity, and Expressiveness

Joseph S. C. Lam

STATE UNIVERSITY OF NEW YORK PRESS

Published by
State University of New York Press, Albany

Printed in the United States of America

For information, address State University of New York Press, State University Plaza, Albany, N.Y., 12246

Production by Cathleen Collins
Marketing by Fran Keneston

Library of Congress Cataloging in Publication Data

Lam, Joseph Sui Ching
State sacrifices and music in Ming China : orthodoxy, creativity, and expressiveness / Joseph S.C. Lam.
p. cm. — (SUNY series in Chinese local studies)
Includes bibliographical references and index.
ISBN 0-7914-3705-1 (alk. paper). — ISBN 0-7914-3706-X (pbk. : alk. paper)
1. Rites and ceremonies—China. 2. Sacrifice—China. 3. Music—China—Religious aspects. 4. China—History—Ming dynasty, 1368–1644. I. Title. II. Series.
BL1812.R57L35 1997
299'.51238—dc21 97-36909
CIP

10 9 8 7 6 5 4 3 2 1

For my mother, Laitak Leung,
who taught her children
to explore.

Contents

Figures

Preface

To study Ming dynasty state sacrifices and state sacrificial music is to expand our current views of ritual, music, and Ming China. Examining Ming documents about the state ritual and music, we find many practices and features that demand more scrutiny and explanations. Why, for example, did Ming emperors and scholar-officials spend incalculable time and effort to negotiate ritual and musical particulars that are comprehensively described in Confucian classics and authoritative court manuals? Why was a decrease of four dishes of sacrificial food a contentious matter? What made short state sacrificial tunes, many of which have only thirty-two notes, an expression of Confucian tenets and practitioners? Why and how did orthodox ritual and music appeal to Ming court citizens continuously? How did they understand their state ritual and music?

As a historical ethnomusicologist, I wish I could do fieldwork in the Ming court, observing the court citizens and asking them why state sacrifices and music played such a central role in their public and private lives. The emperors and scholar-officials cannot be reached now, but they have left a wealth of evidence that they found their state sacrifices and music expressive. They responded to every ritual and musical nuance emotionally and critically.

Ming state sacrifices and state sacrificial music (hereafter Ming state sacrifices and music, or state ritual and music) were expressive. In addition to the projection of orthodox and abstract messages—Confucian ideology on the use of ritual and music, historical memories of the past, cosmology, and so forth—Ming state sacrifices and music are also expressions of a particular time, place, thought, and people. A performance of Ming state sacrifice and music followed not only textual and ritual scripts and musical scores that specify structure and broad meanings, but also a myriad of subtle and creative changes introduced by participants. Thus, individual performances of Ming state sacrifices and music were distinctive within established boundaries; their expressiveness was orthodoxly intelligible, yet creatively appealing.

Dynamic interrelationships of orthodoxy, creativity, and expressiveness in Ming state sacrifices and music are clearly indicated in numerous source materials. Standard documents of the Ming dynasty, such as the *Veritable Records of the Ming* (*Ming Shilu*), provide a wealth of historical data about events and court citizens, demonstrating the complex processes in which ritual and music functioned in the Ming court. Ritual manuals and studies, such as the *Ritual of the Tang Kaiyuan Period* (*Da Tang Kaiyuan li*) of 732 and the *Comprehensive Study of the Five Categories of Rites* (*Wuli tongkao*) of 1753, offer historical and technical information that puts Ming state sacrifices and music in cultural and comparative contexts. Notated musical sources, such as the *Collected Ceremonial of the Ming Dynasty* (*Da Ming jili*, 1370/1530), the *General Record of the Court of Imperial Sacrifices* (*Taichang zonglan*, 1476?), and the *Expanded Monograph on the Court of Imperial Sacrifices* (*Taichang xukao*, 1643?), all of which I discovered in 1984, preserve a large repertory of 322 state sacrificial songs and provide an abundance of music for comparative analyses and discussion.

This study is organized into eight chapters, which can be topically divided into two parts: part 1 (chapters 2 through 4) focuses on Ming dynasty state sacrifices; part 2 (chapters 5 through 7) focuses on music of the ceremonials.

Chapter 1 introduces the subject matter, its issues, and the analytical framework of this study. It begins by defining Ming state sacrifices and music as large-scale and presentational ritual and music and identifying diverse ritual and musical responses among different types of participants and audiences. Then the chapter discusses the dynamics of orthodoxy, creativity, and expressiveness and proposes a hypothesis for analyzing the ritual and music being discussed.

Chapter 2 describes the system of Ming state sacrifices and demonstrates its distinctive features by comparing the Ming state sacrifice to Heaven with those of Tang and Song dynasties.

Chapter 3 reports the ways in which the first Ming emperor, Taizu, subscribed to orthodox knowledge of state sacrifices and music but still managed to institute a distinctive system for his empire. Taizu's establishment of the unprecedented Office of State Sacrificial Music (*shenyue guan*) will be highlighted.

Chapter 4 describes the sericultural ceremonials in the sixteenth-century court of Shizong, the eleventh Ming emperor, demonstrating the ways in which Ming state sacrifices and music were appropriated and transformed into personal expressions. To emphasize personal emotions and interpretations of the court citizens, many of their words are cited in this chapter.

Chapter 5 outlines Ming music theory to explain Ming state sacrificial music and demonstrate orthodoxy, creativity, and expressiveness in musical thoughts.

Chapter 6 narrates the musical events in the Ming court, a drama of conflicting forces that illustrates the complex realities in which state sacrificial music functioned.

Chapter 7 compares the music of four sets of state sacrificial songs and analyzes their orthodox norms and creative features.

Chapter 8 concludes with a discussion of three representative Ming scholar-officials' response to state ritual and music.

Briefly, this study addresses ritual dances, musical instruments, and other related topics; its brevity reflects a lack of relevant data. For example, many Ming documents have preserved pictograms of the dances performed during public worship of Confucius (*ji* Kong), but the pictograms illustrate dances in only one of many Ming state sacrifices. Many Ming documents describe musical instruments, but reveal little about the creative changes, if any, made on the instruments. Extensive discussion of these two and other related topics must wait until more data is found.

Many scholars have helped in the preparation of this study. Professor Evelyn Rawski offered insightful comments that inspired me to formulate my interpretation of state ritual and music in Ming China. Professor Harry Lamley, the editor, provided understanding and encouragement when needed. The anonymous reviewers corrected mistakes, identified gaps in the arguments, and showed ways to improve the text. Mr. Abraham Chan solved most of the computer problems, especially those involving Chinese characters and musical notation. A grant from the Academic Senate and Regents of the University of California, Santa Barbara, financed some of the expenses incurred in the research and writing of this volume.

Chinese Dynasties and Ming Emperors

DYNASTIES

Shang dynasty	1766–1122 B.C.
Zhou dynasty	1122–221 B.C.
Chunqiu period	722–481 B.C.
Zhanguo period	403–221 B.C.
Qin dynasty	221–206 B.C.
Western Han dynasty	206 B.C.–A.D. 24
Eastern Han dynasty	A.D. 25–220
Three Kingdoms era	220–280
Western Jin dynasty	266–316
Eastern Jin dynasty	317–420
Era of North-South division	420–581
Sui dynasty	581–618
Tang dynasty	618–907
Five Dynasties era	907–960
Northern Song dynasty	960–1127
Southern Song dynasty	1127–1279
Yuan dynasty	1279–1368
Ming dynasty	1368–1644
Qing dynasty	1644–1911

EMPERORS

Temple Name	*Personal Name*	*Reign title and years*
Taizu	Zhu Yuanzhang	Hongwu, 1368–1399
Huizong	Zhu Yunwen	Jianwen, 1399–1402
Chengzu	Zhu Di	Yongle, 1403–1425
Renzong	Zhu Gaochi	Hongxi, 1425–1426
Xuanzong	Zhu Zhanji	Xuande, 1426–1436
Yingzong	Zhu Qizhen	Zhengtong, 1436–1450
		(captive 1449–1450; restored 1457)
		Tianshun, 1457–1465
Daizong	Zhu Qiyu	Jingtai, 1450–1457
Xianzong	Zhu Jianshen	Chenghua, 1465–1488
Xiaozong	Zhu Youtang	Hongzhi, 1488–1506
Wuzong	Zhu Houzhao	Zhengde, 1506–1522
Shizong	Zhu Houcong	Jiajing, 1522–1567
Muzong	Zhu Zaihou	Longqing, 1567–1573
Shenzong	Zhu Yijun	Wanli, 1573–1620
Guangzong	Zhu Changluo	Taichang, 1620–1621
Xizong	Zhu Youjiao	Tianqi, 1621–1628
Sizong	Zhu Youjian	Chongzhen, 1628–1645

CHAPTER ONE

Issues, Definitions, and a Hypothesis

PRELUDE

Ritual and music are expressive, eliciting critical and emotional responses from participants and audiences. Current scholarship has clearly established that ritual and music of a particular people express who they are and how they live.[1] Such explanations of ritual and musical expressiveness are nevertheless general and synchronic. They seldom address the commonly observed but hardly explained fact that orthodox ritual and music, which have been standardized and practiced over a long period of time, appeal to individual participants and audiences in not only general but also specific terms.

This fact raises many questions, four of which are central to this study. How and why did Ming state sacrifices and music, which were orthodox, remain continuously and distinctively expressive? Did they ever change, and how? Did performances of Ming state sacrifices and music include personal and creative adjustments introduced by individual participants? Can the orthodox state ritual and music be simultaneously orthodox and creative?

There are many strategies to approach these questions, and there are many ways to answer them; ritual and music are too complex and diverse to be defined and analyzed by a single research methodology. I began by trying to understand Ming state sacrifices and music with general and synchronic theories of ritual and music. I soon found that no explanation of the state ritual and music is effective unless it comprehensively addresses the structural features, the participants, audiences, and performance contexts, and the issues of orthodoxy, creativity, and expressiveness.

Like other orthodox ritual and music, Ming state sacrifices and music were constructed and practiced purposefully, communicating, with an emotive force and through multimedia means, cultural, social, contextual, and personal meanings to participants and audiences.[2] Regardless of whether they are interpreted as artifacts, symbols, structure, and/or processes, the state ritual and music demonstrate not only a prominent orthodoxy (orthopraxy), but also a subtle and noticeable creativity in individual realizations (performances).[3] Operating within prescribed boundaries, the creativity produced features that rendered individual realizations distinctively expressive; the creativity, nevertheless, posed no challenge to the orthodoxy, and generated no abrupt or radical changes.

Such a nature of Ming state sacrifices and music pinpoints a dynamic relationship between orthodoxy and creativity, which in turn explains the continuous expressiveness of the state ritual and music. By appearing to have curbed creative efforts, Ming state sacrifices and music appear to be operating orthodoxly, projecting a sense of properness, timeless continuity, dominating authority, and other known and expected meanings. By exercising creativity within prescribed bounds, however, the state ritual and music manage to become distinctive every time they are performed. Thus, they can be, time and time again, identified, interpreted, manipulated, and appropriated as personal expressions by participants and audiences. In other words, the expressiveness of Ming state sacrifices and music is not only cultural and timeless, but also individualistic and historical.

Thus, to understand Ming state sacrifices and music, one needs to identify their ritual and musical structure as minutely as possible, examine responses of the participants and audiences, and understand the dynamic operation of orthodoxy, creativity, and expressiveness. Toward such an understanding, this chapter defines the state ritual and music, classifies the participants and audiences and their responses, theorizes about the operation of orthodoxy, creativity, and expressiveness, and proposes, in the form of a hypothesis, an analytical framework for examining the state ritual and music.

MING STATE SACRIFICES AND MUSIC AS LARGE-SCALE AND PRESENTATIONAL RITUAL AND MUSIC

As large-scale and presentational ritual and music, Ming state sacrifices and music include many elements that can be affected by orthodox or creative forces. Officiated by emperors, imperial clansmen, and scholar-officials, but participated in by a large number of ritual and musical staffs, and witnessed, directly and indirectly, by a much larger audience, each Ming state sacrifice is in fact an elaborate *ceremonial*—a scheduled and extensive sequence of court ceremonies and activities designed according to the ranking and purpose of the ceremonial being performed. Thus, a Ming state sacrifice would, for example, include: breeding of the required sacrificial animals; the court's abstention (*zhizhai*) from regular activities in the days (ranging from one to seven days) immediately preceding the *sacrificial ceremony* (discussed later in this chapter); inspection of the sacrificial animals; ritual notices to the imperial ancestors; arrangements to ensure the emperor's safety when he performs various ritual duties outside the palace; and preparation of the altar, the sacrificial ceremony, and the celebratory banquet that formally concludes the sequence of ceremonies and activities. The climax of a Ming state sacrifice is of course the sacrificial ceremony offered by the emperor, or his delegate(s), to a particular group of deities on a specified day and at a specified altar. In other words, a Ming state sacrifice is a complex and time-consuming process that entails many highly specialized and interrelated events and involves many variables. For example, the formal process of the Ming state sacrifice to Heaven spans a period of fifty days.[4] If one includes the informal activities, such as the scholar-officials' research on historical models of the ceremonial and discussions to solve various contextual and performance problems, a Ming state sacrifice is indeed an endless process.

Ming state sacrifices are labeled according to the deities they honor; thus, there were state sacrifices to Heaven and to the progenitor of agriculture. However, such labels are nothing more than convenient references, because a Ming state sacrifice would involve many more deities than its title could suggest. It not only worships a *host deity* (*zhengwei*) or group of deities, but also the host deity's *companion(s)* (*peiwei*) and *followers* (*congsi*). For example, the sacrificial ceremony honoring Heaven would worship, in addition to Heaven, the founder of the Ming empire and a pantheon of heavenly deities and natural forces. (See chapter 2 for further details.) The relationships among the host deity and his companions and followers are not unlike those among an emperor and his honorable guests and officials, a fact that underscores the cosmological and social underpinnings of Ming state sacrifices.

A full-blown sacrificial ceremony includes nine progressive ceremonial stages, which are by themselves complex programs of ritual activities. The nine stages are:

1. Welcoming the deities (*ying dishen*)
2. Offering of jade and silk (*dian yubo*)
3. Offering of sacrificial food (*jinzu*)
4. First offering of wine (*chuxian*)
5. Second offering of wine (*yaxian*)
6. Last offering of wine (*zhongxian*)
7. Removal of sacrificial food (*chezhuan*)
8. Farewell to deities (*song dishen*)
9. Burning of sacrificial articles (*wangliao*)

These stages are clearly marked during performances—as they are about to begin, they are announced by an intoner (*changzan*). During each of these nine stages, which are defined according to the main celebrant's actions, many ritual activities would occur simultaneously. For example, the secondary celebrants (*fenxian guan*) would present the supplementary offerings to the followers, while the main celebrant would offer the second and third offerings to the host deity and his companion.

A sacrificial ceremony takes place on an altar proper (or inside the formal hall of a temple), a ritual space that is defined by its particular architectural design and by the presence of one or more spirit-throne(s) (*shenzuo*), which are specifically set up for the occasion. Literally, a spirit-throne refers to a throne-like prop, on top of which stands a spirit-tablet, that is a name tablet that represents the presence of a deity. The area in front of the spirit-throne is the place where various sacrificial victims and offerings are displayed and where ceremonial gestures are performed. (See Figure 1.1.)

A sacrificial ceremony is officiated by a main celebrant who is either the emperor or his delegate, and by a number of secondary celebrants who are either scholar-officials or imperial clansmen appointed by the emperor. These celebrants perform all significant ceremonial gestures, such as drinking the blessed wine, kneeling (*gui*), paying obeisance (*bai*) and prostrating (*fufu*) in front of the spirit-thrones. Assisted by many ritual staffs, the celebrants solemnly execute their ceremonial duties and move around specified ritual positions, such as the obeisant-post (*baiwei* or *banwei*), on and off the altar proper.

It should be emphasized that the celebrants neither perform sacrificial music and dances nor engage in any menial tasks, such as moving ritual paraphernalia. Musicians, dancers, and ritual staffs would furnish those and anything else to help the celebrants perform their duties. The music per-

Figure 1.1.
An arrangement of a spirit-throne and sacrificial offerings in a late Ming state sacrifice to Heaven (*MHD* 82.35)

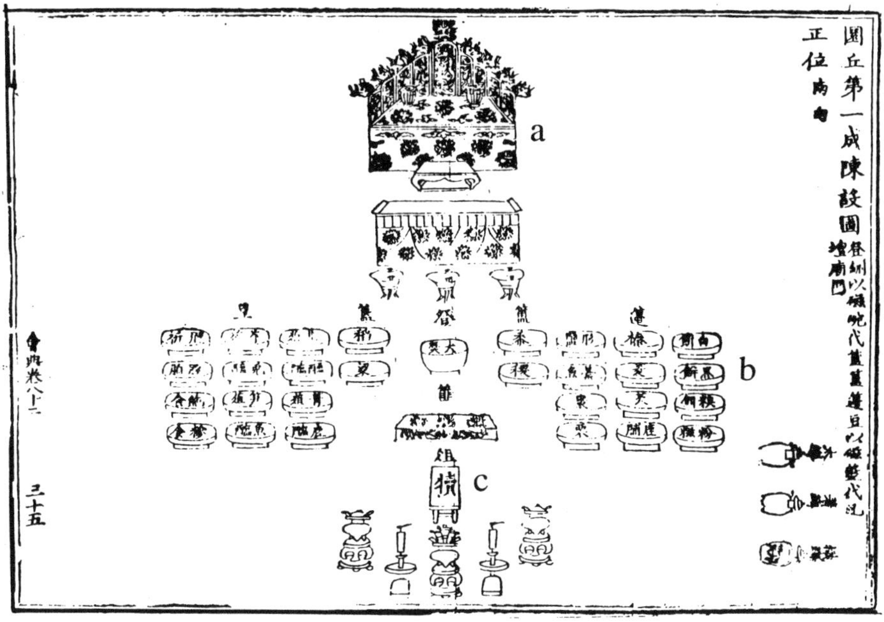

a. spirit-throne; b. dishes of sacrificial foods; c. the sacrificial victim of a bull.

formed to accompany various ceremonial gestures of the celebrants and ritual staffs is the state sacrificial music discussed in this study.

A sacrificial ceremony is witnessed by an audience of court citizens, scholar-officials, and foreign dignitaries who are invited (ordered) to attend the ceremony. Occupying assigned positions on the south side of the altar proper, the audience remains stationary throughout the ceremony. Facing north and thus showing their subordinate status to the emperor and the deities, the audience passively observes and witnesses the ceremonial activities being performed on the altar proper. The performance of a sacrificial ceremony is indirectly witnessed by military escorts and soldiers who guard the altar compound or temple-compounds, and by commoners who would at least notice the celebrants' procession to the altars.

Complex as it is, a sacrificial ceremony is only the climax of a state sacrifice and should not be confused as the ceremonial itself. It is crucial to examine and contextualize the many ceremonies and activities that happen before and after the sacrificial ceremony. The expressiveness of a Ming state sacrifice transcends ritual activities, large and small, which occur at any given point in the ritual process. In fact, the expressiveness of a Ming state ritual is negotiated before, during, and after individual performances. By the same token, much of the expressiveness of a sacrificial ceremony depends on what has happened before its performance, and what interpretations its preparations and performance would solicit subsequently. Essentializing a Ming state sacrifice and its music as clearly defined and independent units is only a theoretical convenience.

As described earlier, Ming state sacrifices and music are fundamentally different from those communal rituals that occur in a relatively short time span, and in which all (or most) members of a community actively participate on a more or less equal basis.[5] As large-scale and presentational ceremonials that once dominated the lives of emperors and scholar-officials, Ming state sacrifices and music are now historical, and their aural, visual, and psychological impacts can only be historically imagined with experiences learned from the Confucian Ceremonial performed in present-day Taipei, Qufu, and other Chinese cities. Among Chinese and current ceremonials that may tangentially serve as comparative references, the death ceremonials of Sun Yat-sen, Chiang Kai-shek, and Mao Zedong come to mind.[6] While the basic features of these death ceremonials are fundamentally different from those of Ming state ritual, which is sacrificial, the gargantuan scale of the three twentieth-century death ceremonials and their webs of cultural, social, political, and personal meanings are not incomparable to those of Ming state sacrifices and music. All reveal dynamic operation of orthodoxy, creativity, and expressiveness.

RESPONSES AND EXPRESSIVENESS OF MING STATE SACRIFICES AND MUSIC

The expressiveness of ritual and music is well-known. Geertz, for example, has demonstrated that ritual are models of and for reality, communicating and affirming culturally important cosmological conceptions and values.[7] Other scholars have shown that ritual and music are multivalently expressive, appealing to individual participants and audiences in diverse but equally persuasive and emotive ways, and transforming the persons into members of real and/or imagined communities.[8] These studies have successfully explained why ritual and music are expressive in general, but they have not yet comprehensively addressed the question of why orthodox ritual and music can remain expressive over a long period of time. To rephrase the question with reference to Ming state sacrifices and music, one asks why and how they continued to appeal to the emperors and scholar-officials who were expertly familiar with what the ritual and music could project, whether Confucian ideology, social values, and/or other elements of the Ming world.

Many issues are involved, and one begins by asking whether the Ming emperors and scholar-officials actually found their state ritual and music expressive. The answer is definitively affirmative. Nominally, the Ming emperors and scholar-officials performed their state sacrifices and music for the deities; and thus, theoretically speaking, only the deities' supernatural responses could demonstrate and validate the expressiveness of the performed state ritual and music. In terms of human reality, however, it is the Ming court citizens who decided for themselves whether their state ritual and music were expressive. They decided, and left a substantial body of public and private evidence.

Ming emperors and scholar-officials spent a tremendous amount of human and material resources to continuously maintain and practice their state ritual and music. The magnificent altars and temples, some of which still stand in Beijing, only give an architectural hint of what was involved. Such use of resources is one of the most eloquent statements that the Ming court citizens found their state ritual and music meaningful and indispensable. Otherwise, why would they build magnificent altars and write revealing essays and poems? Ming court citizens were practical; they did not perform state ritual and music because their culture and society required them to do so. They canceled state ritual and music as needed. They were no different from Song Chinese, who changed their gods, and from modern Chinese, who abolished and reconstructed sacrificial ceremonials as needed.[9]

If Ming emperors and scholar-officials found their state ritual and music expressive, then one can ask what that expressiveness was and how the court citizens identified it. As revealed in Ming documents, Ming court citizens responded to specific ritual and musical elements critically and emotionally. For example, the performance site of Shizong's sericultural ceremonials was a much debated point. (See chapter 4.)

A most vivid illustration of the court citizens' responses to ritual and musical features in actual performances is Liu Ji's (1311–1375) eulogy on the performance of the state sacrifice to Earth in 1370.[10] First, Liu Ji, one of the influential scholar-officials who helped Taizu conquer the Ming empire, described how the emperor and his court observed abstention and prepared themselves for the sacrificial ceremony, and how the weather was undesirably rainy earlier in the night, but cleared up as the time of ceremony approached. Liu Ji then wrote:

> When the emperor ascended to the altar proper in full ritual regalia, all was quiet. Then, the altar proper was illuminated brilliantly by the torches, and filled with the crystal clear tones of state sacrificial music. The incense offered to the deity rose up to the sky without a flutter. All the ceremonial gestures were performed smoothly, and the thousand officials inside the altar compound witnessed the ceremony solemnly and respectfully. What a spectacular sight . . .

Liu Ji's writing makes it clear that the expressiveness of state sacrifices and music elicits two fundamentally different but not unrelated types of responses. First, the court citizens find state sacrifices and music expressive of what they already know—in Liu Jiu's case, the legitimacy of Taizu and the Ming empire. Responding to something familiar and the status quo operative is a basic human reaction, and little explanation is needed here. Second, the Ming court citizens find, in performances of state sacrifices and music, distinctive and creative features that express something unique about the particular time, place, thought, and people.

This second type of response needs to be discussed here, and to illustrate its nature and significance one can examine the issues with the two scenarios that follow. When a state sacrifice to Heaven, an orthodox means of legitimizing a Chinese ruler, is performed in times of unrest, it is clear why and how different court citizens would respond. Those who support the ruler would understand the ritual as a reaffirmation of his mandate from Heaven, and as a demonstration of his power. In contrast, those who do not support the ruler would find the ritual sacrilegious and Machiavellian. The stakes and issues of a state sacrifice to Heaven performed during times of unrest are unmistakable.

When the same state ritual is performed during a time of peace and prosperity, the issues and stakes are ambiguous, however. What purpose does such a performance serve, besides showing the court's gratitude to the deities, reaffirming the emperor's unchallengeable power, and conforming to orthodoxy (orthopraxy). These purposes are official, but they are not as compelling as they may seem—performances of state sacrifices to Heaven can be suspended or slighted. Shizong, for example, lost interest in the state ritual, even though he was most concerned about it in the first part of his long and relatively prosperous reign of forty-four years.[11] Similarly, Shenzong, Shizong's grandson, ignored the practice; he performed the state sacrifice to Heaven only three times in his long reign of forty-eight years.[12] In other words, in peaceful times, court citizens' responses to state sacrifices and music are much more multivalent and personal.

If Ming emperors and scholar-officials do not find something in state sacrifices that appeal to them personally, they would not engage in ritual and musical matters. There is no denial that emperors and scholar-officials could play-act their roles and make "official" responses: in the Ming time, state sacrifices were obviously performed by and responded to with indifference by Wuzong and other emperors.[13] However, the bulk of historical records demonstrates that most Ming court citizens responded with an intellectual and emotional intensity that could not be sustained by expedient reasons or by play-acting. Thus, one has to presume that most court citizens responded sincerely.[14] Furthermore, one has to presume that they found something distinctive and creative in individual performances that engaged their hearts and minds.

Such engagements are specific, not naive intuitions, casual impressions, and predictable reactions to orthodox messages. One should recall that during performances of sacrificial ceremonies, Ming emperors and scholar-officials performed only a limited number of ceremonial activities, such as offering wine, kneeling down, and prostration. They did not sing, dance, or engage in any vigorous and repetitive bodily movements that would induce a trance or alter their physical and mental perceptions.

Ming court citizens were sensitized by the ritual and musical stimuli, but they could not afford to lose control of themselves or their critical eyes and ears. Even an indulgence in coughing was not allowed, and officials who indulged were dutifully reported.[15] Ming emperors and official-scholars did not attend performances of state sacrifices unprepared: directly and indirectly, they were involved in every step in the formulation of the ceremonial programs. They also were familiar with all paraphernalia of the state ritual and music. Unlike the commoners or even scholar-officials at the bottom of the bureaucracy, Ming emperors and scholar-officials were not awed by the richness of the ritual objects. They were ritual and musical experts who would identify creative and distinctive features in the performances, scrutinizing, manipulating, and appropriating them with personal perspectives.

CONCERNED PARTICIPANTS AND CRITICAL AUDIENCES

The arguments previously discussed underscored a well-known fact of ritual and music: their expressiveness depends not only on ritual and musical features, but also on the persons who decode what and how the features express. In other words, the expressiveness of Ming state sacrifices and music has to be analyzed with respect to the participants and their perspectives. Here they are defined as *concerned participants* and *critical audiences*. Ming emperors, scholar-officials, and music masters who are knowledgeable about all aspects of Ming state sacrifices and music act as concerned participants when they actively and directly participate and control preparations and performances of the state ritual and music; however, they may or may not be the actual celebrants. Ming court citizens act as critical audiences when they have neither active nor direct control over preparations and performances of the state sacrifices. They may, however, publicly or privately criticize the events, and their critical comments may affect the concerned participants' ritual and musical views and activities. For example, Shizong and the scholar-officials who conceived and carried out the ritual and musical revisions of the 1530s are the concerned participants of state ritual and music performed at that time; the scholar-officials who, voluntarily or involuntarily, played no direct and active roles in the revision process are the critical audiences. (See chapters 6 and 8). The distinction between the concerned participants and the critical audiences is by no means rigid: Ming court citizens could and did change positions during ritual and musical processes.

This definition of concerned participants and critical audiences is selective, but it allows focused discussion on the responses of the court citizens who were representative of the Ming tradition of state sacrifices and music. This definition also suspends the need to examine, in this discussion, responses of ritual novices, disinterested participants, and passive audiences—that is, people whose responses to the expressiveness of state ritual and music are neither representative of the tradition nor relevant to the issues being discussed here. These responses can, however, be briefly discussed next.

A ritual novice, such as a young prince learning to perform a state sacrifice, may find the performance expressive. Nevertheless, the prince's responses reveal more of his unfamiliarity with the ritual and musical features and less of the ways experts understand and engage in the state ritual and music. Like the novice's responses, the understanding of disinterested participants is neither significant nor relevant. Shenzong's indifference to the state sacrifice to Heaven, for example, was a personal issue, which has little to do with the ritual and musical expressiveness of Ming state sacrifices and music.

Similarly, reactions of passive audiences are secondary to the discussion here. As minor officials, ritual staffs, and soldiers, they were drafted to perform various chores and forced to passively witness the ceremonial activities. They were there simply to serve and to be awed by the imperial ritual and music. Their responses had little influence on the emperors and scholar-officials who controlled the state ritual and music. By the same analysis, the reactions of Ming commoners are negligible: they could only accept (or ignore) the performed state ritual and music as expressions of imperial power and authority; they had no means to demand what should be ritually and musically performed and presented to them. Of course, there were occasions when commoners took actions to appropriate state sacrifices themselves. Such actions, however, demonstrate the commoners' challenge to the throne and are not representative of the ways in which state sacrifices and music normally functioned in Chinese courts.

As a contrast, responses of the concerned participants and critical audiences of Ming state sacrifices and music—Ming emperors, scholar-officials, and music masters—are representative, significant, and informative. They participated in all steps of the ritual and musical process, and they directly and indirectly controlled—researched, negotiated, designed, criticized, manipulated, and appropriated—all ritual and musical features. For these concerned participants and critical audiences, Ming state sacrifices and music constituted not only a means of governance but also one of living. By adjusting and interpreting the state ritual and music to match their own needs, the concerned participants display who they are, what they believe, and what they are doing in particular contexts. In other words, they appropriate the state ritual and music as individual expressions. Their acts of appropriation and expressions are of course clear to the critical audiences who are also ritual and musical experts, and who can immediately tell what is being adjusted. By making positive or negative comments, the critical audiences demonstrate what they have learned, and what they would accept and reject. Through their comments that would eventually become publicly known, the critical audiences would leave their marks on subsequent understanding of the state ritual and music.

THE DYNAMICS OF ORTHODOXY, CREATIVITY, AND EXPRESSIVENESS IN MING STATE SACRIFICES AND MUSIC

Ming court citizens live with state sacrifices and music, constantly manipulating and appropriating the state ritual and music to match their needs and express their ideas. Nevertheless, their acts of manipulation and appropriation have to be creative within bounds. If they ignore the perceived boundaries, they undermine the dynamics between orthodoxy and creativity on which the individualistic expressiveness of the state ritual and music depends.

If *orthodoxy* refers to beliefs and practices that adhere to authoritative and standardized parameters over a long period of time, the expressiveness of Ming state sacrifices and music depends on their being orthodox. To function as an imperial ritual and music that is distinct from those practiced by the commoners, Ming state sacrifices and music can only emulate practices of the past, eschewing fashionable and popular trends. To be intelligible, the state ritual and music must employ elements that are commonly accepted and known in the community of court citizens. To appear authentic and credible, the state ritual and music must appear accurate, which requires faithful application of authoritative and preexistent prescriptions. To be efficacious, the state ritual and music cannot appear compromised; the creative and adjusted features must not contradict or challenge the perceived orthodoxy.

If *creativity* refers to distinctive features that serve a unique purpose and exist in a form that symbolizes and perpetuates that distinctiveness and purpose, the expressiveness of Ming state sacrifices and music also depends on their being creative.[16] The state ritual and music can only be performed creatively: every realization (performance) of a state ritual involves numerous theoretical and practical problems that are unique to individualistic performance contexts and cannot be solved with general prescriptions described in classical documents and orthodox manuals. To become expressions of specific time, place, thought, and people, the state ritual and music must display more than what is orthodox and commonly known; they must show distinctive features as results of those contextual elements and as evidence of interpretation, manipulation, and appropriation by those concerned participants and critical audiences. Furthermore, the distinctive features must be embodied in sensory (visual, aural, and others) stimuli that constitute the multimedia form of the state ritual and music.

However, the sensory stimuli must not render the state ritual and music unorthodox, and thus unacceptable. Only when the orthodoxy of the state ritual and music appears unchallenged, the expressiveness of distinctive and creative details becomes meaningful and relevant. For example, the empress's use of bamboo hooks in Shizong's sericultural ceremonials is meaningless unless the state ritual is considered proper and the orthodox use of gold hooks is known. (See chapter 4.)

Ming state sacrifices and music must be simultaneously orthodox and creative. If the state ritual and music are totally orthodox and without creative elements, Ming court citizens only needed to follow orthodox rules literally and routinely. They did not need to spend time and effort discussing and formulating ritual and musical details. Similarly, they did not need to be critical; they would have nothing to criticize—literal application of standardized prescriptions cannot produce anything that is unknown and open for criticism. Ming state sacrifices and music are, however, not only orthodox but also creative. Even with an abundance of documents, numerous discussions, and carefully guarded and maintained practices, Ming state sacrifices and music could not (and did not) operate with one ultimate and unambiguous set of prescriptions that could be literally and routinely applied over a long period of time and without regard to the people and contexts involved.

From conception to performance, Ming state sacrifices and music involve complex and lengthy activities, and there was a constant demand for and ample room for creativity. Particular contexts of time, place, thought, and people would generate specific demands and problems that could only be resolved creatively. Ming state sacrifices and music were creatively performed as realizations of orthodox prescriptions from the past and solutions of problems in the present.

A HYPOTHESIS TO ANALYZE EXPRESSIVENESS IN ORTHODOX RITUAL AND MUSIC

Being creative within prescribed bounds, Ming state sacrifices and music continuously refresh their expressiveness that is on one hand general and timeless and on the other hand personal and historical. Not only does every performance of a state ritual and music project something well-known and clearly defined, it also expresses something creative and distinctive. Such an expressiveness, which depends on the dynamic tensions between orthodoxy and creativity, is of course not unique to Ming state sacrifices and music, and it also can be found in other large-scale and presentational ritual and music. Toward understanding such ritual and music and their expressiveness, and toward comparison of Ming state sacrifices with other ritual and music, the following hypothesis is presented as an analytical framework.

Concerned participants and critical audiences always find orthodox ritual and music expressive. While they regularly and repeatedly perform these ritual and music according to well-known and clearly defined prescriptions, they also would subtly and creatively change detail features in individual performances, manipulating and appropriating the ritual and music as their personal expressions. The manipulated and personalized features in the adjusted ritual and music complement orthodox forms and contents, generating neither abrupt nor radical changes. At the same time, however, the same features render the adjusted ritual and music continuously expressive, refreshing them with something specific and not prescribed. Being ritual and music experts, concerned participants and critical audiences promptly identify the manipulated and personalized features, interpreting what creativity and purposes are being expressed. Such interpretations always involve the immediate needs of the concerned participants and critical audiences. Without that involvement, the interpretations as well as the creative features that are identified are abstract and ignorable.

Application of the aforementioned hypothesis depends on locating the traces of orthodoxy, creativity, and expressiveness. In this study, I have equated traces of orthodoxy with those inflexible features in Ming state sacrifices and music, which have remain unchanged throughout the Ming dynasty, are described in classical documents, and are usually found in the state ritual and music of the Tang and Song dynasties. Similarly, I have equated creative elements with unique features in individual Ming state sacrifices and music. To locate these traces of orthodoxy and creativity, I have compared corresponding state ritual and music from the Tang, Song, and Ming eras. To show how the Ming emperors and scholar-officials responded to the expressiveness of their state ritual and music, I have relied on what they said and did in their ritual and musical processes, many of which are extensively cited and described in the chapters that follow.

CHAPTER TWO

State Sacrifices in the Ming Court

INTRODUCTION: A HISTORICAL OVERVIEW

> Since ancient times when virtuous rulers built their empires, [there was] nothing they rigorously practiced more than state sacrifices. When they performed the ceremonials, they sought for sincerity and respectfulness as internal [efforts] and prepared the ceremonials fully as external [efforts]. That is [the way] to communicate with the gods. [Now], when I have received the mandate from Heaven [to rule] and have unified the country, the first thing [I will do] is to build the suburban altars and the ancestral temple to advocate the practice of ritual. I realize that we are at an initial stage of the empire and the ceremonials are not completely instituted. [However, without the state sacrifices] how can I communicate with the gods and reach the deities? My ministers, you should select the appropriate [features] of ancient and current practices [to institute state sacrifices for our new empire]. Make sure that they are moderate and proper. Report to me with a proposal.[1]

With these words, Taizu, the founder of the Ming dynasty, formally initiated a unique system of state ritual and music for his empire. Taizu's action was not unexpected. State sacrifices and music, the most prominent and official manifestation of Chinese ritual and music, were not only established means of governance for Chinese emperors and scholar-officials, but also culturally sanctioned channels in which to express their religious, social, and personal concerns. Performed with a wealth of ritual paraphernalia that displayed governmental control of human and material resources, state sacrifices were copiously described in classical documents and enthusiastically discussed and promoted by Confucian scholar-officials.[2] Projecting a representation of the natural and supernatural worlds of the emperors and scholar-officials, state sacrifices revealed the ways in which they understood, in abstract and specific terms, their existence and the roles they played.

As early as the Zhou dynasty, a complicated system of state sacrifices had evolved in which the state sacrifice to Heaven had already assumed a prominent status.[3] Heaven was perceived as a supernatural force that controlled human activities, and its mandate legitimized the power of human rulers. Thus, on one hand, Chinese rulers employed the state sacrifice to Heaven to demonstrate, to his people, his rights and authority bestowed by Heaven, and on the other hand performed the ceremonial to show respect and gratitude to Heaven, requesting continued protection and favor that would sustain his mandate.

For similar reasons, a collection of state sacrifices was offered to a pantheon of deities, such as those of the sun, moon, mountains, and seas, that were believed to be in charge of various operations of natural elements that affected the success of human endeavors. If such ceremonials were religious in nature and political in objective, they also were emotional in their aspiration, since they salved human feelings of vulnerability to unpredictable calamities, both natural and human.

A series of state sacrifices also was offered to imperial ancestors. Originated as expressions of filial piety, these ceremonials, like other state sacrifices, were imbued with supernatural and political attributes.[4] By honoring their ancestors and emphasizing the interrelationships among family members, the sovereigns employed the ceremonials to remind the commoners of their duties to their families, communities, and ultimately to the empire.[5] In other words, state sacrifices offered to imperial ancestors were ritual representations of the authoritarian and patrilineal structure of traditional Chinese society. By presenting the emperors as filial sons, the ceremonials became powerful projections of their legitimacy and political power: Their ancestors, who were virtuous and successful, politically and militarily, founded the empire and bequeathed the thrones to them; filial sons, that is, the sovereigns, were worthy of such legacies. By presenting the imperial ancestors as deified persons, the ceremonials provided a means for the emperors to seek and demonstrate the supernatural protection they would receive from the spirits of their ancestors.[6]

State sacrifices were based on the Confucian and classical ideology that ritual and music are a means through which people can cultivate themselves to become human and proper. Indeed, for traditional Chinese who understood Confucianism, ceremonials were not only expressions of their controlled emotions, but also efforts to sustain proper relationships with fellow human beings and with natural as well as supernatural things. Thus ritual realized and propagated ethical duties: a sovereign should rule like a sovereign; officials should show respect and fealty toward rulers; sons should respect their fathers and so forth. Such a philosophical stand did not disprove, however, the understanding that ceremonials were religious activities. Confucians did not exclude that aspect from their ritual. The Confucian philosopher Xun Zi succinctly described the dichotomy within sacrifices: the superior man looks upon the sacrifices as a fine gloss over matter, while the common people consider it supernatural.[7] Ching K'un Yang, in expanding upon this thought, asserts that the supernatural qualities could not be dismissed from the minds of most Confucians, who preferred to consider rituals as expressions of "human feelings."[8] Because of such ambiguity, Confucian ceremonials were never mere orthodox formalities or intellectual exercises, but essential activities in traditional China. State sacrifices constituted only an imperial and grandiose version of those ceremonials.

As state sacrifices became the ultimate representations of human propriety in traditional China, they also became models of human existence to which all should aspire. In other words, the ceremonials functioned as a means of governance that prescribed the behavior of those who ruled and those who were ruled. If state sacrifices led sovereigns and court officials to excel, performing their duties and becoming effective and respected rulers and officials, the ceremonials also guided the commoners to distinguish what was socially and politically acceptable and what was not. When a court practiced state sacrifices dutifully, it demonstrated its aspirations to emulate Confucian and classic standards of human behavior. Such demonstrations were powerful, as their messages were clear to all and their effects were much more long-lasting than the use of physical force.

State sacrifices were not only a means to rule the commoners, but were also measures to control the emperors. Theoretically, a Chinese emperor was endowed with absolute power, but this does not mean he was absolutely free. He had to behave (or appear to behave) according to the standards represented by the state sacrifices; if he ignored such standards, his legitimacy and authority would diminish. By the same token, scholar-officials should always serve the emperors. However, as the official-scholars were obliged to guide their sovereigns in the practice of state sacrifices, they found an avenue to influence the behavior of their sovereigns.[9] When scholar-officials reproached their rulers for ignoring the state sacrifices, pointing out the occurrence of portents in the form of natural calamities, the scholar-officials struck where the emperors were vulnerable.[10]

The more meanings state sacrifices acquired, the more essential they became to the traditional Chinese court, a process that was further propelled by external forces. Since the Han dynasty, Confucianism became the official philosophy of China. Furthermore, efforts to teach and apply the philosophy were perpetuated by a system of civil examinations that tested Confucian subject matters and was controlled by Confucian bureaucrats. Thus anyone who aspired to become a scholar-official had to study the Confucian classics. In the process, they became Confucians, or at least persons knowledgeable about Confucianism, which emphasized ritual and music. Even imperial clansmen were obliged to learn the teachings of Confucius: although they could amass power through military operations, or inherit the thrones, they had to rule by means of a bureaucracy of scholar-officials. If the imperial clansmen were not Confucians at the time they came to power, they would be converted soon after. An exemplary instance is Taizu, who was born a poor commoner but who learned to manipulate the tenets of Confucianism as a ruler.[11]

The Chinese tradition of state sacrifices did not function in isolation. State sacrifices constituted only one of five categories of court ceremonials (*wuli*), which is outlined in the *Book of Ceremonial* (*Liji*) and other classical works. State sacrifices belonged to the category of auspicious ceremonials (*jili*). The remaining four categories include: celebratory ceremonials (*jiali*) for various secular and celebratory court functions, such as weddings and the crowning of princes; welcoming ceremonials (*binli*) for greeting state guests, especially those who come from foreign countries; military ceremonials (*junli*) for various military functions, such as the return of a victorious general; and death ceremonials (*xiongli*) for funerals and other related activities.

The five categories of court ceremonials complemented one another, but state sacrifices dominated. This fact is copiously described in historical records, vividly perpetuated by the splendid temples and altars created for the sacrificial performances and statistically attested to by the financial expenses incurred.[12] By the time of the Ming dynasty, the Chinese tradition of state sacrifices had operated for more than three millennia and had accumulated many prescriptions for its practice. These prescriptions, which were well-known and well-studied by court citizens, constituted the orthodox boundaries for Ming state sacrifices and music. However, this does not mean that Ming state ritual and music were devoid of ambiguities and creativity. In fact, there were many ambiguous prescriptions, which were creatively manipulated by Ming emperors and scholar-officials.

THE SYSTEM OF MING STATE SACRIFICES

As a system, Ming state sacrifices achieved its most elaborate stage during Shizong's reign (1522–1566) in the middle of the sixteenth century. As enumerated in the *Ming History* (*Mingshi*), a total of forty-six state sacrifices were performed regularly within an annual cycle, which can be classified according to the deities they honored and the ranks they held.[13] The former classification reveals the formal intentions and functions of the state sacrifices, while the latter underscores the ways in which they were performed as great, middle, and small sacrifices.

The former classification divides the state sacrifices into three groups. The first group was performed to honor and express gratitude to a pantheon of deities of natural forces, which controlled (or assisted with) specific operations of the cosmos and/or basic needs of the empire and its people. Among these state sacrifices, those worshipping Heaven stood apart, because the deity was preeminent and because his companions were usually limited to Earth and selected imperial ancestors—the founder(s) of the empire and the father of the current emperor. The rationale for choosing such companions is associative: Earth is the cosmological counterpart of Heaven, while the founder built the empire and the father begot the current emperor. Thus, the ceremonials for worshipping Heaven constituted a distinctive subgroup of Ming state sacrifices, including:

1. The suburban sacrifices (*jiaoji*) offered, singularly or collectively, to Heaven and Earth (see chapter 3)
2. The sacrificial prayer offered to Heaven and the founder, requesting grain harvest (*qigu*)
3. The sacrificial prayer offered to Heaven requesting rain (*dayu*)
4. The great sacrifice to Heaven and the imperial father (*daxiang*)

In addition to the ceremonials associated with Heaven, the group of state sacrifices honoring natural forces also includes those that worshipped:

1. The deities of soil and grains (*sheji*)
2. The deities of imperial soil and grains (*disheji*)
3. The sun (*zhaori*)
4. The moon (*xiyue*)
5. Heavenly and earthly deities (*tianshen dizhi*)—the twelve celestial branches (*taisui*), the time divisions (*yuejiang*), the forces of wind, cloud, thunder, and rain (*fengyun leiyu*) and the spirits of mountains, plains, seas, and rivers (*yuezheng haidu*)
6. The city gods (*chenghuang*)
7. The deities in charge of doors, stoves, gutters, and wells (*wusi*)
8. The deities in charge of horses (*mashen*)
9. The deities in charge of banners and military affairs (*qidu*)

The second group of state sacrifices honored legendary and historical personages considered meritorious for their personification of virtues and/or teaching of the fundamental skills of living. This group includes state sacrifices offered to:

1. The progenitor of agriculture (*xiannong*)
2. The progenitor of sericulture (*xiancan*)
3. Meritorious sovereigns of past dynasties (*lidai diwang*)
4. Teachers of rulers (*shengshi*)
5. The three sage-rulers and masters of medicine (*sanhuang*)
6. Confucius (*xianshi*)
7. Meritorious officials of the Ming (*gongchen*)
8. Deified personages honored in temples in Nanjing (*Nanjing shenmiao*)
9. Deified personages honored in temples in Beijing (*jingshi jiumiao*)
10. Various deified persons (*zhushen*)
11. Wandering ghosts and spirits (*litan*)

The third group of state sacrifices worshipped the imperial ancestors. These state rituals were performed inside the imperial ancestral temple compound (*taimiao*), a large complex of buildings erected around three halls that defined the worship of imperial ancestors.[14] These three halls,

Figure 2.1.
The imperial ancestral temple compound in the late Ming (*MHD* 86.23)

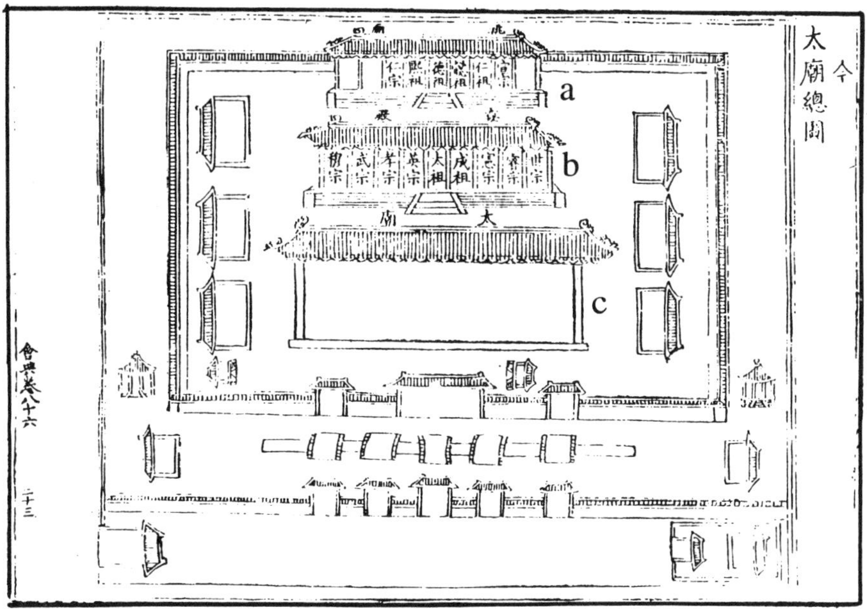

a. the hall of remote imperial ancestora; b. the hall of rest; c. the formal hall of imperial ancestors. The Chinese characters written inside of the "halls" are the names of deceased emperors.

which stand one behind another and mark the central axis of the compound include:

1. The formal hall of imperial ancestors (*zhengdian*) where most of the ceremonials were performed
2. The hall of rest (*qindian*) where the spirit-tablets and personal belongings of the intimate imperial ancestors—i.e. within nine generations of the current emperor—were housed
3. The hall of remote ancestors (*tiaomiao*) where the spirit-tablets of imperial ancestors ten or more generations away from the current emperor were housed[15] (See Figure 2.1.)

Among the fundamental state sacrifices offered to the imperial ancestors are:

1. Individual sacrifices to each of the intimate imperial ancestors (*texiang*), which were performed during the spring
2. Seasonal sacrifices (summer, autumn, and winter) to all of the intimate imperial ancestors (*xiangli*), which were performed in the first months of the seasons
3. Year-end sacrifice to all imperial ancestors (*daxia*)

During Shizong's reign, two additional ceremonials were also regularly performed: seasonal sacrifices to all imperial ancestors (*shixia*) and state sacrifice to the progenitor of the imperial clan (*dadi*). The Ming court also offered state sacrifices to imperial ancestors during these three occasions:

1. Installation of the spirit-tablet of a deceased emperor in the formal hall of imperial ancestors (*shenfu*)
2. Presentation of a deceased emperor's posthumous title (*jian shihao*)
3. Removal of the spirit-tablet of a deceased emperor from the formal hall of imperial ancestors to the hall of remote imperial ancestors (*fengtiao*)

In addition to the aforementioned ceremonials that were periodic, the Ming court also offered many sporadic state sacrifices. For example, during coronations, weddings, military actions, the emperors' departure for trips, and other important events of the empire, the court would perform informational ceremonials (*jigao*) to Heaven, the deities of soil and grains, the imperial ancestors, and other deities appropriate to the occasion.

State sacrifices were traditionally ranked as great, middle, and small ceremonials according to three basic criteria: importance of the deities being worshipped; the court's assessment of the ceremonials; and particular contextual considerations. As reported in the *Ming History*, the Ming system included thirteen great state sacrifices, twenty-five middle ones, and eight small ones.[16] Such ranking of the ceremonials was relatively consistent: great sacrifices were seldom demoted; ambiguities and fluctuations in ranking mostly involved the middle ceremonials and those performed irregularly. For example, ceremonials honoring Heaven were always great sacrifices, and the state sacrifice to Confucius was always a middle ceremonial.

The three ranks of the state sacrifices were general classifications. Ceremonials belonging to the same rank could be further differentiated by the use of various ritual and musical elements, such as the types of sacrificial jade, the colors of the sacrificial silk, and the sizes of the escort for the celebrants. For example, the state sacrifices offered to the progenitors of agriculture and sericulture were both classified as middle ceremonials. However, the former ceremonial involved the sacrificial victims of an ox, a pig, and a goat, while the latter, only a pig and a goat; the size of the altar proper for the former was longer than that of the latter.[17]

The ranking of a ceremonial is significant because it dictates the length of the formal process of ritual and musical activities, types and amount of offerings, and other structural as well as performative elements in the state sacrifices. For instance, the formal process of a great ceremonial, such as the state sacrifice to Heaven, may begin as early as fifty days before the actual sacrificial ceremony. In contrast, the formal process of a small sacrifice, such as the state sacrifice offered to the deities of banners and military affairs, may begin as late as ten days before the sacrificial ceremony.[18]

Another explicit indication of the ranks of the state sacrifices was the number of sacrificial food served in bamboo and wood vessels, or their equivalents (*biandou*). Only the great sacrifices, such as those offered to the imperial ancestors, would present twenty-four kinds of sacrificial food served in those vessels. In contrast, a middle ceremonial, such as that offered to the progenitor of agriculture, would only serve twenty kinds of sacrificial food in the bamboo and wood vessels.

The ranking of Ming state sacrifices was purposeful because it provided a basis for the court citizens to compare the ceremonials and their numerous features, whether the identities of the companions and the celebrants, the numbers of sacrificial food, the types of sacrificial animals, the sizes of the military escort for the emperors' trips to the altars, the exact hours for their departures, and so forth. It was through the differences of the features that Ming state sacrifices became expressive not only of orthodox theories and practices but also of specific and personal messages.

THE MING STATE SACRIFICE TO HEAVEN

Ming state sacrifices were large-scale and presentational ceremonials, and their basic structure and principles of operation can be illustrated by the following sketch of the ritual-musical process of the state sacrifice to Heaven.[19]

Fifty days prior to the performance of the sacrificial ceremony in the round-mound-altar compound (*yuanqiu*), located in the south suburb of the capital, the emperor was asked to officiate at the pending event. Thirty days prior, the music director began rehearsing the music of the ceremony. Six days prior, the emperor informed the ancestors that he would, on the following day, take a trip to the round-mound-altar compound to inspect the sacrificial animals. Four days prior, all participants in the sacrificial ceremony were reminded that the three days of intense abstention would begin on the following day. Three days prior, the emperor went to the temple of imperial ancestors and invited the spirit of the founder to participate in the pending ceremony as Heaven's companion. Two days prior, the emperor offered incense to individual ancestors in the hall of rest inside of the imperial ancestral temple compound, bidding farewell to his predecessors. One day prior, the emperor left for the abstention hall in the round-mound-altar compound. On the same day, ritual staffs arranged the spirit-thrones, musical instruments, and other ritual paraphernalia on the altar proper.

The arrangement was set for a coordinated series of offerings to three groups of deities. On the top tier of the altar proper were the spirit-thrones for Heaven, the host deity and for the founder, the companion; the former was erected in the center of the ritual space, facing south, the latter, to the east, facing west. On the second tier were the spirit-thrones for the sun and the moon, which were placed, respectively, on the east and west sides. On the third tier, the remaining members of the followers were assembled on two spirit-thrones; these followers included the planets and other celestial bodies and the forces of cloud, rain, wind and thunder. In front of the spirit-thrones, various sacrificial items were arranged—wine goblets, silk, jade, sacrificial food, sacrificial victims, candles, incense, and so forth.

By midnight of the day of performance, the emperor was waiting in the great canopy inside the altar compound, while the ritual staffs installed the spirit-tablets on the individual spirit-thrones.[20] As the task was completed, it was reported to the emperor, who then emerged from the great canopy. Donning full ritual regalia, the emperor proceeded to his obeisant-post on the second tier of the altar proper. Then, when all participants took their ritual positions, the sacrificial ceremony formally began with an intoner chanting the words "kindle the torches" and "welcome the deities."

With the altar proper brilliantly illuminated, the first stage of the ceremony began, and the musicians started to play the first piece of music (*yue*, music or music and dance; hereafter, music) for the occasion. Accompanied by the musical sounds, the emperor approached the incense table (*xiang'an*) in front of the spirit-throne of the host deity, kneeled in front of the table, and offered three rounds of incense to the deity. He repeated the same series of gestures in front of the spirit-throne of the companion. Then he returned to his obeisant-post. As he arrived, the playing of music stopped. In silence, the emperor and all officials performed, in their obeisant posts, the four obeisances (*sibai*) to the deities.

The second stage of the sacrificial ceremony began with the intoner chanting the words "offer the jade and silk," which signaled the musicians to begin playing the second piece of music for the occasion. With this music, the emperor approached the spirit-throne of Heaven, kneeled, and offered the jade and silk to the deity. He repeated the same series of ceremonial gestures and offering to the companion. Then he returned to his obeisant-post; at that point, the musicians stopped playing.

The third stage of the sacrificial ceremony began with the intoner chanting the words "deliver the sacrificial food." Then the musicians played the third piece of music for the occasion, while the ritual staffs brought in the sacrificial food and arranged them in front of the spirit-thrones. After the food delivery was completed, the emperor approached the spirit-thrones, offered the food to the deities, and returned to his obeisant-post. Once the emperor reached his post, the music stopped.

The fourth stage of the sacrificial ceremony began with the intoner chanting the words "present the first offering of wine." Then the musicians began playing the fourth piece of music for the occasion, while the emperor approached the spirit-throne of Heaven, accepted a goblet of wine from a staff, and offered it to the deity. Having completed his gesture of offering, the emperor moved to a position where he would listen to a ritual officer's reading of the prayer prepared for the occasion. As he reached his position, the musicians suspended playing of the music. At this point, all present on the altar proper kneeled to listen to the reading of the prayer. After the reading was completed, the musicians resumed playing the fourth piece of music. Accompanied by the music, the emperor and all present performed the prostration to the deities. Then the emperor approached the spirit-throne of the companion, accepted a goblet of wine from a ritual staff, and offered the wine to the ancestor. After the offering, he returned to his obeisant-post, and the musicians stopped their performance.

The fifth stage was the second offering of wine. Except for the reading of the prayer, the ceremonial gestures involved were the same as those in the last stage. The music performed was the fifth piece for the occasion.

The sixth stage was the last offering of wine. After the intoner chanted the title of the stage, the musicians began playing the sixth piece of music for the occasion. Then, surrounded by musical sounds, the emperor offered wine to Heaven and the companion. At the conclusion of the offering, the intoner chanted the words "bestow the blessed wine and meat." Taking that as a cue, the emperor moved to a position where he would drink the blessed wine (*yin fujiu*) and receive the blessed meat (*shouzuo*). Then the musicians stopped playing. In silence, the emperor received the blessed wine and meat, performed the prostration, and returned to his obeisant-post. There the emperor and all present performed the four obeisances.

The seventh stage of the ceremony was the removal of the sacrificial food by the ritual staffs. Throughout the stage, the musicians played the seventh piece of music for the occasion, while the emperor witnessed the activities in his obeisant-post.

The eighth stage began with the intoner chanting the words "farewell to the deities," and the musicians' playing the eighth piece of music for the occasion. Accompanied by the music, the emperor and all present performed the four obeisances. Then, the ritual staffs collected the ritual documents, silk, and food and delivered them to the furnace (*taitan*). The emperor moved to the east of his obeisant-post.

The ninth stage consisted of watching the burning of the sacrificial articles. After the intoner's announcement, the musicians began playing the ninth piece of music for the occasion, and the ritual staffs retreated to the third tier of the altar proper. Then the emperor moved to a position where he would observe the burning. When about half of the wood and sacred articles inside the furnace was burned, the intoner announced the completion of the sacrificial ceremony. After that chanting, the musicians stopped playing and the emperor retreated to the great canopy, where he removed his sacrificial regalia. Then he embarked on his trip back to the palace.

As the ceremonial activities directed to Heaven and his companion occurred on the top tier of the alter proper, the worshipping of the followers occurred on the second and third tiers of the altar. This worshipping activity supplemented what happened on the top tier of the altar and involved only four ceremonial stages. The first stage of this simplified version was the offering of incense to the deities, the offering of the silk, the first offering of wine, and the readings of the prayers. The second and third stages offered wine to the deities; and the fourth stage involved the removal and burning of the sacrificial food and items. The performance of these stages was coordinated with those on the top tier of the altar proper.

The burning of the sacrificial articles was the last ceremonial stage performed inside the altar compound, but it was not the last event in the ritual and musical process of a state sacrifice to Heaven. Upon returning to the palace from the altar compound, the emperor hosted a celebration banquet and awarded the scholar-officials who had assisted in the successful performance of the ceremonial. After the banquet, scholar-officials who were intellectually and emotionally touched by the experience wrote critical comments in memorials, eulogies, personal memoirs, poems, and other writings, which were then circulated and studied publicly or privately.

As described earlier, the sacrificial ceremony in a state sacrifice involves music as an integral component. The music is nominally performed to facilitate communication with the deities, but it is not a medium to deliver prayers or help celebrants go into a trance or other altered mental states. In fact, the music and their sung texts serve to remind the celebrants who they are and what they are doing by commenting on the ritual setting, the ceremonial gestures, and the ritual meanings. (See chapter 7.) The music also creates a ritual-musical soundscape to underscore the identity of the emperor, mark the progression of the ceremonial stages, and create a continuity and commonality among all ceremonial activities, participants, and audiences on and off the altar proper. Indeed, the music is the only element that simultaneously reaches all participants and audiences inside the altar compound.

Such functions of the music are reflected by the timing of the music performed and the number of pieces played. For stages one through three, five, and nine, music accompanies the emperor's movements throughout, commencing at the beginning of each stage (after the intoner's chanting) and stopping at its conclusion, when the emperor has either returned to his obeisant-post, or moved to equivalent positions. In stages four, six, seven, and eight, the relationships between music and ceremonial activities differ only slightly. Music does not always accompany the emperor's actions: It is suspended during the reading of the prayer in stage four and while the emperor is drinking the sacrificial wine and receiving the sacrificial meat at the end of stage six.[21] In stage seven, the music accompanies the removal of the ritual food, while the emperor stays put in the obeisant-post. In stage eight, the music accompanies the participants' four obeisances and the staffs' delivery of the sacrificial articles to the furnace.

MODELS FROM THE TANG AND SONG DYNASTIES

As outlined previously, the fundamental structure of Ming state sacrifices resembles that of the Tang and Song dynasties. In this sense, Ming state sacrifices are indeed very orthodox, their fundamental structures standardized. However, Ming state sacrifices also are very different from their predecessors. In fact, there are so many discrepancies between Ming and earlier ceremonials that they cannot be compared feature for feature.[22] To illustrate the general similarities and to detail discrepancies among ceremonials of the Tang, Song and Ming dynasties, three representative state sacrifices to Heaven will be outlined here. For convenience of discussion, the ceremonials will be sketched according to the use of music and sequence of the nine ceremonial stages.

The Tang dynasty first formalized its state sacrifices in 633 with the completion of the *Ritual of the Zhenguan Period* (*Zhenguan li*), which is now lost. A summary of an early Tang sacrificial ceremony honoring Heaven is nevertheless preserved, and shows basic similarities between the Tang and Ming versions.[23] According to this summary, the ceremony includes the following stages that were performed with music:

1. Welcoming the deities
2. The emperor's procession
3. Offering of jade and silk
4. Offering of sacrificial food
5. Offering of wine and the emperor's drinking of the blessed wine
6. Retreat of civil dancers and entry of military dancers
7. Performance of the military dance
8. Farewell to the deities

The most comprehensive description of Tang dynasty state sacrifice to Heaven is in the *Ritual of the Tang Kaiyuan Period* of 732, an authoritative manual for not only the Tang court but also those of subsequent dynasties.[24] In fact, the manual is one of the references constantly cited in the *Collected Ceremonials of the Ming Dynasty*, which is one of the most important documents on Ming state ritual and music.[25] The *Ritual of the Tang Kaiyuan Period* describes the worshipping of Heaven as a ceremonial of seven phases, illustrating the importance of the various ritual activities performed before and after the sacrificial ceremony and underscoring the state sacrifice as a complex series of ceremonies and related activities. The seven phases include:

1. Abstention
2. Arrangement of ritual positions and equipment in the altar compound
3. Inspection of the sacrificial victims and utensils
4. The emperor's departure from the palace
5. Offering of jade and silk
6. Offering of sacrificial food
7. The emperor's return to the palace

The fifth and sixth phases of this Tang ceremonial, which constitute an equivalent to the sacrificial ceremony of a Ming state sacrifice, include the following ritual program.

It formally began with an announcement by the minister of the Court of Imperial Sacrifices (*taichang qing*). Then the ground orchestra and the civil dancers began to perform the first piece of music of the occasion. Accompanied by the musical sounds, the emperor and officials performed the double obeisances, and the ritual staffs prepared the jade and silk to be offered. As the music was completed, the emperor left his obeisant-post and advanced to another assigned post on the altar. Whenever the emperor traveled among ritual positions, his movement was accompanied by a piece of processional music reserved for that purpose.

Ascending to the top tier of the altar, the emperor took the ritual jade readied for him. Then, to the singing of the second piece of state sacrificial music for the occasion, he approached the spirit-throne of Heaven, kneeled, offered the jade to the deity, performed the prostration, retreated backward, and performed the double obeisances. The emperor repeated the same sequence of ceremonial gestures in front of the companion's spirit-throne, offering silk to the deified ancestor Gaozu (reigned 618–626). As the emperor completed his ceremonial gestures and retreated to his obeisant-post, the musicians stopped singing. Then similar offerings of jade and silk were presented to the other deities installed on the other tiers of the altar. When the offerings were done, ritual staffs delivered dishes of the hide and blood of the sacrificial animals and placed them in front of the various spirit-thrones.

Accompanied by the third piece of state sacrificial music for the occasion, a group of ritual staffs transported various dishes of sacrificial food to assigned places by the staircases of the altar proper. Then a second group of ritual staffs cleared the dishes of animal hide and blood, and a third group of ritual staffs set the dishes of sacrificial food in front of the various spirit-thrones. When this food delivery was completed, the emperor moved to a post where he washed and wiped his hands as well as the wine goblets.

As the staffs prepared ritual wine for the emperor, the fourth piece of state sacrificial music for the occasion was played. During its performance, the emperor approached the spirit-throne of Heaven, kneeled, offered the wine, performed the prostration, and then retreated. When he reached his assigned position and stood, facing north, the music performance stopped. At that point, a ritual officer approached the spirit-throne, kneeled, and began to read the prayer prepared for the occasion. As he finished reading, performance of the music resumed. Accompanied by this music, the officer placed the wooden tablet of the prayer on the spirit-throne of Heaven and retreated. Then, the emperor performed the double obeisances to Heaven. This sequence of ceremonial gestures was repeated in front of the companion's spirit-throne, but a different prayer was read.

As the emperor returned to a position in front of the spirit-throne of Heaven, the fifth piece of music for the occasion was performed. Meanwhile, the ritual staffs prepared a goblet of blessed wine and presented it to the emperor. The emperor accepted the wine, and passed it to a ritual officer, who drank it, spit it out, and then performed the prostration. The emperor performed the prostration, then stood at his position. At this point, ritual staffs delivered trays of cooked food and set them in front of the two spirit-thrones. Then another ritual officer assembled selected pieces of meat (from the third joints of the front legs of the sacrificial animals) onto a tray and offered it to the emperor, who accepted it and then passed it on to his assistant. The emperor then kneeled, drank the blessed wine, performed the prostration and double obeisances, and returned to his obeisant-post. When he arrived at the post, the performance of the fifth piece of music stopped.

As the emperor was stationed at the obeisant-post, the civil dancers left the top tier of the altar proper accompanied by the sixth piece of state sacrificial music for the occasion. The music was repeated as the military dancers entered the top tier of the altar proper and began their performance there. As they performed, ritual officers presented the second and third offerings of wine to the deities.

When the two offerings were completed, the military dances stopped and ritual staffs symbolically cleared the food by moving the containers slightly away from where they were placed. Then a ritual officer announced the bestowal of the blessed meat. Responding to that, the ritual participants performed the double obeisances.

As the seventh piece of state sacrificial music was played, the emperor and all ritual participants performed the double obeisances. Then, accompanied by the imperial processional music, the emperor moved to a position where he would observe the burning of the sacrificial items. During this time, ritual staffs cleared the food and various ritual items and put them into the furnace (*liaotan*), which was filled with wood. The ritual staff kindled the fire. When half of the wood and sacrificial items inside the furnace was burned, the minister announced the completion of the sacrificial activity.

As the above sketch shows, the Tang dynasty state sacrifice was a very complex ceremonial; the prescriptions in the *Ritual of the Tang Kaiyuan Period* are exhaustive—what is outlined here represents only their most fundamental features. It is no accident that Tang state sacrifices were often used as historical models in subsequent dynasties. However, this does not mean the Tang models were literally emulated, a fact clearly demonstrated by the state sacrifice to Heaven of the Northern Song dynasty. As performed by Shenzong (reigned 1068–1085) in 1083, its sacrificial ceremony can be briefly traced as follows.[26]

As the ceremony began, the orchestra played the first piece of state sacrificial music for the occasion, while the dancers performed a civil dance. At the conclusion of the music and dance, Shenzong performed the double obeisances to the deities and proceeded to a position where he washed his hands with a towel. As he completed his ceremonial washing, the orchestral music resumed. Accompanied by this music, the emperor retreated to his obeisant-post.

To perform the second stage of the ceremony, Shenzong climbed the stairs to the top tier of the altar, accompanied by vocal music. After receiving the sacrificial jade from a ritual staff, Shenzong approached the spirit-throne of Heaven. At this point, the musicians began to perform the second piece of state sacrificial music for the occasion. Surrounded by this music, the emperor performed a sequence of ceremonial gestures—he kneeled in front of the spirit-throne of Heaven, put the jade into a silk wrapping, prostrated, rose, delivered three rounds of incense, offered the jade and silk, prostrated, rose, and finally performed the double obeisances to the deity. Then a ritual staff collected the jade, and the music stopped.

As the musicians began to perform the third piece of state sacrificial music, Shenzong approached the spirit-throne of the companion Taizu (reigned 960–975). Accompanied by the musical sounds, Shenzong offered jade and silk to the ancestor with a series of gestures identical to those he had performed earlier. Then he left the top tier of the altar proper and retreated to his obeisant-post.

As the musicians began the fourth piece of state sacrificial music, ritual officials delivered and placed the sacrificial food in front of the spirit-thrones. As this was done, the musicians stopped playing. Then Shenzong moved to a position where he washed the goblets with which he would offer wine to the deities. After the washing, the emperor retreated to his obeisant-post; his movements were accompanied by music.

To offer wine to the deities, Shenzong again climbed to the top tier of the altar. As he approached the spirit-throne of Heaven, the musicians began to perform the fifth piece of state sacrificial music. In front of the spirit-throne, the emperor kneeled, offered three rounds of wine, prostrated, and rose. At that point, the musicians suspended their performance so a ritual officer would read a prayer prepared for the occasion. At the conclusion of the reading, Shenzong performed a double obeisance. Then the musicians resumed their playing, and the emperor offered wine to Taizu with the same sequence of ceremonial gestures. After the offerings, the emperor returned to his obeisant-post. With the emperor stationed, the civil dancers retreated from the altar proper and the military dancers entered. They performed their dance to the music of the sixth piece of state sacrificial music for the occasion.

This sequence of ritual actions was repeated at the second and third offerings of wine to the deities. At the conclusion of the offerings, the emperor proceeded to a position in front of the spirit-thrones, where he would accepted the blessed wine and food. As the musicians began to play the seventh piece of state sacrificial music for the occasion, the emperor performed a double obeisance, kneeled, accepted the wine from his ritual assistant, offered three rounds of wine to the deities, drank the wine, spit it out, and then set the goblet down. At this point, the emperor was offered the sacrificial food, which he accepted and offered to the deities. Then he repeated the gestures of wine offering and returned to his obeisant-post.

As the emperor reached his post, ritual officials cleared the sacrificial food from the top tier of the altar. Then an intoner announced the bestowal of the blessed meat. Amidst the music of the eighth piece of state sacrificial music, the officials performed the double obeisances.

Accompanied by music, the emperor moved from his obeisant-post to a place where he would observe the burning of the sacrificial articles. When half of the wood for the fire was burned, an intoner announced the completion of the sacrificial ceremony. Then the emperor left the altar proper, went to the great canopy where he changed his costume, and proceeded to the green castle (*qingcheng*) where he met his officials and accepted their congratulations. Changing to another ritual costume, the emperor left the green castle in a jade chariot. As the chariot approached the palace entrance, music was performed to welcome the emperor's return. The emperor entered the palace, put on regular clothes, and then held court to grant amnesty to prisoners and to celebrate the success of the ritual performance with his officials.

ORTHODOXY, CREATIVITY, AND EXPRESSIVENESS IN MING STATE SACRIFICES

If the above outlines of the Tang, Song, and Ming sacrificial ceremonies honoring Heaven are broadly compared, they share many common features. All versions are preceded by a series of preparations and related activities, including formal notices, abstention, setting up the altar, and so forth. All versions honor a host deity, his companion, who was always an imperial ancestor, and the deity's followers. All versions include the following crucial ceremonial activities: welcoming the deities, presenting offerings to them, reading of prayers, bidding farewell to the deities, and burning the ritual articles. All versions offer animal victims, jade, silk, cooked food, and three rounds of wine. Communication between the deities and the emperors who officiated at the ceremony is enacted by their acceptance of the blessed wine and meat. In all the versions, the gestures of kneeling, obeisance, and prostration were used to show respect to the deities. And in all the versions, the main celebrants moved around assigned ritual positions—such as the obeisant-post and the post for observing the burning of sacrificial articles.

The above similarities among the Tang, Song, and Ming versions project a thousand-year-old orthodoxy in the practice of state sacrifices. It is a formidable orthodoxy because its roots go back to the ancient times; in this sense, the Tang models constituted an influential but relatively recent development. This view of orthodoxy and continuity is, however, broad and nonspecific. A different side of the ceremonials is revealed if their detail features, ranging from the selection of the followers to the color of the silk offered, are compared one by one. As demonstrated by the aforementioned summaries, such literal comparison is impractical—there are simply too many particular and significant discrepancies among the versions.

The ceremonials cannot be identical. The ritual and musical processes of state sacrifices involve many rounds of deliberations among concerned participants, and no ritual and musical element is merely a detail feature that can be taken for granted. In the Ming court, the institution of a state sacrifice was an imperial prerogative exercised through the scholar-officials. A Ming emperor could not create state sacrifices by himself and without the scholar-officials' help. By the same token, the scholar-officials could not institute state sacrifices through their own wishes; they had to draft proposals requesting that the court launch new ceremonials or make changes in the current ones. Upon court acceptance of these proposals, the emperors would order ritual and musical experts in the Ministry of Rites and/or the Court of Imperial Sacrifices to discuss and research the ritual and musical matters. After favorable conclusions had been reached, or if the emperor insisted, the officials would prepare a preliminary draft on the proposed ceremonial. They would base their arguments and designs on models described in the classics, and/or specified by historical models and traditional practices with which they were familiar. After reviews by the emperor and further negotiations between the emperor and scholar-officials, a final plan would eventually be drawn, specifying all elements of the ceremonial. This process is complicated and accommodates creative efforts to adjust orthodox state sacrifices for immediate and individualistic concerns.

The creativity involved is not exercised to show innovations of the emperors and scholar-officials, but to solve problems at hand. Furthermore, the creativity was deliberately camouflaged to make the state sacrifices look orthodox; being orthodox was one of the factors that made a solution acceptable. A concrete example of such dynamics of orthodoxy and creativity is the round-mound-altar, a magnificent sample of which still stands in the southern suburb of Beijing, which was once the Ming capital. The altar, built by Shizong in 1530, appears to be the very embodiment of orthodoxy because it expresses fundamental ideas in the Chinese tradition of state sacrifice to Heaven. The altar was made circular to represent Heaven, which was thought to be round, and to match the notion that the altar should sit on top of a round mound. The altar has three tiers to show the union of Heaven, Earth, and men, and to demonstrate its hierarchical status as the altar for the most important state sacrifice.

The altar is, however, also a creative edifice, a fact that becomes clear once it is compared with those of earlier times. In the Tang dynasty, the altar to Heaven was square and had four tiers.[27] In Song dynasties, the altar to Heaven was square and had three tiers.[28] In the Yuan dynasty, the altar was square and originally had three tiers. It acquired, in 1310, a fourth tier, by enclosing the four sides of the altar with green ropes. In the beginning of the Ming dynasty, the altar had only two tiers.[29] Furthermore, between 1378 and 1529, the Ming court worshipped Heaven inside of a sacrificial hall. The altar that is now standing in Beijing is a creative product of Shizong's efforts to emulate ancient altars.

The detail alterations in Ming state sacrifices only mirrored the changing needs of the concerned participants and critical audiences. In other words, the ceremonials could not be merely orthodox formalities, because every change, even a seemingly minor one, can transform the ceremonials into individualistic expressions of a particular time, place, thought, and people. An illustrative example is the changes in the Ming state sacrifice to Confucius. In 1476, Zhou Hungmo, the chancellor of the national university, introduced the following changes in the ceremonial: the dance was changed from the six-row format—thirty-six dancers arranged in six rows (*liuyi*)—to an eight-row format (*bayi*), and the number of food served in bamboo and wood trays was increased from twenty to twenty-four. In 1530, Shizong had the dance reverted to the six-row format, and the number of food decreased to twenty. He also stopped the thousand-year-old practice of honoring Confucius with the title of the Most Accomplished and Virtuous King of Civility (*Dacheng zhisheng wenxuan wang*).

Beyond the issues of honoring Confucius with appropriate titles and ceremonials—a key concept in the Confucian practice of ritual and music—the aforementioned alterations also were specific expressions of Shizong and Zhou, two concerned participants. They did not have doubts or conflicts about the ideological and social meanings of the ritual and musical features. And they both knew how it was performed; Taizu proclaimed, in 1393, the ceremonial throughout the empire. Nevertheless, Zhou pushed to have Confucius honored regally. In doing so, he revealed the orthodox understanding that the sovereign occupied the most exalted position in the human world, and thus Confucius could only be appropriately honored when he was ritually given such a position. Zhou also pinpointed an impropriety: Confucius was titled a king since the beginning of the Ming empire, but not offered dance and sacrificial food appropriate to that regal status.[30]

In Shizong's mind, it would be improper to address Confucius as a king and to honor him with regal ceremonials. Shizong argued that the philosopher was never a ruler and that he would not usurp a status that was not his. Thus the emperor changed the dance and sacrificial food and took away the title. What Shizong did was not without theoretical support. However, the emperor's action was a sharp contrast to his bestowal of imperial honors on his biological father, who died a prince. The contrast was not unnoticed among scholar-officials. Whether or not Confucius should be honored as a king is theoretical and may never be definitively solved. However, the issue is urgent in any performance of the ceremonial, and decisions must be made by the concerned participants. Zhou and Shizong made theirs, interpreting and appropriating the ceremonial in the ways in which they intellectually and emotionally desired. Thus the Ming state sacrifice to Confucius was not merely a ceremonial honoring the philosopher, but also an expression of Shizong and Zhou. The two men had effectively appropriated the ceremonial; all historical descriptions of the Ming ceremonial make reference to the changes they introduced.

Considering the ways Ming state sacrifices can be manipulated and appropriated, it is no surprise that Ming court citizens were critical of every ritual and musical nuance. It is these nuances, which may appear trivial and insignificant to the casual observer, which render the ceremonials expressive.

CHAPTER THREE

Taizu's Words and Deeds of State Sacrifices and Music

PRELUDE

On December 13, 1367, shortly before the formal beginning of the Ming dynasty, Zhu Yuanzhang, the future Taizu, inspected the newly constructed round-mound-altar. Immediately, he noticed that it did not completely conform to ancient prescriptions, but grasped why the edifice had to be creative in certain aspects.[1] Responding to the expressiveness of the edifice, Taizu launched a discussion, with Xiong Ding (1322–1376), his diarist (*qijuzhu*), about the virtue of sincerity required in the practice of state sacrifices. Taizu's response was not accidental; it resulted from many years of studying to become an emperor.

In 1367, Taizu was not yet an emperor, but he had already mastered the Confucian ideology of using ritual and music as a means of governance and self-cultivation.[2] Thus, in the process of launching his system of state sacrifices and music, he was able to assume the role of a virtuous sovereign and moral leader, lecturing frequently about the issues of ritual and music and commenting on how they were to be practiced. As documented, Taizu's lectures and comments demonstrate how, on the one hand, he internalized classical understanding and, on the other hand, adjusted and appropriated that understanding to tailor state sacrifices and music to suit his needs.[3]

Taizu emphasized certain fundamental principles: using ritual and music as a means of governance, as communication with supernatural forces, as expressions of personal emotions; adjusting ritual and music to serve present needs; performing ritual and music with sincerity and respectfulness to ensure their efficacy. Such principles are, needless to say, orthodox and ubiquitously described in Confucian writings. As lectured by Taizu, however, the principles took on the distinctive nuances of the emperor, revealing the ways in which he responded to state ritual and music. Taizu's understanding was simultaneously orthodox and creative, a fact that can be demonstrated with a review of ritual and musical concepts preserved in Confucian classics such as the *Record of Music* (*Yueji*), the *Book of Ceremonial* (*Liji*), and the *Analects of Confucius* (*Lunyu*), and in the *Veritable Records of Taizu* (*Taizu gaohuangdi shilu*).[4]

CLASSICAL CONCEPTS ABOUT RITUAL AND MUSIC

About the cosmological (and supernatural?) nature of ritual and music, the *Record of Music* declares: Ritual and music embody all intentions and emotions between Heaven and Earth, display virtues of the deities, adjust their ranks, nurture all animate and inanimate beings in the cosmos, and guide the interactions among sovereigns, officials, fathers, and sons.[5] About the expressive nature of music, the document says: Sounds arise from the human heart/minds that are aroused by external things; when organized, these sounds, which represent emotions, become musical tones (*yin*); when the musical tones are performed with dances, music (*yue*) results;[6] thus music making cannot be dishonest.[7] About using ritual and music as a means of governance, the classic states: Being cautious about elements that affect people, the ancient sage-kings employed ritual to guide the minds of people, music to cultivate their characters, laws to unify their behavior, punishments to deter their wrongdoing; ritual, music, laws, and punishments have the same ultimate goal; they come from the way of governance, and they all serve to manage people's heart/minds.[8] To maximize the effects of ritual and music, the classic proclaims: Even for a moment, people cannot forget ritual and music; when their heart/minds are not harmonious and devoid of music, vulgar and deceitful thoughts will occur; when their behavior is not solemn and respectful, erratic and indolent thoughts will appear.[9] Regarding the timing when new systems of ritual and music should be introduced, the classic says: When a sovereign has accomplished his military goals, he has music made by his court officials; when his empire is stabilized, he institutes ritual.[10]

The Book of Ceremonial comprehensively describes all aspects of ritual, of which only the following concepts need to be highlighted here.

About the urgency of ritual, the classic says: Ritual is the means through which the ancient sage-kings accepted Heaven's mandate to rule the populace; thus, those who lose the practice of ritual will perish, and those who acquire it, flourish.[11] About the ways ritual should be practiced with respectfulness and sincerity, the document begins with the admonition, "Do not be without respectfulness (*wu bujing*)"; it then elaborates: A scholar-official (*junzi*) practices ritual with sincerity and respectfulness and takes the utmost care to implement the prescriptions.[12] About the importance of understanding the meanings behind ritual, the classic states: What is most important in the practice of ritual is to understand its meanings; when one loses sight of such meanings but engages in ritual activities, he is merely performing the tasks of ritual staffs (*zhushi*); when one knows the meanings of ritual, practice it with respectfulness, he is applying the means with which sovereigns rule their empires.[13] About creating ritual to meet changing needs, the classic states: Ritual results from proper reasoning; thus, when one harmoniously coordinates all the reasons that are present, he may create a new ritual [or adjust a preexisting one], even though it does not exist in the times of the ancient sage-kings.[14]

The Analects of Confucius includes many philosophical comments about ritual and music, among which the following are pertinent here. About the nature of ritual and music, Confucius said: "Ritual, oh, ritual! Does it mean no more than the offering of jade and silk? Music, oh, music! Does it mean no more than the sounds of bells and drums?"[15] He also said: If a person does not cultivate *ren* (the most desirable Confucian virtue), how can he practice ritual, and how can he make music?[16] Confucius offered many explanations about how a sovereign can cultivate himself, one of which is prominently echoed in Taizu's thoughts on ritual and music—the sovereign should cultivate himself with respectfulness.[17]

TAIZU'S WORDS ON STATE SACRIFICES AND MUSIC

As Taizu proclaimed himself emperor in 1368, his empire was not yet totally consolidated; battles were still being fought in the north and west. Nevertheless, Taizu concluded that he had achieved his military goal of controlling China, and it was time, as specified by the classics, for him to formally institute a system of state sacrifices and music. Such an institution is a political necessity. The ritual and music thus instituted would not only mark the beginning of his empire by demonstrating his power and authority, but also provide a socio-ethical model for his people, guiding the empire to operate as the ideal society of ancient times.

Determined to become a virtuous emperor by emulating the ancient sage-kings, Taizu had prepared to launch his system of state sacrifices and music as soon as the timing was right, a fact that is clear from a 1364 discussion with Song Lian (1310–1381) and Kong Keren (fl.1360s), two noted Confucian scholar-officials of the time. In that discussion, Taizu commented that Han Wendi (reigned 179–141 B.C.), the virtuous second emperor of the Han dynasty, missed an opportune time to institute a system of state sacrifices and music, so the Han empire failed to become an ideal society.[18] To avoid making Han Wendi's mistake, Taizu appointed, in 1367, Tao An (1312–1368), a ritual expert, to chair a committee of Hanlin academicians to discuss state sacrifices and music.[19] In the following decade, Taizu spent much time and energy instituting state sacrifices and music. Before he established the system he desired, however, he had to make many changes to find what he thought was "right" for the new empire. Many times, Taizu had to teach his officials what ritual and music were about.

Arguing that ritual and music were, as a means of governance, more fundamental than laws and punishments, Taizu explained their functions and warned against treating them as empty formalities. Speaking to officials, in 1384, Taizu declared that:

> The way to rule the world consists only of ritual and music. If [the ruler] has mastered ritual but not music, he has neither the means to cultivate the people's heart/minds nor [the measures that] originated from the way of governance. If [the ruler] has understood music but not ritual, [he] has nothing that can activate the laws or establish the great rule of avoiding extremities. Ritual and music must be practiced simultaneously; only then governance will become pure and good. There is a notion that in addition to ritual and music, there must also be laws and punishments. In my opinion, they only supplement ritual and music as [a] means of governance.
>
> If a government rules with laws and punishments only, dispensing with ritual and music, those above will have a strict and severe control, but they will not have created a mood of peace; those below will have intentions to shirk and will not have the sincerity to resist wrongdoing. In short, ritual and music are like

> the staples of a peaceful reign, while laws and punishments are only the medicines to cure the abuses. When you, my ministers, are conducting official business, pay special attention to ritual and music, and do not take them as empty ceremonials.[20]

Taizu's understanding and involvement with ritual and music was not merely an intellectual and imperial application of the Confucian means of governance—his involvement was also religious. Taizu employed ritual and music to communicate with the deities and ancestors who gave him the mandate to rule and helped him build his empire. His 1367 prayer to imperial deities of Heaven and Earth explains such supernatural functions of ritual and music:

> Regarding the sovereign of our Chinese people, Heaven [last] sent the appointed person (*zhenren*) from the [Mongolian] desert to come and rule China after the mandate of the Song emperors had ended. As [a direct line of Mongolian] rulers, the father, the son, and the grandson lasted more than a hundred years. Now their mandate has ended. Their lands are being fought over by the people and the warlords. Only to me, your delegate, has Heaven given wise and virtuous persons as assistants. Thus, [I can] suppress the various warlords, so that people can live peacefully in their lands.
>
> Now the [pacified] land is over twenty thousand miles in diameter, and all my officials have told [me] that the people have no sovereign [to take care of them], [and they] definitely want [me] to assume the title of emperor. I, your delegate, dare not refuse, but I also dare not dispense with the report to [you], imperial deities of Heaven and Earth. On January fourth next year, I will set the altar to the east of Mountain Zhong, and prepare a sacrifice to declare [my acceptance] to you, as the selection is made by your mind. If I can be the ruler of the people, deities of Heaven and Earth will come [to the altar] on the day of the informing ceremony, and the weather will clear and be bright. If I should not be emperor, there will be strong gales and unusual signs to tell me, your delegate.[21]

Taizu had total confidence in his candidacy, and the fine weather that occurred at his informing ceremony only confirmed his belief, rendering his mandate clear to all his court citizens and commoners.[22] As Taizu relied on supernatural forces to confirm his power, he also realized he could not control the deities, and the fear of losing the mandate crossed his mind. Thus, Taizu strove to show his gratitude and make himself worthy of the supernatural grace by having state sacrifices and music performed diligently. After performing the state sacrifice to Earth in 1369, he commented on the delicate relationship between rulers and Heaven:

> The mandate of Heaven [is something] I do not dare to know. The ancients have said that the mandate of Heaven does not change, but they have also said that it is uncertain. When the uncertain mandate, which is difficult to keep, is given to a proud, indulgent, licentious and incompetent ruler, there is no way that he will not be destroyed. I have read books and found that when [certain] past emperors did not strive for total sincerity or respect in their [performance of] sacrifices, it led to extreme evils. Then, the mandate of Heaven changed. Whenever I think about this, my heart is admonished.[23]

Similarly, in a speech he made after he worshipped Heaven in 1371, Taizu explained why he performed the ritual and music diligently: "Now, I offer annual sacrifices to Heaven at the round-mound-altar on winter solstice and to Earth at the square-marsh-altar on summer solstice. This is in accordance with the ancient ritual practices that show thanks to Heaven and Earth."[24]

Taizu's religious belief in the deities and the communication through ritual was genuine and emotional. In 1373, he prayed to the deities and blamed a previous military loss on his failure to report promptly, and to ask for divine protection:

> Last year, I sent the army to conquer Daxing. . . . During that time of military maneuver, I, remiss in informing you, the Gods, of [the action], and suffered your displeasure. Now I am sending generals . . . to defend the [northern] border. If the barbarians come to disturb us, I will command the generals to lead the army to forcefully subdue [them] to maintain peace in China. Now the army is marching again and I report to you.[25]

As the prayer shows, Taizu believed in ritual communication with the deities, especially Heaven. Thus, to ensure that he alone could communicate with Heaven, he declared, in 1370, prayers to Heaven an imperial prerogative, forbidding commoners to communicate to the deity directly.[26] Arguing that the commoners' prayers to Heaven were "sacrilegious and an usurpation" of imperial authority, he decreed that commoners might only offer sacrifices to their ancestors, to the kitchen god on New Year's Eve, and to the deities of grains in spring and autumn.

Taizu's understanding and use of state sacrifices and music was explicitly more religious and emotional than what is described in the Confucian classics. His views and actions allude to his early experiences. Taizu was once a mendicant monk who was exposed to religious (supernatural) ideas and practices of the time; his dramatic rise from an orphan to an emperor shaped his emotional existence.[27] In fact, Taizu not only offered sacrifices to show respect and gratitude to the deities, he also performed ritual to express personal and religious emotions. A vivid illustration is his 1366 praying to the God of the Big River, seeking supernatural assistance in the battle against Zhang Shicheng (1321–1367), his archrival, that was to ensure his lordship over China. Emphasizing the supernatural power of Heaven, and his own benevolent efforts to nurture the people, he tried to persuade the river god to support him:

> God, [you] follow the clear orders of Heaven, and are in charge of the river. [Your] investigations and judgments are disinterested when you are performing Heaven's commands. I was born in Haoliang and was a commoner. Because of the revolt, I joined the rank and file and became a commander. Since that time, my soldiers and people increased and more territories were acquired. Thus, I ascended to the throne of a king (*wang*), and built the nation of Wu in Jiangnan. [There] I opened up land, broadened my domain, purged the states of the fierce and the ruthless; [I] cared about the soldiers, nurtured the people, and eradicated governments which had become corrupted. By now, eleven years have passed. At this point, Zhang Shicheng of Gusu provinces [and his army] is situated at my southeast border, and has always caused bloodshed.
>
> I have heard that, in all times, when the people wanted to have peace, there would be only one sage-ruler; when the people wanted to be sad, there were many warlords. I cannot

> afford to have more dealings with Zhang . . . [and I have to] have a decisive battle with him, so that I can give peace to the people. [I understand that] the final decision is made by Heaven, but the actions are done by men. [Like] the deep abysses and enormous mountains silting up rivers and lakes; [these momentous] things cannot be made by human efforts in brief times. To fight the decisive battles with Zhang, I ordered the commanders to lead the armada away from the neighboring land and to enter Lake Taihu through the winding rivers. I inform God of my intention.[28]

Emperor Taizu made it clear that he had to win the battle by his navy and strategy, but he also needed the river god's help and impartiality. If the prayer was a religious activity, and the motive, military and political, the immediate effect on Taizu himself was probably more of an emotional catharsis. The god of the river may or may not have helped with the battle, but the prayer was obviously a means to soothe Taizu's anxiety over the military outcome, which would make or break his quest to control China. He won.[29]

Among all of Taizu's state sacrifices, those offered to the imperial ancestors were particularly revealing of his emotional being and personal memories of his parents, whose grace and guidance, Taizu believed, helped build the Ming empire. In a 1368 decree, he said, "I had been originally a commoner of Huaizuo, but I had received the grace of Heaven and the assistance of ancestors," so that I was able to build a new empire.[30] Nevertheless, Taizu's memories of his ancestors were filled with sadness, which were often refreshed and released by sacrificial activities. Returning from a sacrifice to the ancestors in May 1367, Taizu wept without stopping and told Diarist Zan Tong (fl. 1350–1374), "My father died on the sixth of this month; my brother died on the ninth; my mother died on the twenty-second. In one month, there were three successive deaths in the family. When life encounters such [bad luck], how can one bear it? It is an eternal pain and the extreme of frustrated feelings."[31]

Even near the end of his life, Taizu's emotions and gratitude toward his ancestors persisted. In April 1398, when Taizu was leaving the formal hall of imperial ancestors after performing the seasonal sacrifices there, he pointed to the trees and told his attendants, "Years ago, I planted these trees; without my realizing it, they have now become a forest. The trees by the imperial tombs of my ancestors should also be like this now."[32] As the trees triggered a rush of filial emotions in Taizu, tears fell from his eyes.[33] Next month, in May 1398, after performing a ceremony honoring his ancestors, he described how the spirit of his father helped him:

> I just returned [to the palace] after performing the ceremony of setting the spirit-tablets of the ancestors in the newly finished ancestral temple. I rested and dreamt my father was calling to me about trouble in the southwest. I awoke up and went to meet with the officials. There was in fact a report of such charges. The ancestors are divine and are watching from above; there is no time when they are not present.[34]

Taizu understood the nature and functions of ritual and music thoroughly, and he practiced them with religious fervor and complex emotions. Thus, his demand of sincerity and respectfulness in ritual and musical performances reflected not only orthodox prescriptions but also personal involvement. On January 3, 1368, the day prior to the performance of the sacrificial ceremony in the south suburb of the capital, and of his ascension to the throne, he warned the officials:

> People should devote their whole hearts to Heaven. If there is insincerity, be it as thin as a hair, indolence will take advantage. If there is a lack of respectfulness, be it short as the twinkling of an eye, selfish desires will fill the gap. To reach Heaven and Earth and to impress the deities takes only sincerity and respectfulness. People should not think that Heaven is high and far away and that the spirits and gods are hidden so that human beings can [afford to] have a negligent attitude. Though Heaven is high, it watches closely; though the spirits and gods are hidden, they would appear if they want. [If one] understands that the principles of [serving] Heaven and [of serving] people are similar in kind, then the respectfulness and sincerity in his heart will not allow the smallest negligence. Now, that the time of the great sacrifice is approaching, all the officials involved in the event should be careful.[35]

Acting as an emperor and moral leader, Taizu used the authority of Confucius to lecture on ritual sincerity and respectfulness. In 1373, he addressed the officials of the Court of Imperial Sacrifices:

> The way of worshipping the gods is with sincerity and respectfulness. Confucius said: 'Worship the gods as if they are present.' Be there but one hair short of complete sincerity and respectfulness, the deities will not accept [the offerings], so that all the sacrificial animals and offerings become but meaningless things. Then, how can one perform the sacrifices? Since I assumed the throne, I dare not be negligent in the way of serving the gods. I always warn myself to ensure sincerity. You, officials of the Court of Imperial Sacrifices whose duties are to prepare for the ceremonials, should cultivate yourselves and be cautious in the implementation of my worshipping of the gods.[36]

TAIZU'S CREATIVE DEEDS IN STATE SACRIFICES AND MUSIC

Taizu's emphasis on ritual sincerity and respectfulness dictated that his state sacrifices should satisfy his needs, not simply follow orthodox models. Taizu could not be sincere if he did not follow his heart's desires in implementing the state ritual and music. Thus, Taizu promoted the virtues as a classical and authoritative justification for his creative implementation of the state ritual and music. When ordering sacrificial paraphernalia for the imperial ancestral temple in 1368, for example, Taizu asked that the articles be designed as if they were to serve living ancestors; he explained:

> If the present world cannot function like ancient ones, the ancient worlds cannot operate like ours. When ritual follows the emotions of the participants, there can be justified changes. [Indeed,] what is esteemed is the appropriateness of the adjustments. [And because of the changing times,] there must be adjustments. Recent generations have stubbornly followed ancient models [of ritual], and preferred to use [antiquated] utensils such as the bamboo baskets and wooden platters in sacrifices to their ancestors. [However,] as [the ancestors] did not use those utensils when they were alive, [asking them] to use those utensils now that they are dead seems meaningless. [This is why] Confucius said: "Serve the dead as if they were alive; serve those who have disappeared as if they are present."[37]

The officials followed the imperial wish. They plated silver utensils with gold; they prepared wine decanters and goblets in sets of eight, red lacquer bowls and trays in sets of 240. They also prepared complete sets of cloth hangers, pillows, straw mattress and other daily utensils for the imperial ancestors.[38] Taizu's sacrificial utensils are both orthodox and creative. He followed orthodox requirements to prepare the right types and numbers of ritual utensils for the imperial ancestral temple. He was nevertheless creative in understanding Confucius' words literally—that the dead ancestors should be served as if they were living—and had the ritual utensils designed as though they would serve daily purposes. The presence of such ritual utensils, not the orthodox bamboo baskets and wooden trays, was distinctive and expressive of Taizu's intentions and interpretations.[39]

Taizu's creativity with state ritual and music is most apparent in his drastic changes of the suburban sacrifices that exploited the ambiguities and conflicts inherent in the practice of the ceremonials. To understand Taizu's creative exploitation, the basic problems and ambiguities of the suburban sacrifices should be briefly introduced here. Literally, suburban sacrifices refer to the sacrificial ceremonies performed at altars built in suburbs of the capital. Thus the term refers to at least four ceremonials:

1. The state sacrifice to Heaven, the sacrificial ceremony of which is performed at a round-mound-altar built in the southern suburb of the capital
2. The state sacrifice to Earth, the sacrificial ceremony of which is performed at a square-marsh-altar built in the northern suburb of the capital
3. The state sacrifice to the sun, the sacrificial ceremony of which is performed at an altar built in the eastern suburb
4. The state sacrifice to the moon, the sacrificial ceremony of which is performed at an altar built in the western suburb[40]

Two of these four sacrificial ceremonies were usually celebrated on specific days: to Heaven on winter solstice and to Earth on summer solstice. The sacrificial ceremonials offered to the sun and moon were observed in spring or in both spring and autumn; the actual days of performance varied.

As practiced throughout Chinese history, the suburban sacrifices were always dominated by the one worshipping Heaven. Thus, suburban sacrifices may be narrowly interpreted as those offered only to Heaven.

Whether the suburban sacrifices are perceived broadly or narrowly, however, the nature of the ceremonials can become ambiguous in actual realizations: A sacrificial ceremony offered to Heaven not only worships Heaven, but also some combinations of the following deities or deified persons as Heaven's companions and followers—the Earth, sun, moon, founders of dynasties, fathers of the current emperors, and a pantheon of other heavenly and earthly deities.

As worshipping these deities involves numerous adjustments and coordination among different state sacrifices and among different ceremonies that constitute a complex ceremonial, the nature of the suburban sacrifices is always a contentious subject. In other words, the practice of the suburban sacrifices was never a straightforward application of orthodox prescriptions but an intricate process in which the concerned participants juggled diverse and often conflicting considerations—theoretical definitions, historical examples, particular contextual restraints, personal needs, and so forth.

The concerned participants must arbitrarily decide for themselves how they want to realize the suburban sacrifices: even with the comprehensive prescriptions in ritual manuals, there are still no easy and definitive answers about how the ceremonials should be practiced. An illustrative example is the issue of whether worshipping Heaven and Earth should be performed as one or two ceremonials. This is a dilemma for Chinese court citizens, because it represents conflicting elements in what should be a cosmologically coordinated world. Every court citizen would know that Heaven, the yang (male, father) element, is distinct from Earth, the yin (female, mother) element; thus it is appropriate to honor the deities separately. However, the court citizen would also know that yin and yang operate as a pair of cosmological elements, and the father and mother function as a united family; thus it is inappropriate to honor the deities separately.

Taizu and his officials soon encountered the problems of the suburban sacrifices in their efforts to institute a perfect system of state ritual and music. From 1368 to 1369, the first two years of the Ming dynasty, they honored Heaven and Earth with individual ceremonials. However, they soon found it was insufficient to venerate the sun, moon, deities of the twelve horary branches, and time divisions as Heaven's followers. Thus the officials proposed to install individual state sacrifices to the sun and moon. They reasoned that, as natural forces, the sun and the moon ranked only after Heaven and Earth, and that, to appreciate the operation of the yin and yang forces of the cosmos, sacrifices should be offered to the sun and moon on summer and autumn equinoxes.[41] Furthermore, to complete the worship of heavenly deities, the officials proposed a supplementary sacrificial ceremony to honor the stars in the altar to the moon. As the proposal was theoretically sound and developed from classical ideas, it was accepted and implemented. Such implementation of the suburban sacrifices was however orthodox in concept but creative in practice. Many details, such as worshipping the deities of the twelve horary branches and the time divisions as Heaven's followers, were Ming innovations.

Performing the suburban sacrifices as a series of four ceremonials was theoretically desirable and expressive of the court's pursuit to emulate ancient models. Nevertheless, the performances tested the energy of the emperor. In 1377, Taizu opted to combine the state sacrifices to Heaven and Earth into one ceremonial and scheduled its performance in spring at the altar compound in the southern suburb. The gist of his arguments was simple yet powerful: If Heaven and Earth were like father and mother to him, it would not be proper to separate them in the south and north altars, so that they could never join with one another.[42] Needless to say, Taizu's wish of honoring Heaven and Earth together was promptly implemented, as the practice had many historical precedents.

Taizu also introduced a change of venue and date, which attested to his creativity and personal concerns: He decided to perform the combined ceremonial indoors and on a spring day. For the last ten years, he had been bothered by the ominous signs of unexpected rain, capricious wind, and shady clouds that appeared during performances of state sacrifices. Correlating fine weather with ritual success, Taizu believed state sacrifices could not be efficacious if they were performed during undesirable weather, so he ordered the new timing for the ceremonial and the building of a large hall to accommodate its performances. To justify his creative schedule and venue, Taizu challenged the validity of the orthodox timing, questioning why Heaven and Earth, the most yang and yin elements, were, respectively, worshipped during winter and summer solstices, the most yin and yang days.[43] To rest his case, Taizu criticized stubborn adherence to orthodoxy and charged as follows:

> [Scholars have] theorized that the worship of Heaven and Earth emphasized [sincere] substance over elaborate [forms], but they followed ancient models stubbornly, and resisted changes. Until today, sacrifices to Heaven and Earth do not vary among different

> participants. If ritual followed ancient practices without changes, I would question, whether people should also hang on to their ancient ways and resist any changes. If people hang on to their ancient ways [of living], then they should drink natural water with cupped hands, eat raw meat and blood, and live in nests and caves. Are [such ways of living] possible now? I don't think so.[44]

Taizu's arguments convinced his court, and his wishes were fully realized in 1380, when a new hall of great sacrifices (*Dasidian*) was built on the old site of the round-mound-altar in the south suburb of the capital. Performing state sacrifices during the spring and indoors was not an idea totally without precedents; state sacrifices to imperial ancestors were always performed indoors, and spring was the time for many ceremonials.

Still, Taizu's solution of the combined ceremonial blurred the orthodox boundaries between indoor and outdoor sacrifices and stretched the perceptions about what suburban sacrifices should be. It is noteworthy that Taizu did not implement his changes by sheer imperial force but by attacking the conflicts over ritual intentions and form and stressing the orthodox emphasis on sincerity. Even the Son of Heaven had to camouflage his creative efforts in state sacrifices and music. Taizu's solution began a new stage in the system of Ming state sacrifices and music, which lasted until 1530, when they were drastically revised by Shizong, the eleventh Ming emperor, who was passionately concerned with ritual matters. Thus, the Ming performance of the combined sacrifice in spring inside the hall of great sacrifices represented and perpetuated Taizu's efforts to institute a proper but highly personal system for his empire. As a ritual architecture, the hall of great sacrifices and its copy in Beijing, which existed until 1530, stood as a creative and expressive testimony of Taizu's success in establishing the Ming empire. (See Figure 3.1.)

If Taizu's combined ceremonial and the hall of great sacrifices lasted only 151 years, his creative institution of the Office of State Sacrificial Music (*shenyue guan*) continued until 1911, when imperial China collapsed. Since the Han dynasty, state sacrificial music was always directly controlled and practiced by officials and musicians of the Court of Imperial Sacrifices (*taichangsi*). In 1379, Taizu changed that tradition by establishing a new office and by entrusting its administration to Daoist monk/musicians. In fact, the emperor's trust of the Daoists was so strong that he allowed the title of the office to reflect its Daoist association. The last word in the Chinese title of the office, that is "*guan*," usually means a Daoist

Figure 3.1.
The temple compound for the Ming state sacrifice to Heaven and Earth (MHD 81.22)

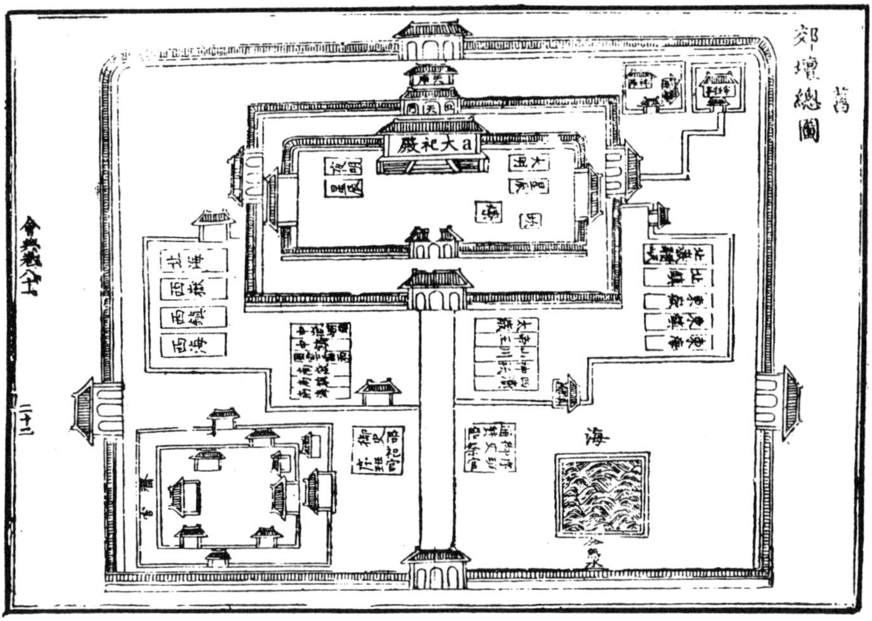

a. the hall of great sacrifices. The Chinese characters written in front of the "hall" represent supplementary altars.

temple. Taizu also allowed for the continuity of the Daoist-musical tradition in the office by giving the Daoist-officials the privileges of accepting apprentices.[45] To ensure that the Daoists performed their musical duties, the emperor had the office located inside the altar compound in the southern suburb of the capital and built the hall of great harmony (*Taihe dian*) to accommodate musical rehearsals.

Realizing that many emperors in the past only employed Daoists to perform private ceremonies to achieve longevity/immortality, Taizu declared that his employment was different, stressing that he recruited them because they were "purified." In his mind, the superlative Daoist monks were superhuman: they cultivated their bodies and minds in isolated places, observed the sky days and nights, rectified wrongs in the world, and performed benevolent deeds; they could spiritually roam between the limits of the cosmos, and they could always communicate with the deities.

Knowing that his appointees were not as powerful as those superlative ones, Taizu was still convinced that they had acquired a purified mental state and could well serve the deities and manage the musical affairs of the office.[46] Thus, he described his appointments as assigning superhuman (*xian*) officials to take care of music for the deities. If Taizu's action was creative, his correlation of the Daoists with sacrificial music was cosmologically sound and not without historical precedent.[47] To many Confucian scholar-officials, however, the appointments entrusted a means of governance and self-cultivation into the hands of their rivals, the Daoists. Consequently, the Confucian scholar-officials in the Ming court were always dissatisfied with the music and the Daoist monk/musicians. The rivalry between the Confucians and Daoists became a distinctive element in the history of state sacrificial music in the Ming court.

TAIZU'S LEGACY OF STATE SACRIFICES AND MUSIC

Taizu's creative interpretation and application of the Confucian ideology and orthodox prescriptions of state sacrifices and music led to a unique system, which became, after Taizu's death, an orthodox legacy for his descendants. Detail changes and adjustments were made only when necessitated by contextual factors. In 1399, when Emperor Hui, the second Ming ruler and Taizu's grandson, offered the state sacrifice to Heaven and Earth for the first time after his ascension, he installed Taizu as Heaven's companion in that ceremony. The change was simple, expected, and expressive: it showed Emperor Hui's gratitude to his grandfather, who founded the empire and bequeathed the Ming throne to him. The adjusted state sacrifice also became Emperor Hui's personal expression, not just a ceremonial instituted by his grandfather.

Chengzu, the third Ming ruler, brought great changes to the empire by seizing, in 1402, the throne from Emperor Hui, his nephew, and by moving the capital, in 1421, from Nanjing to Beijing. Nevertheless, Chengzu kept Taizu's system of state sacrifices and music. As reported in extant court documents, he made only two detail changes. To show his gratitude to the deity of Mountain Tianshou, who lorded over the mountains situated to the north of Beijing, Chengzu installed the deity as a follower in the state sacrifice to Heaven and Earth.[48] He also left the state sacrifice to the meritorious sovereigns of past dynasties in the hands of the Nanjing officials. The changes were subtle but expressive. The presence of the deity of

Mountain Tianshou indicated not only the new site of the Ming capital but also the fact that Chengzu built his military power in that area.

Chengzu's understanding of the state sacrifices and music was essentially similar to Taizu's: The state ritual and music were not only means of governance and self-cultivation, but also of personal expressions. In May 1421, a few months after Chengzu settled in the new capital, Beijing, three halls in the palace were destroyed by fire. The incident was considered an omen, warning Chengzu that he might have offended the deities and might lose their protection. Extremely disturbed, he immediately issued a decree to request help by listing all possible wrongdoings, the first of which concerned, significantly, the state sacrifices:

> [Because] of the fire at the three halls, my heart is frightened, and I do not know what to do. It has been suggested that there may have been negligence in the performance of the sacrifices to Heaven and the other gods, or violations of the founder's legacy, or abuses in the government. . . . If there are wrongs in my deeds, you must itemize them without concealment, so that I can strive to reform and to revive the favor of Heaven.[49]

Chengzu's words echo Taizu's understanding of state ritual and music with a new nuance—Taizu's legacy should not be violated. Indeed, Taizu's system of state sacrifices and music remained essentially intact until 1530, when Shizong managed to implement a drastic revision. Shizong's ideas and applications were, however, fundamentally similar to those of Taizu's; the dissimilarities and Shizong's creativity lie more in the ritual and musical particulars than in the basic structure of the ceremonials or their orthodox principles. In fact, Shizong was successful because he presented his revisions as accurate applications of orthodox prescriptions.

CHAPTER FOUR

Shizong's Sericultural Ceremonials

PRELUDE

As the founder of an empire, Taizu had the license and opportunity to project his creative understanding into his state sacrifices and music. His descendants were in less favorable positions: they had to deal with the orthodoxy of not only the Confucian tradition but also that of Taizu's legacy of state ritual and music. However, most Ming emperors had little reason or need to overhaul Taizu's system; they were satisfied with very subtle changes, ritual or musical, structural or performative. Shizong's case was different: he drastically revised, in the 1530s and 1540s, Taizu's system of state sacrifices and music, producing new and adjusted ceremonials, eliciting strong emotional and critical responses from all who were concerned.

Shizong's revised state ritual and music were deliberate results of complex processes in which the emperor, his supporters, and rivals conducted rigorous research, negotiated with vehement arguments, acted with strategic maneuvers, and made their bids to appropriate the state ritual and music. Thus, Shizong's revised state ritual and music were neither straightforward applications of orthodox prescriptions nor uninhibited realizations of creative and emotional impulses; they were simultaneously orthodox and creative, and expressive of specific meanings in Shizong's court. To illustrate this nature of the revised state ritual and music, and the process in which they took shape, the institution of Shizong's sericultural ceremonials will be described here.[1] To convey the emotional and expressive nuances in the participants' understandings of the state ritual and music, long passages from the *Veritable Records of Shizong* (*Shizong suhuangdi shilu*), the primary source of this discussion, will be quoted.[2]

The genesis of Shizong's sericultural ceremonials can be traced to the beginning of the emperor's reign. Shizong, who had been born a prince in the princely establishment in Anlu of the Hubei province, was handed, in 1521, the Ming throne when his predecessor and cousin Wuzong died without an heir. Once Shizong accepted the throne, his genealogical relationships with Wuzong and his biological father became a serious ritual problem. As argued by Yang Tinghe (1459–1529) and other senior officials of the time, Shizong should have abandoned his own genealogical line and accepted that of Wuzong's to become an heir to the imperial line. Such an arrangement would, however, entail many ritual and psychological adjustments, including, for example, changing the ritual status of Shizong's biological father to that of an imperial uncle. Being particularly sensitive to ritual propriety and emotionally attached to his biological father, Shizong resisted that arrangement. His position was clear from the very beginning. When he arrived at the capital gates in April 1521, he refused to enter the city immediately and to be welcomed as an heir apparent (*huang taizi*); he wanted and was received as a reigning emperor.

To underscore both the legitimacy of his emperorship and his own genealogical line, Shizong tried fervently to honor his deceased father with ceremonials and titles. Needless to say, the emperor's efforts would also consolidate his own political power and authority in the court. After many confrontations with court officials who opposed his efforts, the ritual-political crisis of 1524, labeled the Great Rite Controversy, erupted.[3] The court became divided and morale was low as supporters of the emperor were promoted and opponents rebuked.

Eventually calm prevailed for a few years, but the issues of the status and nature of ceremonials and titles honoring the emperor's biological father remained touchy. Realizing that ceremonials were an effective means to demonstrate and exercise his authority and power, Shizong wanted to revise and appropriate the Ming system of state sacrifices and music to match his needs and understanding of the issues. At the same time, Taizu's system of state ritual and music also needed to have its expressiveness updated after one and one-half centuries of use. Indeed, appeals to revise the state ritual and music had emerged. As early as June 1527, Liao Daonan (?–1547) had proposed some revisions.[4] In December 1529, Minister of Rites Li Shi (1471–1538) requested that the *Collected Ceremonial of the Ming Dynasty* be published as a reference work to guide discussions of ritual and music. The immediate trigger to

Shizong's revision of the 1530s and 1540s, however, came from an official's proposal to institute the sericultural ceremonials.

The sericultural ceremonials were, of course, no more than an excuse to begin revising the Ming ritual system drastically. Shizong wanted to reorganize the suburban sacrifices, splitting the combined sacrifice to Heaven and Earth into two independent ceremonials, each with its own companions. Shizong's desire was inseparable from his efforts to honor his biological father, because the selection of companions for the ceremonials would involve imperial ancestors and would have direct and indirect impacts on the ritual status of the father. Indeed, as the revision unfolded, Shizong eventually honored his father as Heaven's companion in the state sacrifice to Heaven and to the imperial father (*daxiang*), a ceremonial that was supposedly an emulation of an ancient ritual practiced in the hall of brightness (*mingtang*).[5] Thus, issues in Shizong's revision rapidly transcended questions of ritual propriety and ambiguity, but developed into ideological conflicts and clashes of political strategies and factions. Indeed, the state sacrifices were not merely a realization of Confucian ideology and values, but also of the means and expressions of the intellectual, emotional, and political struggles among the court citizens. While many scholar-officials sincerely supported or loyally opposed the emperor's actions, the issues often were confused by misunderstandings and sycophantic sought for personal gains. In such an environment, the sericultural ceremonials came into being.

SHIZONG'S SERICULTURAL CEREMONIALS

On February 12, 1530, Xia Yan (1482–1548), then a chief supervising secretary of the Ministry of Personnel (*like du jishizhong*), who had little direct contact with the emperor, proposed to the throne to institute the sericultural ceremonials.[6] Positioning himself as a scholar-official aspiring to implement the Confucian ideology of ritual and music, Xia Yan presented his proposal as a means to help the emperor achieve his goal of becoming a virtuous and exemplary ruler. Xia Yan had earlier reported similar ideas to the court but this time he appealed to the throne directly, claiming he was inspired by the emperor's recent performance of the state sacrifice to Heaven. Presenting detailed observations, Xia Yan's memorial is theoretically persuasive and emotionally revealing. It reads:

[After being] dispatched [by the government] to investigate the farming land near the capital, I have recently proposed to employ the various imperial lands as places to process silkworms and as gardens to cultivate mulberry trees. [I have also requested the government] to order officials from the appropriate bureaus to plant mulberry trees [in those lands] in preparations for the sericultural ceremonials within the palace. [So far], no actions have been carried out.

Ten days ago, Your Majesty performed the great sacrificial ceremony to Heaven in the southern suburb, and I was privileged to be in your company, although I am only a lowly official. I looked up to Your Majesty and found Your Majesty performing the sacrifice to the deities respectfully and seriously. [Even before that day, Your Majesty showed the same sincerity and emphasis in ritual matters.] Your Majesty postponed the date of the seasonal sacrifices to the imperial ancestors until after that performed in the suburbs; [Your Majesty] worshipped Heaven before the celebration on New Year's Day; and [Your Majesty] prayed, last winter, for snow in the altar [in the southern suburb]. [Before the recent sacrifice to Heaven], Your Majesty avoided the grand halls in the palace, fasted with simple meals, reduced the number of military escorts for the trip to the round-mound-altar, and declined to have officials keep company with you during the sacrificial ceremony. That Your Majesty was penitent for the empire was clearly [expressed] in the text of the prayer. The officials, who assisted with the sacrificial ceremony, witnessed Your Majesty's solemn and public efforts to serve Heaven and to care kindly for the people; [they knew Your Majesty's efforts were] done in all possible earnest.

As my overwhelmed emotions [caused by witnessing Your Majesty's performance] subsided, I humbly thought that my earlier proposal to institute the sericultural ceremonials may also contribute to Your Majesty's efforts in paying respect to Heaven and caring for the people. Besides, [the proposed actions] would carry on the founder's institution of state sacrifices, and would remedy the present lack of the sericultural ceremonials. Since the industries of agriculture and sericulture provide food and clothing for all, it is not proper to exclude

> singly the sacrifice and the ritual exercises [related to sericulture]. [Furthermore], because the ceremonials of agriculture and sericulture are models for future generations, it is improper to neglect [one of] them.
>
> If Your Majesty accepts my proposal, please order the officials in the Ministry of Rites to meet and discuss the matters, and command the scholar-officials to research and design [the performance procedures]. Once they are properly practiced, the whole world and all future generations will look upon them in admiration.[7]

Shizong was pleased with the proposal because it would advantageously support his wishes to revise the ritual system, expanding the suburban sacrifices into four independent ceremonials. Immediately, he showed Xia Yan's memorial to the Grand Academician Zhang Cong (1475–1539) and sent an edict to the Ministry of Rites, commanding the officials to study historical models and implement the proposal. The emperor also explained that he was interested in the ceremonials as a means to realize his desire to emulate benevolent sovereigns of ancient times. His move was shrewd; he acted as if he was following up on a meritorious appeal by an official.

Zhang Cong and other officials of the Ministry of Rites quickly responded. They immediately drafted a plan according to orthodox prescriptions of sericultural ceremonials and presented it to the emperor. The officials said:

> [We propose to] build the altar to the progenitor of sericulture outside Anding Gate, [the northernmost gate of the capital], with a design similar to that of the [altar to] the progenitor of agriculture. On the four sides of the proposed altar, there will be the terrace of picking mulberry leaves, the workshops of sericulture, and the abstention halls. The location and design of the terrace of picking mulberry leaves will be patterned after the field for the exercise of farming inside the altar compound for the progenitor of agriculture; the abstention halls, after those in the round-mound-altar compound but on a smaller scale. By the abstention halls, there will be twenty-seven workshops of sericulture where the silkworms will be washed.

> [The exercise of picking mulberry leaves] should imitate that of farming. After the empress's picking of two silkworms, the wives of the three dukes (*sangong*) will pick five; the wives of the other nobles and the nine chief ministers will pick nine. As the final acts of the exercise, a score of women selected from among the commoners will receive the leaves and wash the silkworms inside the workshops of sericulture.[8]

As drafted by Zhang Cong and his colleagues, the plan for the pending sericultural ceremonials was sketchy and predictable; it was a quick response to an imperial command and impartial attempt to formulate a ceremonial according to orthodox and historical models. The officials' recommendations, however, showed no creativity to solve contemporary and practical problems. Huo Tao (1487–1540), Supervisor of the Household Administration of the Heir Apparent (*zanshifu zanshi*), found the recommendations faulty because he realized the issues of protocol and other practical complications caused by the physical distance between the palace and the chosen site. He pointed out that the empress and her entourage could not stay overnight outside the palace and that they could not go to the site, perform the ritual, and return to the palace within one day. Thus, he declared that Zhang Cong's recommendations had only "external appearance but no substance": The empress and the court ladies could not take the trip and perform the recommended ceremonials, even though it was their personal participation that would render the ritual meaningful. Huo Tao pleaded for the selection of a site near the palace.[9]

Shizong was not pleased, and he refuted Huo Tao's arguments by reiterating an orthodox and theoretical understanding of the issues:

> Agriculture and sericulture are sources of food and clothing, and are the preparatory steps towards an ideal empire. That an emperor farms in the southern suburb and an empress cultivates silkworms in the northern suburb is an institution which does not change in ten-thousand generations. How can you, who have long understood ritual, say what you have said? Moreover, going to the suburbs to perform sacrifices is an institution practiced since ancient times. It is not to be measured by long or short distances. If the sericultural ceremonials are performed inside the palace, I am afraid, they cannot become models for later generations.[10]

The Ministry of Revenue also opposed the proposed site, describing it as conveniently flat and wide, but inconveniently wanting water that was needed to wash the silkworms. Citing Tang and Song practices of performing the ceremonials inside the palace, the ministry recommended a site in the Western Imperial Garden that was located south of the palace, where there was water from the Lake of Pure Nectar and the Beautiful Island (*Taiyi qiongdao*).

Concerned about his plans to expand the suburban sacrifices, the emperor rejected the ministry's proposal. He contested, "In the ritual system of the Zhou dynasty, the ceremonials of farming and sericulture were respectively performed in the southern and northern suburbs. That the Tang people may have been satisfied with an imperfect solution should not be taken as a precedent." Then he accused the officials of being inconsistent in their choosing a site for the future altar, and he commanded them to reexamine the issues and report to him. Shizong was determined that the ceremonials be performed in the northern suburb, but he knew that his motives were being questioned and that a ritual-political battle was developing. Thus, he issued a long edict, defending his views by trying to fend off further criticisms. His edict reads:

> The saying "*yimou wucheng*" means that one needs not solve a matter when one has doubts and has reached no conclusions. Xia Yan's proposal to institute the sericultural ceremonials and your memorials of yesterday have presented [the pros and cons about the matter] in great detail. This matter [of the ceremonials] has been on my mind for a long time. I am pleased with Xia Yan's proposal, and I do not have any doubts about the conclusions. This is why I am writing to tell you that I have decided and I have not been misled [by Xia Yan]. Regarding Huo Tao and his ideas, I have sent him my comments. However, I am afraid, once his memorial is made known, discussion will inevitably reach a point where his comments will be used as an excuse to attack the government and to cause trouble.
>
> As stated in Xia Yan's proposal, the industries of agriculture and sericulture would provide food and clothing for the people. [Thus,] it is not proper to leave out [the sericultural ceremonials]. As the ceremonials of agriculture and sericulture are models for all future generations, it is improper to neglect [one of] them. This explanation has all the reasoning needed and

there are no other [motives]. What[ever proposals or arguments] that I have accepted are just that, not anything else.

Besides, the institution of ritual and music by the sovereign is the pure and ancient way [of governance]. This is why Confucius has said similar words to teach all later generations. If people's good nature persists, [the words of Confucius] should [be followed] without any changes. However, people's [improper] desires are getting completely out of control.

Now, five criticisms have been lodged against me. First, the founder's institution [of ritual and music] had been completed and has been followed by all subsequent emperors now departed; [thus], why should I add [new ceremonials]? Second, the founder did not make these [sericultural] ceremonials, and all the deceased emperors dared not propose them. Why do I dare to create them? Third, if the empress will not even adventure to go beyond the Meridian Gate, how could she go as far as the northern suburb? If these [activities] were not something the ancestors did in their times, why should they be instituted now? Is it not an offense to the legacy of the ancestors? Fourth, did the founder not know that ritual and music derive from the creator of an empire? His saintly planning and sage considerations already had finality. [The institution of ritual] does not need my actions and it is not something I should do. Thus am I not being presumptive? Fifth, when people inside the palace were asked about [the proposed ceremonials], some answered that the implementation would be difficult; some said that they had never heard of the ceremonials in the previous reigns; some would just knit their brows [to show their doubts].

For the time being, [what] evil people [might say] cannot go beyond these five accusations. If they do, then, [they] would use the fear of calamities and portents [as an excuse]. Beyond these, no other arguments can be fabricated. This is why I order you, my officials, to discuss [the matter] and respond with a well prepared proposal.[11]

After such strong words, the officials conceded and replied with the following solution on the problem of the distance and with a fourfold plan to implement the proposed ceremonials:

Some officials wanted to have the ceremonials performed within the palace because they were afraid that the distance [to the altar compound] was too far. We, your officials, were concerned about this [point] in the beginning. [We have now found a solution.] It is true that the distance is far if [the ladies] leave the palace from the Daming Gate [i.e. the central and southern-most gate of imperial city] and go to [the altar] outside the Anding Gate. [However,] if the ladies leave the palace from Tonghua [or] Xuanwu Gates [i.e. the east and northern-most gates of the palace, the distance is not that far, and] such changes will not nullify [one's efforts in emulating] ancient practices.

After examining the matter thoroughly, we propose a fourfold implementation of the ceremonials. The first [is] the addition of the exercise of processing the silkworm cocoons. If there is one for the picking of mulberry leaves, but none for the processing of silkworm cocoons, the series of ceremonies is incomplete; [thus, we recommend the addition of the latter.] Once the cocoons have matured, they will be transported from the northern suburb to within the palace by appointed officials. A site inside the palace will be cleared for building the appropriate workshops to process the cocoons and weave the silk threads. The "three-bowl-hand" (*sanpen shou*) ceremony will be performed as the finale of the silk-processing exercises.

The second [is] to fix the directions [and other problems] of the altar compound. The altar of the progenitor of sericulture and the terrace of picking of mulberry leaves will be modeled entirely after the altar of the progenitor of agriculture and the field of the farming exercises. The altar of the progenitor of sericulture faces north; the terrace of picking mulberry leaves faces east. [This design] follows Tang practices.

The third [is] to design the utensils for picking mulberry leaves. According to Tang practices, once the empress arrives [at the terrace], she is presented with gold hooks [to perform the ritual act; however, we do not recommend this]. Since the silk-processing exercises are for appreciating the difficult tasks of the females, [the use of] gold hooks seems extravagant. We recommend that bamboo hooks be used and be made like those used by the commoners; they should not be too ornate to insure that the ritual message is not lost.

> The fourth [is] to choose the administrators for the altar compound [and for the trip of the empress]. During the empress' trip to the [northern] suburb, all requisite decorum and formalities must be directed by the palace attendants; [this is] to implement solemn and strict standards [of behavior] of the inner court. We beg the selection [and appointment] of honest and mature eunuchs from the Directorate of Ceremonial as administrators.[12]

The emperor accepted the proposal, but made a couple of recommendations:

> I recommend that, as a convenience, the empress leave the palace from Xuanwu Gate to perform the sacrificial ceremony to the progenitor of sericulture. I would order officials of the inner court to prepare 10,000 soldiers; 5,000 of them will guard the altar compound and the others will be escorts on the road. A site in the West Imperial Garden will be opened for the building of the workshops for the ceremonies of [processing of the cocoons] and weaving of the silk thread, the latter of which concludes the silk-processing exercises. The design of the altar compound will follow that for the progenitor of agriculture; however, the scale of the former will be decreased to nine-tenths of the latter. The numerical [proportions of the altar compound] will use [ratios of] even numbers. The abstention halls need not be built. Only the halls for donning the sacrificial costumes, the workshops for sericulture and for the cocoon processing will be built in accordance with ancient prescriptions.[13]

Thus, the sericultural ceremonials approached realization. Before being implemented, however, responses from other officials arrived. In a memorial, Minister of War Li Chengxun requested that the government realize ritual aspirations into concrete actions. His memorial is idealistic, but it demonstrates how well Ming scholar-officials knew historical practices, and how ritual and daily realities could be merged through creative and associative interpretations. Li's memorial reads:

> It is not that the ceremonials of agriculture and sericulture had not been performed since the three ancient dynasties, but rather that they had all been done hastily, and were unworthy of being

described. The only exception was during the second year of Han Wendi, when the farming exercises was decreed, together with a fifty percent reduction in land taxes. Thus, at that time, [production of] food and clothing increased and punishments were seldom needed. I beg Your Majesty to take that as a model. Through these two things, Your Majesty can think of the commoners' extreme difficulties in procuring food and clothing. All [Your Majesty's actions] should emphasize the basics of [governance] and suppress trivialities.

During banquets or leisure times, when Your Majesty notices things like draperies, costumes and [materials used in] chariots, Your Majesty should consider whether any brocades show extravagances and licentiousness, [the production of which brings] suffering to the female workers. When Your Majesty observes equipment, chariots, etc., Your Majesty should reflect upon any presentation of pearls, jades, and extravagant things that are wasteful and harmful to the farmers' [economy]. When Your Majesty enjoys rich [meals of] meat and other foods, Your Majesty should remember the barren years and famines, and those people who have no food and clothing and cannot peacefully remain in their fields. When the officials report criminal cases and ask for judicial decisions, Your Majesty should ponder whether there is so much more punishment than cultivation of virtues that the innocent people do not know what to follow. Your Majesty should inspect the officials inside and outside of the court, promote those who truly care for the people, and dismiss those who are treacherous and have no integrity.

The unoccupied lands in the field for the ceremony of farming can be used for farming; the embankments of government roads can be used to grow mulberry trees. [These measures] should be carried out in places near the capital, and along the coast, and should be extended to the whole empire.

[Your Majesty should] order the officials who recruit workers to encourage the tilling of deserted lands by taxing them lightly, and entice, with loans of oxen and seeds, those farmers who have fled and lost their fields. Everything that is beneficial to farming and sericulture should be done; everything that is harmful to them should be abolished. Then, when

> there is ample food and clothing, propriety and courtesy can arise, the civilizing of the people will flourish, and punishing, will be restrained.[14]

The emperor sent the memorial to the responsible offices for discussions. By March 1530, the construction of the altar compound was underway, and plans for the ritual buildings took shape.[15] The altar of the progenitor of sericulture was to be square. with 30.6 feet on each side and two tiers rising to a height of 3.06 feet.[16] There would be flights of stairs on all four sides. On the altar's east, west, and north sides, mulberry and cudrania trees would be planted. The hall for banquets and repose would not be built. The Office of the Ceremonial Administrator (*zhangli fang*) would be renamed the Imperial Office of Sericulture (*cangong lingchu*). The terrace of picking mulberry leaves would be a square of 16.45 feet on each side and 1.65 in height. [In the altar compound], there would be five sheds for chariots. The walls surrounding the square [altar] would measure 940 feet long on each side. Inside the West Imperial Garden, only the houses for weaving silk threads were to be built.

Construction, however, was unable to proceed without further complications. The Directorate of Astronomy requested permission to suspend construction and postpone performance of the sacrificial ceremony until the next year. The directorate argued that, according to Zhou dynasty prescriptions, the sericultural ceremonials should be performed on an auspicious day in spring, and that no such day was available in the current year. To appease the emperor, the directorate declared that the ceremonies of picking the mulberry leaves and processing the cocoons could still be performed inside the palace during the current year.

The emperor's reply was equally solicitous and resorted to supernatural elements. Revoking the power of his imperial ancestors, and effectively foiling the official's request, the emperor contended, "I have reported [the performance of the sacrifice] to the ancestors, and I dare not stop it [now]." Then the Ministry of Rites asked permission to simplify construction by using reeds, straw matting, bamboo and wood to build a temporary altar compound. The emperor granted the request, responding as though he were the most considerate of sovereigns: "There are quite a number of bamboo and straw buildings, and even these are not constructed without expense. Consider the financial situation and build only one or two of them." The finished altar compound, however, was not as simple. Two altars, the hall for donning the sacrificial costumes, and the workshops of sericulture exercises, were constructed.[17]

On March 8, 1530, the Ministry of Rites presented to the throne the performance procedures for the sericultural ceremonials, describing the ritual programs step by step.[18] Still there were other particulars that required additional attention from the emperor. Commoners whose homes occupied land needed for the building of the altar compound's east exit were resettled, and their damages were generously compensated. Special permits (*yapai*) that allowed the court ladies to enter the compound were designed; their size was one-third smaller than that of the permits used by the male officials. Gardens of mulberry and cudrancia trees were planted in the spare lots near the newly constructed altars and houses.[19]

The emperor realized that the sacrificial ceremony honoring the progenitor of sericulture should be performed with music and dance, and there was a shortage of palace musicians and dancers. Thus, he ordered the Ministry of Rites to solve the matter. By March 19, 1530, the office replied with a long memorial, specifying the reasons and the process by which they devised their creative solutions. The memorial reports:

> The sacrifice to the progenitor of sericulture has been practiced since the Zhou and Han dynasties, but its music and dance features are not recorded in the classics. [Thus, we chose to] consult the description of the sericultural ceremonials as practiced during the Kaiyuan period of the Tang dynasty. [According to that description,] on the day of the sacrifice, the director of the Imperial Office of Music (*taiyue ling*) would place the musical instruments south of the altar proper and within the inner wall of the altar compound. The instruments would be arranged as an imperial orchestra (*gongxuan*) and the various female musicians would take their positions behind [the instruments]. [From such a description, we] have learned that the sacrifice to the progenitor of sericulture uses female musicians.
>
> From the *Compendium of Administrative Law of the Six Divisions of the Tang Bureaucracy* (*Tang liudian*), [we have noticed that] the director of the Imperial Office of Music was charged with [the duties of] training the musicians, and [making the music] match the [proper] pitch standard for the state sacrifices. [We have also found that] the dances, accompanied by the imperial orchestra, were of the eight-rows format. . . . [However],

> the *Compendium* describes only the costumes for the sixty-four civil dancers and the sixty-four military dancers, but not those for the female musicians.[20]
>
> The *Treatise on Music* (*Yueshu*) by the Song scholar Chen Yang [which was presented to the throne in 1104,] has also been consulted. [That treatise] includes an illustration for the sacrifice to the progenitor of sericulture, with a diagram of the placement of the imperial orchestra and singers. However, the treatise includes no [illustrations of the] dances. . . . Due to the insufficient [musical and dance] personnel in the palace, [we recommend] changing [the format of the dances in the sacrificial ceremony] from the eight-rows format to that of the six-rows. . . .
>
> [Now,] we have examined all of the books on the ceremonials, [and realized that even though] the employment of music and dance was a regular practice in the sacrificial ceremonies, [information on musical and dance practices is rare and sometimes unreliable]. The [musical] practice of the Zhou and Han dynasties cannot be consulted [now]; the practice of the Song [dynasty] cannot be used as a source of reference, because the ceremony was officiated by delegated officials. [Thus] only the [practices] described in the records of the Kaiyuan period approximate ancient [ones]; the discussions and arguments [about music and dance] in Chen Yang's *Treatise on Music* are however more clear. Therefore, [we conclude that even if we] use only singing and omit the dances, [our sacrificial ceremony would] still conform to the ancient practice. Besides, [the reduced format and the omission of dance] would indicate that [the status of] the sericultural ceremonials is slightly lower in rank than those offered to the progenitor of agriculture.[21]

The emperor agreed. Deciding that the dances were no concerns for women, he accepted the officials' recommendation of using music only. As he called off the dances, the emperor, however, was keen to request the Ministry of Rites design a specialized headdress and costume for the female musicians. The office recommended a black headdress and costume, the design of which was similar to those used by musician-dancers for the state sacrifice to the progenitor of agriculture. The officials proposed the color black for specific reasons: the northern suburb is in the direction of yin, whose color [association] favors black; matching geographical direction and music with their corresponding color is a means to ensure effective communication with the deities, and to project appropriate meanings of the ceremonials.

By April 3, 1530, preparations for the sericultural ceremonials were near completion, and officials of the Ministry of Rites made plans for rehearsals and sought imperial approval on the final details. To prevent mistakes in the performance of the newly instituted ceremonials, explanatory diagrams on the exercise of picking mulberry leaves were distributed to court ladies so they could learn the proper actions in a short time. Since there was no longer a wall separating the ritual houses of the inner court ladies from those of the outer court ladies, a new housing arrangement was made. Finally, the place for the exercise of picking mulberry leaves was named.[22]

Then, on April 24, 1530, the empress performed, for the first time in the Ming dynasty, the sacrificial ceremony to the progenitor of sericulture and other related ceremonies.[23] It was the first and only performance in the northern suburb, but it was not the end of the process of instituting the ceremonials. By April 30, 1530, official conclusions were reached about Li Chengxun's memorial, translating some of his idealistic requests into practical programs. Farming land would be assigned to registered residents of the altar compound and other commoners living in the Shuntian and other specified areas; they would work on the land to produce for themselves and the court, and they would be charged with low taxes.[24]

On May 24, 1530, the Ministry of Rites presented a schedule and plan to perform the final events of the sericultural ceremonials. The ministry requested that the emperor order the supervisor of sericultural affairs to select from among the female workers involved in the sericultural ceremonials ten women who could reel silk from the cocoons and another ten who could weave. The ministry also requested the construction and provision of all the necessary machinery for reeling silk from the cocoons and weaving. The office scheduled the events as follows. The Directorate of Astrology would select an auspicious day for the reeling of silk from the cocoons. Prior to that day, the supervisor of sericulture would send the chosen women into the workshops for weaving silk. On the day of the ceremony, the empress would leave the palace [to go to the house for weaving silk]. [During the trip], the guards and escorts would be deployed as usual. After the empress's arrival at the house, one inner court lady would be ordered to perform the ritual finale. Then, to complete the exercises, [the silkworm cocoons] would be distributed to the female workers [for reeling]. The silk thus reeled would be sent to the Directorate for Imperial Apparel and other offices in charge of weaving and dyeing, and would be used for making sacrificial costumes. Reports of the above events would be presented to the court. The female workers would be paid according to regulations.[25]

By this time, effects of the sericultural ceremonials and political complications of Shizong's ritual and musical revision openly emerged. Deng Xian, a censor of examinations in Nanjing of the Jiangxi Circuit, criticized the ceremonials, opposed the expansion of the suburban sacrifices, and requested clemency for Huo Tao, who had been punished.[26] A few months later, in November 1530, Gong Yao, the supporter-general of the State of Ruichang Princely Establishment, submitted a laudatory memorial, extolling the emperor's observance of sacrifices and requesting similar measures for the imperial clansmen.[27] Gong's memorial was discussed. His request that imperial clansmen be allowed to build altars for ceremonials of agriculture and sericulture was denied. His other suggestions that did not infringe upon imperial privileges were accepted.

By the end of 1530, the sericultural ceremonials were established and the process from inception to the first complete sequence of ceremonies had been performed. However, a crucial issue—the empress's trip to the northern suburb—remained unresolved, and it appeared again when the date of the sericultural ceremonials approached in 1531. Once again, the officials tried to persuade the emperor to have the empress perform the ceremonials inside the palace. To convince him, they cited the success of the previous year and pointed out that the construction of the altar compound was incomplete. In his memorial of February 19, 1531, Li Shi, the Minister of Rites, promised that once construction of the altar was finished, proper action would again be discussed.[28]

The emperor was not so easily convinced, suspecting that the officials wished to suspend the ceremonials because unexpected wind and haze arose during the last performance. Trying to keep his sericultural ceremonials as he had wished, the emperor demanded an urgent discussion and report. The officials replied, still trying to convince him to have the ceremonials moved. This time, they used the classics to persuade the emperor:

> We have [consulted] the *Rites of Zhou* and found that [there was an ancient practice of] sending delegates to officiate at the ceremonials. [Even if] the delegates officiate, and Her Majesty performs only the exercise [of preparing the silkworms] inside the

> palace, [the silk thus reeled] is [still] used for the making of sacrificial costumes. [This is because through those ceremonies] the difficulty of women's work is experienced, and the significant meaning of the ancient practice [of the ceremonial] is conveyed. Thus, complete conformity with the ancient practice does not [mean] that the empress [must] go to the northern suburb [to perform the ceremonials] annually.[29]

The emperor rejected the officials' interpretation. Once again, he used as his excuse the weight of his deified ancestors: "I have informed the ancestors that the empress's sericultural ceremonials had been codified as annual events." Less than a month later, nevertheless, the fate of the ceremonials took a dramatic turn. The emperor had a change of heart. During the morning of March 22, 1531, the emperor informed Zhang Cong and Li Shi that he would discuss moving [the performance of] the ceremonials to the West Imperial Garden. By late afternoon, the emperor went to the garden and summoned the two officials to meet him in the old Renshou Palace. Their conversations and activities that afternoon were conciliatory, revealing the fluidity with which decisions about state ritual and music were made and why the concerned participants would understand every nuance of the ritual and musical features.

The emperor said:

> I think the [ceremonials] of farming and sericulture are important affairs. [However], in order to save effort and time, I would like to build the altar of soil and grains in front of the Renshou Palace, and the altar of the progenitor of sericulture at its back. My ministers, [I ask you] to check and see if it can be done or not.

> Zhang Cong said:

> I received Your Majesty's summon this morning, but I did not know Your Majesty would come to the site this very day. [I will go to the site right now.]

Then he kneeled, asking permission to leave for his assignment. The emperor was pleased and went to Zhaohe Palace, where he waited for [the return of] the two officials. They returned and reported:

> The houses in the back of the Renshou Palace [can be used] as they are; with [new] decorations, they are worthy as the workshops of sericulture. The site for the altar of soil and grains, as chosen by your Majesty, is facing the right direction.

The emperor said:

> As for the altar compound of the progenitor of sericulture, [I want you to] build an additional hall of donning the sacrificial costumes and several other small houses. [The efforts] should be economical.

Then the emperor offered wine and food to the two officials who had retreated to the rear chambers in the west side of the palace. Shortly afterward, the emperor asked an imperial commissioner to deliver delicacies to the officials. When the two officials reentered the hall to express their gratitude to the emperor, he asked them to approach his couch. Looking at Li Shi, he said:

> As for the altar compound in the northern suburb, you do not need to ask me; you can immediately send official word to the Ministry of Work to have it demolished.[30]

Thus, Shizong's sericultural ceremonials moved to a new site. Thereafter, the ceremonials were performed within the palace annually, until they were suspended in 1559. Compared to events and arguments involved in Shizong's other efforts in revising the Ming system of state sacrifices and music, the story of the sericultural ceremonials is relatively straightforward and simple. Nevertheless, it illustrates how the institution process was an interplay of conflicting elements, including those of orthodoxy and creativity, and how numerous personal and creative touches rendered the ceremonials unique expressions of Shizong's court.

ORTHODOXY, CREATIVITY, AND EXPRESSIVENESS OF SHIZONG'S SERICULTURAL CEREMONIALS

The institution process of Shizong's sericultural ceremonials followed established court procedures. The idea was initially proposed by an official,

Xia Yan, and was accepted by the emperor and senior officials. Then the court began to research ritual and practical matters. Soon, draft designs and recommendations for the ceremonials were presented and discussed among the emperor and officials. Eventually, the ceremonials took shape with the officials' final recommendations and the emperor's approval.

In their efforts to emulate ancient and appropriate models, the officials studied established practices described in the classics and other reference works from the Zhou, Han, Tang, and Song dynasties. Operating within the intellectual framework of Confucianism and the Chinese tradition of state sacrifices, the emperor and the officials designed the sericultural ceremonials according to ancient models. Structural features of the ceremonials, such as the sacrificial ceremony, the altars, the offering of jade, silk, wine, and victims all followed orthodox prescriptions. Other ritual and musical elements, such as the timing of the ceremony, the use of escorts, the building of supplementary ritual buildings, and the arrangement of musical instruments, followed established associations among direction, color, size, gender, social, and other cosmological elements.

This formidable presence of orthodox elements did not however obliterate the need for creative solutions to numerous practical demands. In fact, there are so many innovative solutions that individual features of the Ming version cannot be compared with those of earlier models.[31] The Ming version is unique because it included many prominent features that had no documented precedents in the past: the office of the sericultural affairs, its patrolling over the court ladies, the routing of the empress's trip, the omission of dance in a state sacrifice, the diminished size of the altars and their proportions of even numbers, the entrance permits, the empress's use of bamboo hooks, and the black color of the headdress and costumes of the musicians. One by one, these detailed features combined to render the Ming ceremony distinctive.

To commoners and minor officials who played no roles in the institution of the sericultural ceremonials, the empress's performance of the sacrificial ceremony on April 23, 1530, was probably a grand manifestation of imperial privileges, governmental actions, and religious and Confucian ideas. The sheer size of the altar compound, the 10,000 military escorts, and the unique sensory stimuli of the black costumes and female voices probably overwhelmed the commoners and minor officials. They were taught an imperial lesson of sericulture and Shizong's emphasis on it.

To the concerned participants, such as Zhang Cong and Li Shi, and to the critical audiences, such as Huo Tao and Deng Xian and those who opposed or doubted Shizong's efforts, the performance of the ceremony projected much more specific expressions, which can only be understood within the contexts of Shizong's court. The orthodox elements in the ceremony gave Zhang Cong and his colleagues the satisfaction that their research and efforts to design the ceremony according to established models had materialized. Distinctive features, such as the specific routing of the empress's trip, the use of female musicians, and the empress's bamboo hook, represented not only the officials' creative solutions to theoretical and practical problems, but also the back-and-forth negotiations among themselves and the emperor.

To the critical audience who did not agree with the emperor's ritual revision, the ceremonials elicited different responses. Atypically, the sacrificial ceremony had no dances and used a number of musicians who did not correspond to the imperial status of the empress; the ceremony was a violation of the legacy left by the founder of the empire, which had been kept intact for 151 years. To those who remembered the emperor's ruthless treatment of Huo Tao and Deng Xian and who questioned the emperor's sincerity and intentions in revising the Ming system of state sacrifices and music, the ceremony was morally wrong. To these critics, the sericultural ceremonials were not merely an orthodox state sacrifice but an expression of many undesirable thoughts, actions, and people in Shizong's court.

CHAPTER FIVE

Ming Music Theory

PRELUDE

Many music treatises from the Ming dynasty have been preserved, documenting a unique body of music theories that aspire to explain music comprehensively. In reality, the theories focus on state sacrificial music, discussing its features in musical, ritual, and cosmological terms, and justifying its use as a means of governance and self-cultivation. Only a minority of the theories involves musical compositions or performance practices. Labeling this body of music theory as *Ming music theory*, this chapter presents it as an explanation of Ming state sacrificial music and as a demonstration of the ways in which Ming theorists formulate creative solutions to orthodox issues of music. Toward that goal, this chapter is divided into three parts: The first part introduces historical roots and social contexts of Ming music theory, analyzing the factors that rendered it orthodox; the second part introduces orthodoxy and creativity in Ming music theory by describing its established scheme of theoretical issues and representative solutions; the third part highlights the creativity and expressiveness in Ming music theory by describing a Ming theorist's two contrasting views on an identical theoretical issue.

HISTORICAL ROOTS AND SOCIAL CONTEXTS OF MING MUSIC THEORY

Historical roots of Ming music theory go back to the times when Confucius and other ancient philosophers formulated their concepts about music, and when the concepts were reinterpreted by Han dynasty scholars.[1] For example, the twelve absolute pitches (*shi'erlü* or *lülü*), a fundamental concept for identifying and discussing musical sounds, are first mentioned in the *Tales of the States* (*Guoyu*), a document from the Chunqiu period. Similarly, the first formula to calculate the twelve absolute pitches is recorded in the *Master Guan's Treatise* (*Guanzi*), which is attributed to the Chunqiu philosopher Guan Zhong. Many cosmological-musical concepts in Ming music theory, including the correspondence among musical sounds, the operation of yin and yang elements, and the warning of the portents, are based on the theories of Dong Zhongshu (179–104 B.C.) and other Han scholars. The *Record of Music*, a standard reference for Ming theorists, is arguably a Han edition of music thoughts from the Zhanguo period.[2]

The purview and structure of Ming music theory are results of a long scholarly tradition. Since Confucianism became the official ideology for scholar-officials in the Han dynasty, a body of Confucian texts, such as the *Rites of Zhou* (*Zhouli*), *Book of Ceremonial*, *Record of Music*, and *Classic of Odes* (*Shijing*), became a canon of authoritative texts on music, delineating a classical purview and a common source of data and premises for music discourses. Then, a scheme of theoretical issues evolved, offering a structural framework to discuss music.

By the Song dynasties, the scheme of issues was firmly internalized in a body of music knowledge that served as a foundation for Ming music theory.[3] In fact, a number of Ming music treatises were written as exegeses of Cai Yuanding's (1135–1198) *A New Treatise on Regulating the Pitch Pipes* (*Lülü xinshu*), a most famous work from the Southern Song. Similarly, Chen Yang's *Treatise on Music*, an encyclopedic compendium on music that was presented to the Song court in 1104, is a reference frequently cited by Ming scholar-officials. References to theoretical and historical treatises of the Song dynasties are standard features in Ming treatises.

Ming music theorists were scholar-officials like their Song predecessors: a number of Ming theorists, such as Wang Tingxiang, Ji Ben, and Han Bangqi, actually occupied high positions in the Ming court. Like their Song predecessors, Ming theorists adopted a classical and scholarly approach to discuss music. They developed their theoretical ideas and arguments by citing passages from the classics and by making references to historical precedents. They also camouflaged their original ideas as commentaries and "correct" understanding of ancient theories. A vivid illustration of such scholarly practices is the *Collected Works on Music*

(*Yuelü quanshu*) of Zhu Zaiyu. The collection refers to all classical works and music treatises known at that time; its list of references is a comprehensive bibliography of music scholarship in late sixteenth-century China.[4] Superficially, Zhu's collection presents theoretical discussions that are no different from those in many other Ming music treatises. However, the collection is in fact a monument of musical and theoretical creativity: it proposes many new musical solutions, including one of the first, if not the earliest, theses on well-tempered tuning in the world.[5]

Ming music theory was purposefully discussed within the social network of scholar-officials. Music was not only a means of governance and self-cultivation, but also a required knowledge for career advancement. Music issues could be tested in public examinations through which scholars could qualify for official positions in the government.[6] Thus, music theory was an intellectual and a practical concern for the scholar-officials, and they actively exchanged music ideas with their colleagues. Through oral discussions, personal letters, informal essays, formal treatises, and other means of communication among the scholar-official-theorists, music theory spread throughout the Ming world.

To effectively realize their theories as proper music that would contribute to the well-being of the Ming empire, Ming theorists had to present their formal treatises to the court and had their theories applied to state sacrificial music. As an embodiment of proper music, the genre was directly controlled by the emperor and performed only in the court. If direct presentation to the court was not possible, however, the theorists would seek approval and confirmation in their local and personal circles, asking senior scholars-officials to recommend their works and ideas. Through political and social connections, the theorists' ideas can become influential in local, if not national, musical scenes.

As described earlier, Ming music theory was entrenched within historical, cultural, and social boundaries. Nevertheless, it was still a creative and expressive product of its time. That it relied heavily on music theory of the Song dynasties reveals not only the Ming theorists' Confucian perspectives, but also their deliberate glossing over the "barbarian" music of the Yuan dynasty, which was temporally closer to the Ming.

Ming music theory developed with ritual and musical activities in the Ming court. Focused interest in music theory appeared just before the turn of the sixteenth century, when Ming state sacrificial music was becoming more and more of a concern in the court. Ming music theory blossomed by the mid-sixteen century, when it was given a tremendous stimulus by

Shizong's ritual and musical revisions in the 1530s and 1540s. In fact, thirteen Ming music treatises were compiled within the emperor's reign (1522–1566), and two of them—Zhang E's *Musical Score and Dance Illustrations for the Sacrifice to Confucius* (*Dacheng yuewu tupu*), and the *Music Books of Li Wencha* (*Lishi yueshu*, ca. 1545)—were authored by Shizong's music masters.

By the late sixteen century, Ming interest in music theory had peaked. It was, however, at that time that Zhu Zaiyu completed his *Collected Works on Music*. In a way, Zhu's collection is a late blossom of the efforts to solve music problems of the 1530s. It should be noted that Zhu himself acknowledged the lessons he learned from his father and other theorists who were active during Shizong's reign. By the early seventeenth century, when the Ming empire was approaching its end, interest in music theory was renewed. Revision of state sacrificial music was once again proposed as a means to help revive the collapsing empire.

Late Ming music theory shows two distinctive features. First, late Ming music treatises tend to emphasize factual data. Being influenced by a scholarly trend of critical evaluation of source materials and data, the emphasis led to chronicles of music events in the court and treatises that are essentially compilations of earlier writings.[7] A representative chronicle is Chen Renxi's *A Collection of Ming Documents and Treatises* (*Huang Ming shifalu*, 1630); its chronological description of state sacrificial music in the Ming court is accurate and thorough. Two representative compilations of preexisting writings are Zhang Xuan's *A Collection of Notes on Ming History* (*Xiyuan wenjianlu*) and Huang Yuliang's *Monograph on Music History and Theory* (*Yuelü zhi*). Second, late Ming music treatises include more information on the practical matters of music. The trend first appeared in Zhang E's *Musical Score and Dance Illustrations for the Sacrifice to Confucius* of 1520, which is the earliest extant writing that includes practical notes on the performance of musical instruments and dances. References to performance practices and notational illustrations appeared more regularly and extensively in treatises of the late sixteenth century, such as Li Zhizao's *A Proposal for the Performance of the Confucian Ceremonial in Schools* (*Panguan liyueshu*) of 1618.

Both treatises of Zhang and Li use the songs of state sacrifice to Confucius as musical illustrations. This focus on the songs is not accidental. It not only reflects a continuous demand and practice of the songs that were publicly distributed in 1393 but also a shortcoming of

Ming music theory.[8] Ming theorists probably had limited access to state sacrificial music, the genre that most vividly represented the Confucian ideology on ritual and music. State sacrificial music was an imperial prerogative, and only people with imperial sanction had the chance to practice or witness it directly.[9] As a result, many Ming theorists had no choice but to discuss music in general and cosmological terms. To illustrate their theoretical ideas with actual examples of music, they had to rely on the songs sung during the state sacrifice to Confucius.

THE SCHEME OF ISSUES IN MING MUSIC THEORY

The contents of Ming music treatises are diverse, ranging from technical explanations on the physical measurements of a musical tone to philosophical desideratum and cosmological interpretations that have little physical relevance to musical sounds. Beneath this diversity, however, is an established and integrated scheme of issues. The foundation of that scheme is a Confucian belief: Music is a means to cultivate people's virtue, so they can acquire *ren*, the highest and most representative virtue in the Confucian world, and can become *junzi*, cultivated people who would strive to make their society ideal.[10]

This Confucian belief was authoritative, as it came from Confucius' words. Confucius proclaimed that Shao, the dance-music attributed to the sage-ruler Shun, was the most perfect music, and that vulgar music of the Zheng State (*zhengsheng*) should be banned.[11] Confucius also proclaimed: "How can people without *ren* make music?"[12] The argument displays a convincing, albeit associative, logic: How can proper music be made by people who are not proper?

The belief is supported by a number of corollaries that are self-serving but are not unrelated to certain empirical observations of musical behavior: 1) music comes from the heart-minds (*xin*) of people, and expresses genuine human feelings that are activated by external stimuli;[13] 2) music appeals to and affects supernatural, human, and inanimate beings because music exists and operates through the cosmic *qi* and the yin and yang forces, and through the correspondence among correlated entities;[14] 3) proper music would cultivate the good nature in all human beings, guiding them in their self-cultivation and construction of their ideal world; proper music also would harmonize the supernatural, human, and inanimate operations of the cosmos, rendering it orderly and ideal; 4) the antiquity was a golden time, and Shao, the proper music of the time, was both an indication and cause of the success.

The Confucian belief and its corollaries led to an idealized view of music and its power. Thus, Ye Liangpei wrote in his preface to Xu Zhen's *An Illustrated Commentary to Cai Yuanding's "New Treatise on the Regulations of the Pitch Pipes"* (*Lülü xinshu fenzhu tusuan*) of 1541: "Since ancient time, the sovereigns' methods of ruling the world, of changing the habitual tendencies and moods of the populace, of achieving peace and of accomplishing cultivation of virtues have all been based on music."[15] If the ideology is not supported by tangible results, however, the problems lie in the people and their musics. If people are not cultivated by music, they are not practicing proper music—their music is improper and/or produced by those who have not acquired *ren*.

Given the belief in the idealized power of music, it was no wonder that Ming theorists wanted to use music to solve problems in their world. Such a practical purpose, however, dictates the acceptance of an orthodox scheme of theoretical issues. Discussion must begin with the premise that *guyue*—namely the proper music of antiquity that is symbolized by Shao and should be used as the model for all subsequent works of proper music—existed and generated the golden reigns of antiquity. Then, the premise leads to a set of logical and interrelated issues: the musical attributes of *guyue*, the time and reasons why it was lost, the rise of improper music, and the arguments that *guyue* could be reconstructed at the time of the discussion.

As these issues involve many unknown and unverifiable historical facts, Ming theorists formulated different solutions. For example, in his *Proper Music and Entertainment Music* (*Yayue yanyue*) of 1530, Zhang Yu contested that *guyue* vanished right after the reigns of the sage-ruler.[16] Huang Jiqing's solutions, as presented in his *Some Limited Views of Music Theory* (*Yuelü guanjian*), are, however, more representative.[17] He stated that *guyue* became corrupted in the beginning of the Eastern Zhou dynasty and was lost after the death of Mencius, when people could no longer understand what proper music was. However, Huang declared that the *Classic of Odes*, the *Rites of Zhou*, and other classical texts had preserved essential details of *guyue*. Based on these descriptions, the ancient musical instruments that were still being used in the Ming time—such as the wooden box (*zhu*) and wooden tiger (*yu*)—Huang argued that it was possible to reconstruct proper music in his time. Huang's emphasis on the musical instruments was typical. Many Ming music treatises include

Figure 5.1.
Four illustrations of musical instruments from the *Huang Ming taixue ji* (5.46b)

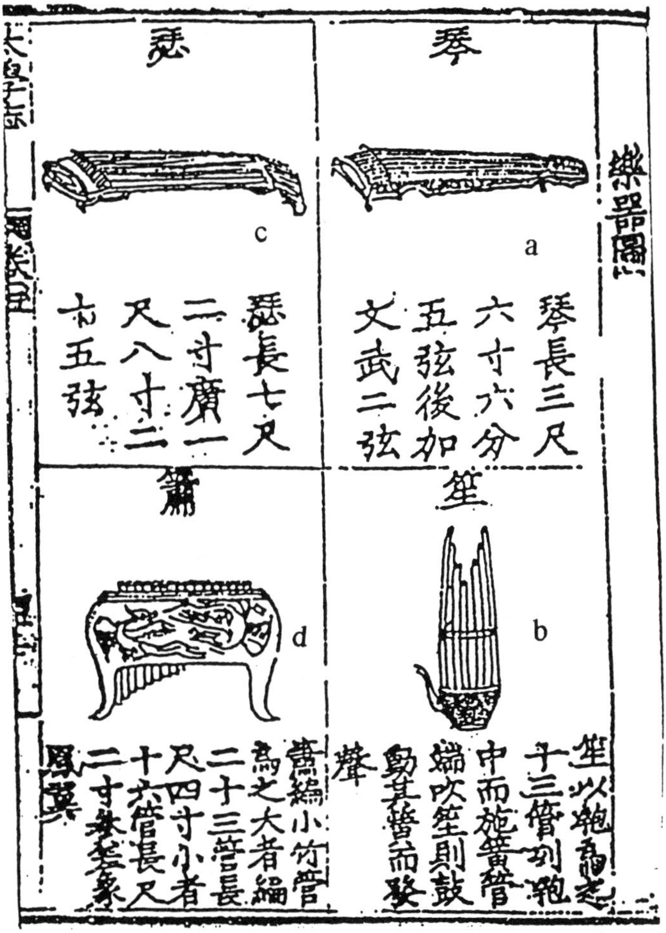

a. seven-string zither (*qin*); b. mouth-organ (*shenq*); c. twenty-five string zither (*se*); d. panpipe (*paixiao*). The Chinese characters describe the organological features of the instruments.

extensive descriptions about the materials and designs of the musical instruments, their historical origins and uses, their associative meanings, and any other relevant matters.[18] (See Figure 5.1.)

Once the issues on sources and methodology to institute proper music through reconstruction (emulation) of *guyue* were established, Ming theorists had to convince the government to implement their ideas. In other words, the theorists had to address the issue of why the Ming court would successfully reconstruct the music when earlier dynasties had failed. Zhang Yu, for example, argued that by Emperor Shizong's time, the Ming dynasty had accumulated sufficient merits to deserve the revival of *guyue*. Wang Sizong, the author of *Huangzhong as the Originating Tone* (*Huangzhong yuantong*) of 1566, considered the late Ming an opportune time because the emperor had taken the initiative to revise music.

To realize the reconstruction of *guyue*, however, Ming theorists had to solve another sequence of interrelated issues, which included the origin of music, pitch standards, making pitch pipes, and other prerequisites in the production of a system (or repertory) of music. As succinctly pinpointed by Ji Ben in his *Treatise on the Essentials of Music Theory* (*Yuelü zuanyao*) of 1539, "To make music, one must make sounds harmonious; to make sounds harmonious, one must adhere to the [correct] pitches because they are the foundation of music."[19]

What those pitches are and how they are found, however, are complicated issues, and Ming theorists offered many solutions. The most representative one is the Ling Lun legend, which first appeared in Lü Buwei's *Spring and Autumn Annals* (*Lüshi chunqiu*), a Zhanguo document. As described by Lü, Ling Lun produced a set of twelve absolute pitches, six yang and six yin ones, by cutting bamboo pipes to imitate the sounds of male and female phoenixes; he first cut the *huangzhong* pipe, that is the first of the twelve pitch pipes, into a length of nine *cun*, and then used that pipe as a basis to make and measure the remaining eleven pipes. The legend is appealing. It ascribes the authority of deciding the pitch standard to a supernatural bird and proposes the use of pitch pipes, measurable physical objects, to generate the musical pitches.

The legend also reinforces Ming theorists' efforts to correlate the music pitches and pitch pipes with various cosmic and human activities.[20] Such correlations are crucial issues for Ming music theorists, because they believed the correlations rendered the music semantically meaningful and musically powerful. However, the correlations bring further theoretical issues that the Ling Lun legend cannot answer. What measurements were used in antiquity? And how and why musical pitches derived from a supernatural source can be measured and verified by human standards? Ming theorists knew that throughout history, the standards of linear measurement had fluctuated and that the Ming measurement may not match that of antiquity. Ming theorists also realized the contradictions in using human standards to verify the accuracy of pitch pipes that imitated sounds of supernatural phoenixes.

A solution to this dilemma is the *houqi* exercise, which was first described by scholars of the Han dynasty.[21] The arguments for *houqi*, which literally means "watching for the *qi*," are simple and convincing if one believes in *qi*. Since *qi* is thought to disperse across the land at a different level each month, *qi* is the most reliable means to confirm the length of each of the twelve pitch pipes. In other words, one can verify the accuracy of the pipes by observing how they correspond to the movement of *qi*.

As outlined in the *Collected Ceremonial of the Ming Dynasty*, the *houqi* exercise takes place within a space surrounded on all sides with a three-tiered wall that is sealed after all necessary implements have been installed.[22] Within the space is a round, canopied shallow excavation into which soil-filled trays are placed, each aligned to one of the twelve points of the compass. Twelve pipes, each of an appropriate length, are buried at an angle in the soil to a depth that fixed their exposed ends on a plane with one another. Each pipe is then filled with ashes and covered with a piece of raw-silk cloth. On a prescribed day in each of the twelve lunar months, a *qi* is thought to cover the earth to a specific height, generating sympathetic ethereal vibrations that would joggle the silk cloth and ashes in a specific pipe, leaving a mark that shows the exact height the *qi* had covered. That mark is considered an indication of the accurate length of the pitch pipe being examined. For example, the *qi* that arrives on winter solstice was considered to cover a height of nine *cun*. That measurement is what an "accurate" *huangzhong* pipe of nine *cun* should match. As music theory, the *houqi* exercise is more speculation than practice, and there are many variations in its application. Nevertheless, in its time it provided a means to use the cosmic *qi* to confirm the measurement of the pitch pipes.

With or without *houqi*, however, Ming theorists had to confront the issues of physical measurements—length, diameter, and volume—of the pitch pipes and their resultant pitches. Indeed, like their predecessors, many Ming theorists spent a bulk of their efforts to discuss the issues in physical and cosmological terms.[23] Only a few of the theorists would entrust the matters to natural courses. Cao Kui, for example, concluded that human calculations and measurements of the pitches are useless because the attributes of music cannot be analyzed with mere human intelligence; Cao argued that a person, virtuous and pure, would know the principle of the pitches intuitively.[24]

Most Ming theorists addressed the issues in cosmological, physical, and mathematical terms. Cosmological measurements and correlations were used to confirm the accuracy of physical measurements and mathematical calculations: The "accurately measured" elements of music must operate synchronously within the cosmological construct. Thus, in addition to physical and linear measurements, Ming theorists discussed the dimensions of pitch pipes and pitches with various cosmological concepts that always involved, singularly or collectively, operation of *qi*, the yin and yang forces, the five elements, the mutations of the hexagrams, and various interpretations of physical and cosmic numbers.

A representative of the theorists who focused their calculations on the manipulation of yin and yang forces and cosmic numbers was Wan Gong, author of *A Manual of Ceremonies and Music for the Temple of Confucius* (*Wenmiao liyueshu*) of 1583. He held that the measurements of length, width, and weight have numbers that reflect the stretching and shrinking of the yin and yang *qi*. Furthermore, Wan asserted, all operations are based on mutations of nine and three, because that is how everything came into being. Applying such concepts to his musical theories, Wan considered the proper length of the *huangzhong* pipe to be nine *cun*, and its bore as three *fen* (one *fen* is one-tenth of a *cun*), that is, nine and three.[25]

Cosmological measurements and interpretations do not however solve physical problems: the materials with which the pitch pipes are made, standards for their measure, their measurements, and their production.[26] Like Wan Gong, most Ming theorists used traditional ideas to answer these problems: use bamboo to make the pipes; the *huangzhong* pipe measures nine *cun* in length, nine *fen* in outer circumference, three *fen* in inner diameter, and has a volume of 1,200 millet grains; the remaining eleven pipes are to be derived from the *huangzhong* pipe through the method of *sanfen sunyi*, which means, literally, the addition and subtraction of a third. In practice, the method refers to a process in which the twelve absolute pitches are generated through cycles of fifths and octave replacements: when the length of a pitch pipe is shortened by a third, the sound it produces will be a fifth higher than that produced with the full length; similarly, when the pipe is lengthened by a third, the sound it produces will be a fourth lower. Through octave replacements, cycles of fifths can be lined up as a series of twelve absolute pitches within an octave.[27]

The method is simple, but it produces a major hurdle in traditional Chinese music theory, which has tormented music theorists since the Han dynasty and which is traditionally called the problem of "going without return" (*wang erbu fan*). Theoretically, once the measurements of the *huangzhong* pitch pipe are decided, the remaining eleven pitches and pitch pipes can be generated according to the *sanfen sunyi* method, then music making can proceed. Indeed, such was the case for most Chinese theorists and musicians. However, since the Han dynasty, critical theorists have realized that there is a major flaw in the method: The thirteenth pitch (or the twelfth fifth) generated by the method matches neither the originating pitch nor its substitute, which is an octave higher—by modern measurement of pitch levels, the thirteenth pitch is about twenty-four cents higher than the octave of the originating pitch. This discrepancy between the two pitches contradicts the fundamental premise that the twelve absolute pitches operate as a self-contained and circular series of pitches, each of which can be freely and equally transposed.

The discrepancy between the two pitches would not be a serious problem if it was just a musical inconvenience. But it was not. It conflicted with the cyclical operations of the cosmic and natural elements, such as the annual cycles of the four seasons and the twelve months. In the cosmologically coordinated world of Ming theorists, the conflict led to an ominous deduction: If the twelve absolute pitches operate in a noncircular way that is cosmologically invalid, there is a mistake in either the pitches or the cosmological system. Obviously, Ming music theorists, like their predecessors in earlier dynasties, prefer to find the mistake in the calculation of the twelve absolute pitches.

Ji Ben's view on the issues is representative. Presuming that the yin and the yang *qi* rotate in full circles endlessly, while stretching and shrinking within their own progressions, Ji could not accept any musical theory (and calculations) that allowed the thirteenth pitch to break the circular operation of the twelve absolute pitches.[28] Thus, he had to criticize the Song theorist, Cai Yuanding, who proposed the addition of six extra notes, a solution that was widely accepted among Ming theorists.[29] In return, Ji Ben had to construct a system of yin and yang operations and calculations that dissolved the problem. The Ming theorist who succeeded in solving the problem of "going without return" with a musical and practical answer was Zhu Zaiyu, who proposed a theory of equal temperament. Zhu's proposal was a musical breakthrough, and it is now widely, and deservedly, studied by Chinese and Western Chinese scholars.[30]

The problem of "going without return" leads to complex and often convoluted discussions of pitches, modes, and other compositional features. The basic points of these discussions can nevertheless be briefly summarized as follows.[31] All sounds available for music making are classified into the twelve absolute pitches and their octave substitutes, each a fixed pitch (i.e. a pitch with a fixed pitch level), labeled by a specific bisyllable name: *huangzhong*, *dalü*, *taicou*, *jiazhong*, *guxian*, *zhonglü*, *ruibin*, *linzhong*, *yize*, *nanlü*, *wuyi* and *yingzhong*. Thus, a Ming theorist would refer to a particular musical sound by classifying and naming it as one of the twelve absolute pitches; for example, a musical sound that matches the fixed pitch level of a *huangzhong* will be called a *huangzhong*. If the theorist wants to specify the use of the higher octave substitute of the *huangzhong* tone, he would describe it as a *qing* (clear) *huangzhong*. As the average range of tones most often used in music making is about an octave and a third, only four octave substitutes are needed. They are the four high tones (*siqing*), that is, the *qing huangzhong*, *qing dalü*, *qing taicou* and *qing jiazhong*. This classification of fixed pitches is analogous to the Western analysis of musical sounds into octaves and the dividing of an octave into twelve semitones, each a fixed pitch and named as "C", "C#," and so forth. (See Figure 5.2a.)

In a specific musical composition (or passage), however, only a maximum of seven out of the twelve absolute pitches would be employed, and each of the seven pitches can be understood as being either a fixed pitch or relative tone (a tone whose pitch level is variable, but whose intervalic and sequential relationships with other tones are standardized). This understanding is analogous to the Western practice of describing a musical sound as either a "C" or a "do", and of classifying musical intervals in whole-tones and semitones. (See Figure 5.2b.) Thus, to refer to the seven pitches used in a musical composition, a Ming theorist can describe them as either a series of seven relative tones (*qisheng*) or a series of seven fixed pitches (*yun*).

In the first case, the theorist would label the tones as *gong*, *shang*, *jue*, *bianzhi*, *zhi*, *yu* and *biangong* to specify their intervalic and sequential relationships; except the intervals between the fourth and fifth tones and between the seventh and the octave substitute of the first tone, all intervals in a series of seven relative tones are whole-tone ones. This series of seven relative tones is analogous to the Western series of fa, sol, la, ti, do, re, mi. (See Figure 5.2c.) Oftentimes, the use of *bianzhi* (ti) and *biangong* (mi), which entail the occurrence of semitones, is considered undesirable, thus only five tones will be used. A Ming theorist would call them the five

Figure 5.2a-d.
Music Components

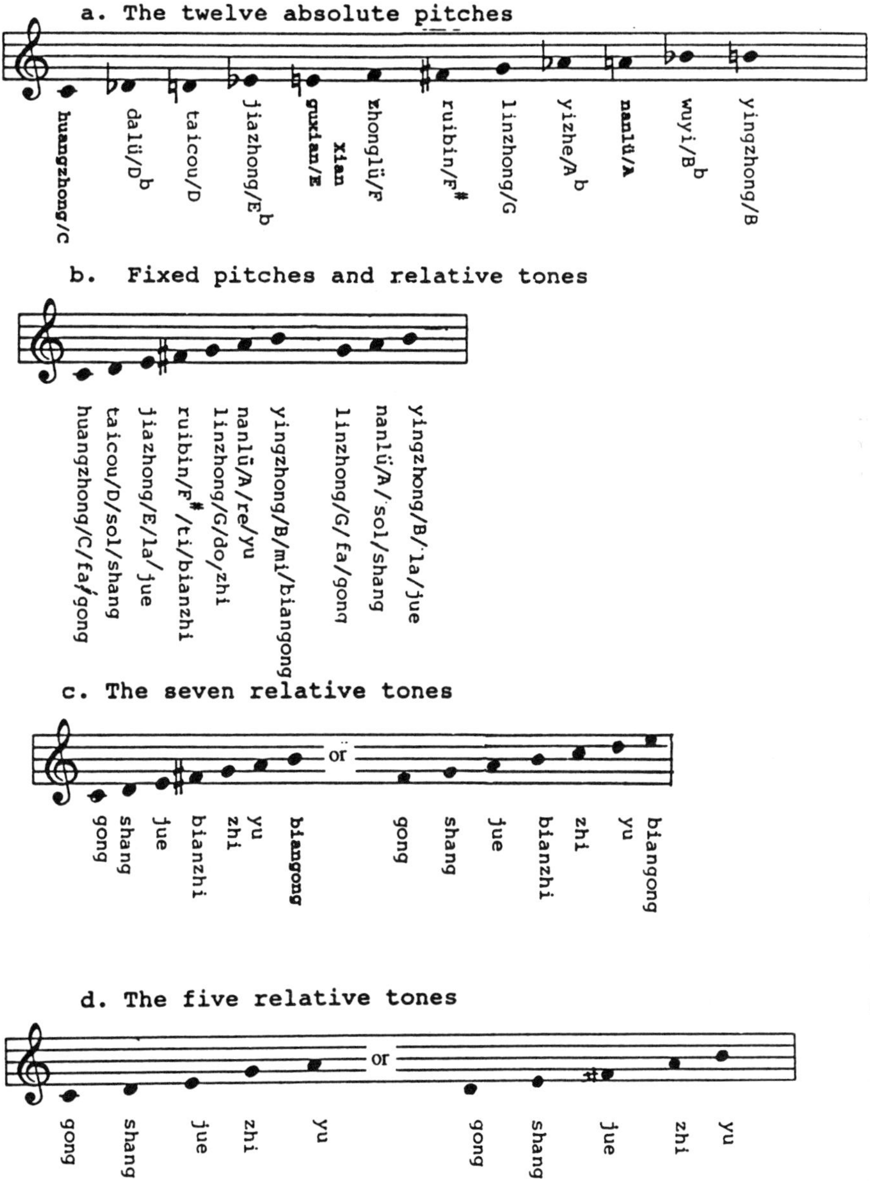

relative tones (*wusheng*): *gong*, *shang*, *jue*, *zhi*, *yu*, that is, fa, sol, la, do, re in Western music. (See Figure 5.2d.)

Thus equipped with a set of terms to specify and discuss individual sounds, Ming theorists would discuss them as constituents of musical modes (*diao*). As revealed in Ming music treatises and Ming state sacrificial songs, a mode is a tonal structure that can be discussed as either a class of fixed pitches or a class of relative tones. In both cases, however, the pitches/tones in a mode are given specific and hierarchical roles and used accordingly, so the resultant music reveals particular patterns and projects a distinctive musical identity. Ming theorists discuss musical modes in many ways, including structural features, usage in particular genres, and various musical and nonmusical associations.

Ming explanations about the basic components of music are involved, but not unclear. Confusion, however, is rampant, because Ming theorists, like their predecessors in earlier dynasties, lived in a world of associative thinking and cosmological concerns, and they could not confine their discussions of music within its technical and empirical boundaries. Arbitrarily, the theorists matched their theoretical and current ideas with historical thoughts and practices and grafted microsystems of musical components into the greater structure of cosmological schemes, generating tangled webs of musical facts and fiction. However, the presence of such webs of associations renders music a powerful tool of Ming thoughts and lives. For instance, the realization of modes and tones in state sacrificial music became a grave matter that could not be casually overlooked. When detected, mistakes in the modes and tones would result in the responsible musicians' persecution. (See chapter 6.)

With the basic components of music explained, compositional concerns follow, three of which were particularly pressing: 1) the relationship between the contour of a melody and the word-tones of the text that is set to the melody;[32] 2) the prescription of syllabic text setting; and 3) the melodic patterns (*juge*). The first issue concerns the conflict between the desire to make a melody "musical" according to particular musical parameters, and the necessity of making the text intelligible when it is sung—Chinese words are unintelligible without the appropriate linguistic tones. If the word-tones are followed or imitated literally, the text will be clearly intelligible, but melodic contours may not satisfy musical criteria; if the word-tones are disregarded, the melody can flow more freely, but the text may be unintelligible. The issue is a central concern not only for Ming theorists, but also for all Chinese musicians. Much of traditional Chinese music is sung

Figure 5.3.
Wang Sizong's embellished song for honoring Confucius

with texts, and the conflict (or a lack of it) is immediately noticed by Chinese audiences.

Ming theorists' solutions to the problem ranged from ignoring the problem altogether to forcing the melodic contour to match the ascends and descends of the word-tones. Liu Lian, the author of the *Original Meaning of the Classic of Music* (*Yuejing yuanyi*) of 1550, for example, composed his melodies by following the word-tones of his text. As a contrast, Wang Sizong, the author of *Huangzhong as the Originating Tone* (*Huangzhong yuantong*) of 1566, offered a more musical solution. While theorizing that melody should follow the word-tones, Wang postulated that the linguistically specified tonal ascends and descends are relative and cannot be rigidly correlated to individual musical pitches. Thus, Wang wanted to "blend" the word-tones into the melody, arguing that it would be incongruous for the melody to follow the word-tones slavishly.[33] He proposed that ornamental notes be lightly sung between the structural tones of each musical phrase. To illustrate his solution, Wang provided a musical composition, a first in Ming discussion of musical structure and ornamental notes.[34] (See Figure 5.3.)

Wang's solution is ingenious, because he realized that the conflict between word-tones and melodic contour is aggravated by the prescription of syllabic text setting: to reconstruct or emulate *guyue*, composers are orthodoxly required to set individual Chinese characters in song texts to individual musical tones; the syllabic style was considered a distinctive feature of ancient music. In other words, the composer has to match the melodic contour and word-tones as soon as the two components occur; the composer cannot use two or more musical notes to generate a match or dissolve the conflict. Wang's proposal suggests the use of ornamental note to dissolve the conflict.

Ming music theorists were not unaware of the crippling effect of the prescription of syllabic text setting, its spurious authenticity, and the use of nonsyllabic music in the past. However, Ming theorists desperately needed a feature that would authenticate their claim of reconstructing and/or emulating *guyue*. Thus, Ming theorists such as Zhang Yu and Ji Ben tended to raise their doubts about the prescription, but then meekly accepted it as a traditional practice: the prescription led to music that sounded "ancient," that is, different from most genres of Ming music that boasted ornate melodies.

Discussions of word-tones and syllabic text setting lead to another compositional concern: the shaping of melodies according to particular patterns. For Ming theorists, seven of these patterns were classical because they were described in the *Record of Music* and because they arose from performance experiences.[35] Wan Gong, for example, advised novice musicians to learn the patterns thoroughly, so they would sing with expression and without mumbling the texts.[36]

Nevertheless, as musical performance and compositions overlap and influence each another, the melodic shapes/patterns also are issues (and tools) for composing and describing (analyzing) music. Thus, Zhu Zaiyi illustrated the patterns with examples from actual music and prepared theoretical tables of melodic phrases for different rhymes and tones.[37] Zhu's musical example is particularly persuasive because it comes from the first song of the Ming state sacrifice to the imperial ancestors, a fact that vividly demonstrates the closer relationships between theory and practice in the late Ming.[38]

Zhu's classification of the musical patterns is not theoretically rigid, as the distinction between some patterns is ambiguous. For example in Figure 5.4, numbers 2 and 3 have, respectively, the same contour as numbers 7 and 6. Only when their different registers are taken into

Figure 5.4.
Zhu Zaiyu's illustrations of melodic patterns

1. *Juzhong ju*—going up straight, like following the ruler:

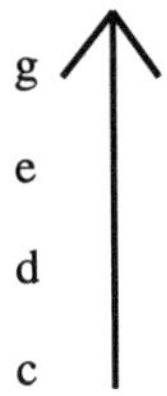

2. *Juzhong gou*—hook in the phrase:

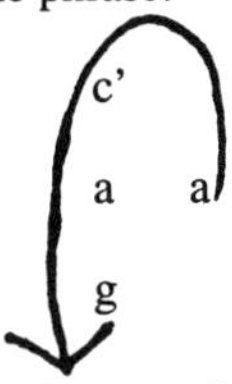

3. *Duan ru guanzhu*—going down straight, like a string of pearls:

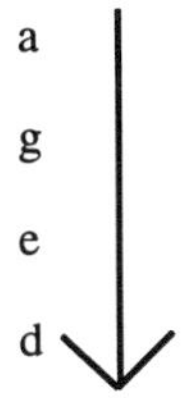

4. *Xia ru zhui*—falling down to a very low range:

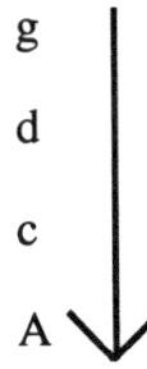

5. *Qu ru zhe*—folded and twisted:

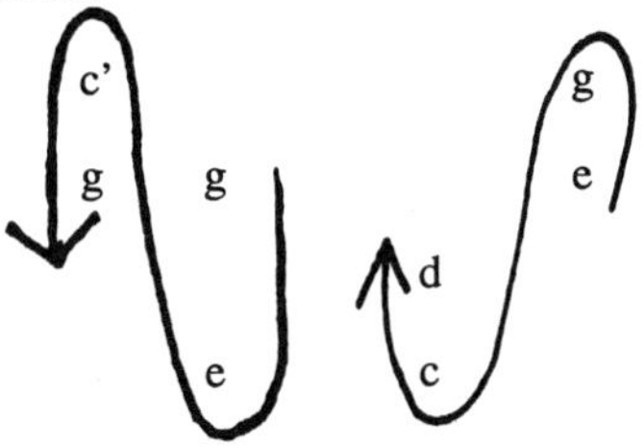

Figure 5.4. continued.
Zhu Zaiyu's illustrations of melodic patterns

6. *Shang ru kang*—holding high:

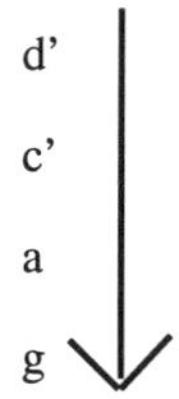

7. *Zhi ru gaomu*—stops like a tree in hibernation; the music ends, but there is more to be said.

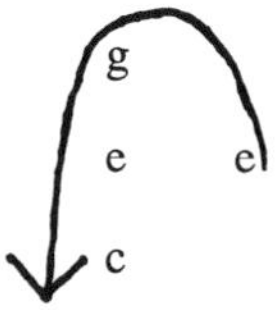

consideration do the patterns qualify as being distinctive. Rather than theoretical failures, however, Zhu's patterns indicate Ming theorists' efforts and creativity to explain every theoretical and practical problem. Even in the late twentieth century, and with the help of computers, the classification of melodic patterns remains elusive.

Zhu's emphasis on the melodic patterns and his use of actual music as illustrations attest to the growing attention to practical problems of music making. Since the mid-Ming, theorists began to describe the playing of instruments with diagrams, *gongche* notation, finger positions on stringed and wind instruments. (See Figure 5.5.) Rudimentary as many of these descriptions are, they are concrete evidence of Ming theorists' determinations to pursue accurate and practical music knowledge.

In fact, such determinations also lead the theorists to address a related mode of expression, namely dance, which is an integral part of state sacrifices and music. In addition to citations from the classics and references to historical precedents, Ming music theorists such as Han Bangqi, Li Zhizao, and Zhu Zaiyu produced numerous pictograms to show stylized dance gestures, each of which is to be performed with individual words in the song text and with musical notes in the melody. (See Figure 5.6.)

Figure 5.5.
A late Ming illustration for playing the horizontal flute (Li Zhizao, 5.27)

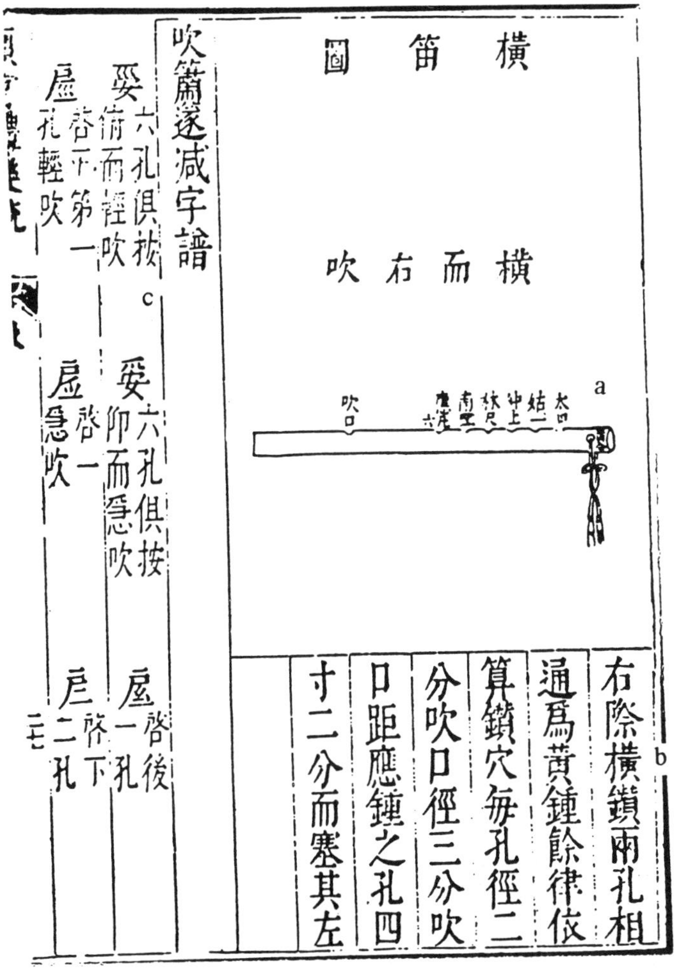

a. the flute and its finger holes
b. organological description of instrument
c. instructions for blowing and covering the finger holes

Figure 5.6.
Four dance pictograms from the
***Huang Ming taixue ji* (5.53b)**

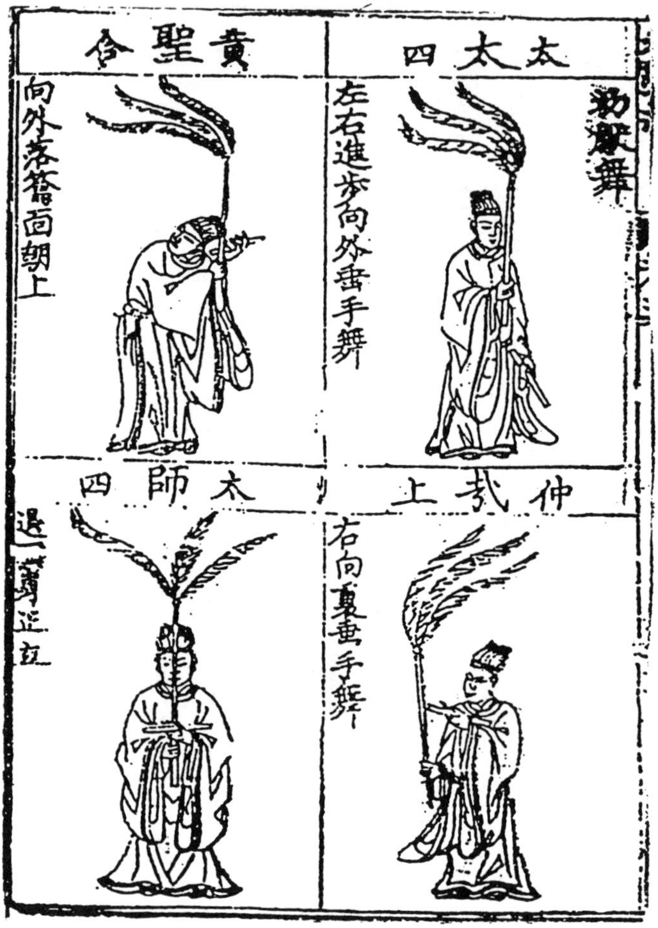

The pictograms should be read from top to bottom and from right to left. Each gesture corresponds to one word in the text and to one note in the melody.

ORTHODOXY AND CREATIVITY IN JI BEN'S MUSIC THEORIES

As sketched earlier, Ming music theory proceeds along an established scheme of issues, even though individual theorists offered a wealth of diverse solutions. It is true that the differences among most of the solutions are subtle, but the cumulative force of such differences sustains Ming music theory. Living in an authoritarian world dominated by a Confucian ideology and orthodox prescriptions, Ming theorists could only operate within clearly established boundaries. In this sense, their operations were highly successful. Not only did they do their best to explain music, they also revealed who they were, how they theorized, and what their musical and intellectual lives were about. The case of Ji Ben is illustrative.

Ji Ben (z. Mingde; h. Pengshan, 1485-1563) is not one of those flamboyant theorists who commanded attention in the imperial court. He represents the creative and energetic Ming scholar-official who strove to do his best, and he pursued music and music theory as a lifelong interest. Versatile and prolific, Ji Ben authored eleven books containing some 120 chapters. Besides music, his interests included history, astronomy, mathematics, geography, military arts, agriculture, and poetry. His long and eventful career was distinguished by his quest for truth and generosity to others.[39]

As outlined in the prefaces of his two extant music treatises, *A Treatise on the Essentials of Music Theory* (*Yuelü zuanyao*) and *A Supplementary Treatise on Music Theory* (*Lülü bieshu*), Ji's involvement with music began early in his career. As a young man enrolled in the national university in Nanjing, he had a futile discussion with Chancellor (*jijiu*) Zhang Mao (1466 js.) about Cai Yuanding's music theories. The event triggered Ji to study music theory actively, leading him into an intensive study of Cai's ideas and the writing of a monograph. Completed in 1505, when Ji was only twenty years old, the monograph is titled *Calculations of the Twelve Absolute Pitches* (*Lülü suanfa*) and was published with a prefatory endorsement by senior scholar-official Yang Lian (1452–1525).

Such a monograph not only testifies to Ji's youthful creativity but also underscores the orthodox and contextual elements in Ming music theory. Ji's monograph discusses the well-established issues of measuring and explicating the absolute pitches and pitch pipes, a fact that illustrates the ways in which Ming theorists relied on their predecessors from the Song and earlier dynasties. Ji's interest in music theory was genuine, and he continued to study. In 1515, he revised the monograph of 1505 and changed its title to *A Treatise on the Essentials of Music Theory*.

Then, Ji Ben was discouraged, rejecting what he had written as inadequate descriptions of the meanings and features of proper music. He abandoned the monograph for more than two decades, but he did not forget music theory. In 1539, when Wang Ting visited Changsha where Ji was living and inquired about Cai's theory, Ji showed the visitor his old treatise. Wang thought it so worthy that he persuaded Ji to publish it again and provided a laudatory preface for the new edition. This edition revived Ji's confidence and led him to further music studies. By 1554, he produced a second treatise, *A Supplementary Treatise on Music Theory* (*Lülü bieshu*), which includes drastically changed interpretations on certain musical features. Such interpretations are creative, expressing not only distinctive ideas but also the theorist's own intellectual and personal growth in an orthodox world.

Ji's new and old understandings of the five-tones and seven-tones are illustrative. In his first treatise, he defended the seven relative tones by invoking the authority of the *Standard History of the Former Han* (*Hanshu*). Since that document described how the sage-ruler Shun wished to hear the seven initials (*qishi*), Ji speculated that the seven relative tones were already in use at that time.[40] To support that speculation, he refuted the description in the *Encyclopedic History of Institutions* (*Tongdian*) that the two bian-notes, namely *bianzhi* and the *biangong*, were added during the Zhou dynasty. Ji charged that the description was a fabrication and an arbitrary paraphrase of the classics, which provided no specifics about the nature of sound and music theory.[41]

In his second treatise, which was written when Ji was a much older man, he executed an about-face and disavowed the seven-tones, basing his arguments on the authority of the *Classic of Documents* (*Shujing*) and *Mencius*. He concluded that music uses only the five relative tones and traced what he considered the mistaken belief in the two bian-tones to descriptions in the *Chronicle of Zuo* (*Zuozhuan*) and the notions of "*qitong*" and "*qishi*" in the *Tales of the States* and the *Standard History of the Former Han*. Furthermore, Ji also characterized the four high tones as being unworthy of mention.[42] What and why Ji changed await further investigation, but what the changes have made clear is that changes and creativity in musical thought are possible even within an established scheme of issues that is thoroughly constrained by musical, ideological, and cosmological considerations.

That Ji Ben changed his understanding of a musical issue was not accidental. It represents his and other Ming theorists' efforts to clarify every technical and nontechnical feature of music. Indeed, they used every available means: The cultivating nature of music, the historical examples, the classical documents, the concept of the *qi*, the dualism of *yin* and *yang*, the five-tones, the syllabic text setting, the performance practices, and so forth. Ming theorists discussed music urgently, because their ultimate goal was not mere music making but the building of an ideal world in a perfect cosmos.

Such a goal underscores the Ming theorists' world of harsh realities, Confucian ideals, orthodox premises, and creative energy. There were inequalities and injustices in the theorists' real life, yet its social structure and intellectual principles, as symbolized by the state sacrifices and music, were never fundamentally challenged; its faults were attributed to improper operation of the elements. If Ming music theory failed to make proper the state sacrificial music of its time, that too was due to the improper observation of musical elements. Thus, it is no surprise that Ming theorists spent their creative and intellectual energy pursuing proper and authentic musical elements. The theorists did not overhaul the orthodox scheme of theoretical issues, because it was a cultural legacy that well-served their Confucian needs and correlative mode of thinking, the modi operandi of the time. Skepticism existed, but sparked no fundamental changes until the modern era.[43] By the same token, creativity emerged within orthodox boundaries: it produced individualistic solutions but posed no fundamental challenge to the established scheme of music theories. Thus, Ming music theory is simultaneously orthodox and creative; it explains not only music but also people living within physical, social, temporal, and intellectual boundaries.

CHAPTER SIX

State Sacrificial Music in the Ming Court

The history of state sacrificial music in the Ming court is a drama of conflicts: orthodoxy versus creativity; theory versus practice; Confucian scholar-officials versus Daoist monk-musician-officials; and state sacrificial music versus entertainment music. Through expected and unexpected turns, the drama reveals that the expressiveness of the state sacrificial music is inseparable from its concerned participants, critical audiences, and contexts. The expressiveness comes not only from the creative features of the music and its physical sounds, but also from the ways in which the music represents its producers and consumers.

When Taizu instituted his system of state sacrificial music, he followed the steps of earlier Chinese rulers in their use of music as a means of governance and self-cultivation. Taizu, however, did not follow those steps casually: He had to coordinate his intellectual aspirations to follow orthodox prescriptions with his practical considerations of what was needed and possible at the time. Otherwise, Taizu could only produce a system of state sacrificial music that would neither serve the needs of his court, nor be accepted as proper music.

Taizu genuinely aspired to make his state sacrificial music as proper as possible; thus, he directly participated in the institution process and actively provided a strong leadership to guide his officials. This institution process began three years before the formal beginning of the Ming dynasty. In November 1365, just after capturing Jinling, the site of the capital for his new empire, Taizu appointed a music manager (*dianyue guan*) to prepare for the institution of state sacrificial music.[1] Taizu's order was not premature: He was confident of his pending control of China, and he knew that state sacrificial music had been created and performed as a demonstration of political legitimacy in the rival court of Ming Yuzhen (1331–1366).[2]

Taizu's appointment of the music manager was followed by other direct involvement with state sacrificial music. On July 28, 1367, he ordered a rehearsal of the music by the palace gate, where musician-dancers (*yuewu sheng*), labeled "Daoist children" in Ming documents, had assembled.[3] During the rehearsal, Taizu struck a tone on the stone-chimes and asked Zhu Sheng (1299–1371), one of the two academicians (*daxueshi*) leading the troupe, to identify the sound.[4] The official failed to identify the tone, mistaking it as the relative tone of *zhi* (sol), even though it should have been *gong* (do). As Zhu Sheng always claimed music erudition, his failure was unexpected. Taizu was annoyed, and Diarist Xiong Ding had to pacify him by explaining the difficulties in understanding the tones of the stone-chimes and supporting his explanations with reference to the classics. Taizu listened and then engaged in a discussion about the harmony (*he*) of music. At the conclusion of the discussion, Taizu ordered the musicians to sing. Singing, the emperor believed, was a means to demonstrate the harmony of music to audiences.

The incident reveals much more than a rehearsal or an official's failure to identify a tone. It encapsulates the ways music was practiced and understood in the early Ming court, and reveals, in particular, Taizu's understanding of orthodox music theory. Like Confucian scholar-officials and music theorists of his time, Taizu knew that the power of music could only be activated with accurate and proper use of the twelve absolute pitches, the seven and/or five relative tones, and other musical elements that corresponded to various human and cosmological elements. Thus, Zhu Zheng's misidentification of the tone struck a wrong chord in a music system whose components theoretically were all accurately and properly placed.

The discussion between Taizu and Xiong Ding neutralized that disturbance but exposed the extent to which the two men internalized the theoretical and practical contents of the orthodox music knowledge. The discussion also demonstrated musical and theoretical continuity between the Ming and earlier times. Although Taizu and his scholar-officials eventually created a system of state sacrificial music that was uniquely theirs, they did not and could not start from scratch. They had to follow Yuan, Song, and earlier models, which they learned as they were becoming warlords and scholar-officials. Clear evidence of such learning and continuity is the Ming songs for the state sacrifice to Confucius that are developed from Yuan models. (See Figure 6.1.)

As his empire was to be formally launched, Taizu promptly established an office to take care of his state sacrifices and music. In August

Figure 6.1.
Yuan and Ming versions of the first song in the state sacrifice to Confucius (*TCXK* 5.33a; Zhu, *Lülü jingyi*, waibian 3.31)

1367, the Office of Imperial Sacrifices was instituted.[5] The office, the origin of which can be traced back to the Qin and Han dynasties, included, besides many ritual and administrative officials, a music director (*xielü lang*) who ranked seventh in a bureaucratic hierarchy of nine grades. In the next month, a candidate was found for the position. Leng Qian (ca.1310–ca.1371), a Daoist musician, was summoned to court, installed, and instructed to set ritual texts to music so they could be sung.[6] One month later, Taizu ordered the gathering of appropriate materials to build musical instruments.[7] For example, stones for the stone-chimes were brought from a place called Sizhouling and paulownia wood for the seven-string zither, the *qin*, from Huzhou, a place in present Jiejiang province. Care in the selection of raw materials was orthodox; proper music could only be produced by musical instruments made with proper materials.

By November 8, 1367, Leng Qian's responsibilities had expanded. He was asked to rectify the songs for the state sacrifices to the four imperial ancestors and to tune the stone-chimes, bell-chimes, and other musical instruments to their proper and accurate pitches.[8] What Leng Qian actually did to the songs remains unclear: he may have composed the music anew or edited preexisting ones. What is clear, however, is that the songs for the imperial ancestors are, as preserved today, stylistically different than those for the state sacrifice to Heaven. (See Figures 7.4 and 7.7 in chapter 7.) Both sets of songs were however composed during the years of 1367 to 1368.[9]

Leng Qian was probably not the only music master working in the court. Perhaps this was one of the reasons why the music and related matters in the state sacrifices honoring the imperial ancestors took shape quickly. By November 13, the dances that were to be performed with the music were choreographed.[10] The civil and military dances in the state sacrifices were to be performed by sixty-four Daoist children. Also in the same month, Taizu not only ordered an investigation into the arrangement of musical instruments in the imperial orchestra, but also asked his officials to search for and bring to court music masters who understood the "essence of music."[11] One by one, Taizu took the steps in the orthodox process of launching a system of state sacrificial music in the beginning of a dynasty.

With the music bureaucracy in place and the musical instruments built, Taizu's attention then turned to the composition of state sacrificial music, initiating a sequence of actions that radiated from the emperor to his scholar-officials and music masters. The sequences had to begin with Taizu, the emperor, as he alone had the authority to have state sacrificial music composed. Only after Taizu had ordered the composition of the music, his Confucian scholar-officials could begin writing lyrics for the state sacrificial songs, describing Confucian understanding of the ceremonials and meanings of individual ceremonial stages. Once the lyrics were composed, they were sent to the music masters who would then set the lyrics to melodies. The music masters' composition of the melodies was less an exercise to show off their musical and creative talents, but more an application of orthodox prescriptions and practices.

Taizu's attention to the composition of state sacrificial music was traditional, but his request and specifications for the creation of a new kind of escort music was atypical: He demanded music and dance to accompany his return from the altars back to the palace and specified that the lyrics of those songs teach people to be sincere and respectful in their worshipping of the deities. Responding to Taizu's commands, thirty-nine songs for returning to the palace (*huiluan ge*) were produced and presented to the throne in October 1373.[12] Following standard practices, Hanlin academicians wrote the admonitory texts while officials of the Ministry of Rites composed the music and designed the dances.

The thirty-nine songs were part of Taizu's efforts to adjust the state sacrificial music produced in the beginning years of his empire. He was not totally satisfied with the music and lyrics produced, even though they were produced according to orthodox theories and practices. Taizu was convinced that natural and astronomical movements warned him of imperfections in his state sacrifices and music.[13] Thus, in May 1375, Taizu declared that the Hanlin scholars' texts for all of the sacrificial songs offered to Heaven and Earth were too literary and florid in style and should be substituted by his own texts that were written in a simpler language.[14] Then, he had his new texts set to new tunes and premiered them in the winter of 1375.

Taizu's texts were supposed to be definitive and would serve their ritual-musical purposes as long as the Ming dynasty lasted. Such was not the case, however, because an extensive revision of state sacrifices soon occurred in the following years of 1375 to 1379, and the individual sacrifices to Heaven and Earth were combined into one single ceremonial. The ritual and musical revision necessitated a new use of Taizu's songs: two of them were dropped, and seven out of the nine songs that Taizu originally composed for the state sacrifice to Heaven became the songs for the newly formulated ceremonial for Heaven and Earth. In their adjusted forms, the songs premiered in the winter of 1377, when the ceremonial was first celebrated inside of the palace. The songs were first heard in the south suburb of the capital in 1379, when the hall of great sacrifices, located within the altar compound for the sacrifice to Heaven and Earth, was completed.

The ritual and musical revision of 1375 to 1379 led to Taizu's establishment, in February 1379, of a heretofore unknown institution, namely the Office of Sacrificial Music (*shenyue guan*), which was headed by Daoist monks who supervised the practice of state sacrificial music, trained the Daoist musician-dancers, and administered their affairs. The office was set up within the altar compound for the state sacrifice to Heaven and Earth and included various facilities for the musician-dancers, one of which was the hall of perfect harmony (*Taihe dian*), the rehearsal hall for state sacrificial music.[15]

The institution of the office is a Ming innovation, but it was not unrelated to earlier practices—Daoist monks and their involvement with court ritual music existed in previous dynasties.[16] Taizu's institution also did not appear to be a challenge to the traditional existence of state sacrificial music and the bureaucracy that supported it. Taizu did not abolish the Court of Imperial Sacrifices that was traditionally the office responsible for state sacrificial music. What Taizu did was formalize a preexisting practice that forced the Confucian scholar-officials in the Court of Imperial Sacrifices to share their musical responsibilities with Daoist monk-musicians. Needless to say, Taizu's action affected Ming state sacrificial music tremendously. He not only subjected the ideologically Confucian music to Daoist officials, but also left a permanent reminder of his own experiences—Taizu was once a young monk.

By 1379, the Ming system of state sacrifices and music had been codified in the form that remained essentially unchanged for the next 151 years. Taizu's efforts to institute state sacrificial music were successful. Through the involvement of Confucian scholar-officials and the construction of conventional musical instruments, orthodox ideas and practices of state sacrificial music were put into place. Through the newly composed repertory of tunes and the ideas and practices they embodied, a unique tradition of Ming state sacrificial music was created. Through the newly created Office of Sacrificial Music, the tradition was guaranteed to be continued through generations of Daoist teachers and disciples.

Until 1530, Taizu's legacy of state sacrificial music was considered proper and sacrosanct and was faithfully maintained by succeeding Ming emperors. Subscribing to the same Confucian ideals, Taizu's descendants had little reason to challenge the propriety of their progenitor's system. Furthermore, as descendants, they were expected to respect Taizu's system as an ancestral legacy and to preserve it faithfully. Indeed, the authority of Taizu's legacy was so great that even minor changes were meticulously recorded and introduced when the need for them could not be ignored. Revisions made by the fourth Ming sovereign, Renzong, are illustrative. To address Taizu as an ancestor and a founder, Renzong made minor adjustments in the first and fourth songs of the state sacrifice to the imperial ancestors. The changes (one phrase in the first song and four phrases in the fourth song) are carefully recorded in court manuals of state ritual and music and are clearly marked in the musical scores. Either the old text is written side by side with the new one, or the new text is inscribed in smaller characters following the original one. That there is only one musical setting for both texts suggests that there were no melodic changes. (See Figure 6.2.)

In time, however, it became more difficult to sustain Taizu's system. New ideas about ritual and music occurred, and dissatisfaction with the current system emerged.[17] In August 1450, Liu Xiang, an instructor (*zhujiao*) in the Directorate of Education (*guozi jian*), criticized the lack of proper music in the state sacrifice to Confucius and the sole use of entertainment music in the celebration banquets in the palace.[18] He made two recommendations to Daizong, the seventh Ming emperor. First, poetic music (*shiyue*), secular songs set syllablically to texts chosen from the *Classic of Odes*, should be composed and used at banquets to cultivate virtue.[19] Second, new performance methods should be adopted for the music in the state sacrifice to Confucius: the music should be performed with a

Figure 6.2.
The presentation of old and new texts
in the *TCZL* (2.17)

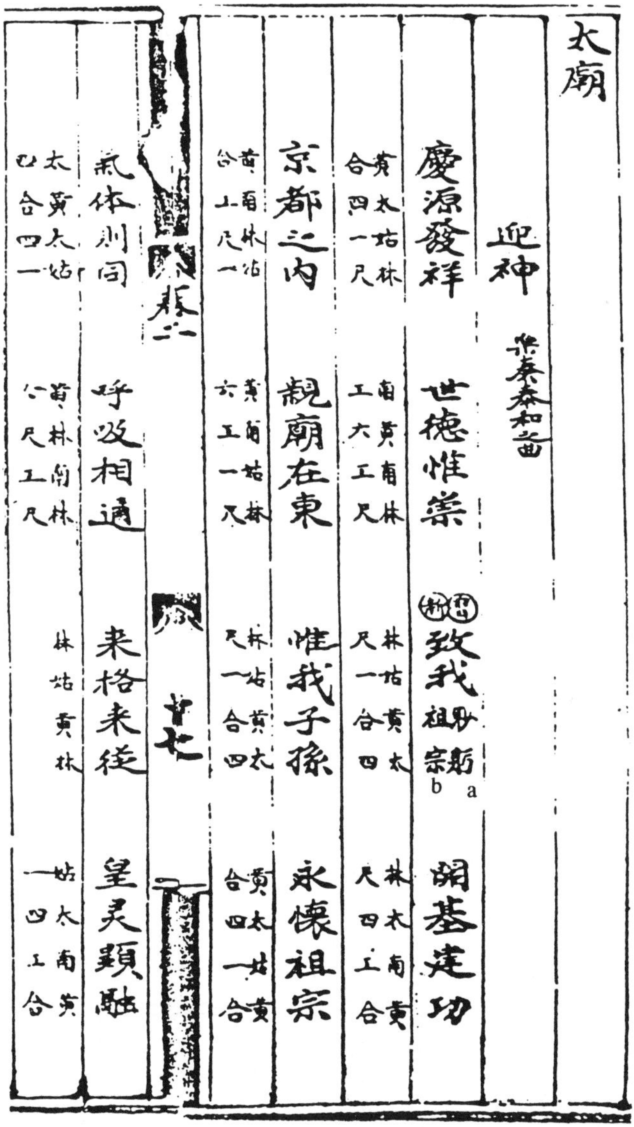

a. old text; b. new text. Columns 3, 5, and 7 show the song text; columns 4, 6, 8, give the *lülü* (right side and *gongche* (left side) notation.

tempo that was not too brisk; its phrases should neither begin suddenly nor end waveringly. Liu Xiang's appeal produced no verifiable results.

Scholar-officials such as Liu Xiang seriously desired to remove what they considered musical imperfections. They were, however, countermanded by others who held the present system as proper, and they wanted to preserve it as an unchangeable legacy. The conflict between the two groups of scholar-officials underscores the tensions between the idealistic (creative) pursuit of proper ritual and music and the conservative (orthodox) inertia to maintain the status quo. Liu Xiang represented the idealistic, and he was persistent. Despite his earlier failure, he appealed to the throne, again, in November 1464.[20] This time he recommended changing the songs for the state sacrifice to the imperial ancestors, because they were directed specifically to Renzu, Taizu's father. The emperor requested a discussion by officials of the Ministry of Rites, who vetoed Liu Xiang's suggestions. They argued that specific references to the ancestors had been corrected already and that the songs could be properly used henceforth.

Eleven years later, in August 1475, Chancellor Zhou Hongmo of the Directorate of Education proposed to honor Confucius with a new title and with the most exalted type of state sacrifices.[21] In other words, Zhou requested that the dance in the state sacrifice to Confucius be performed in the eight-row format and that the number of sacrificial food served in bamboo baskets and wood trays be increased from twenty to twenty-four. Zhou's proposal was not successful. One year later, in September 1476, Zhou appealed again and this time his proposal was partially accepted.[22] Confucius' title, the Most Accomplished and Virtuous King of Civility, did not change; neither did the number of forty-four musicians, required to play the music for the ceremonial. Only the number of dancers was raised to sixty-four, and the number of sacrificial food was increased to twenty-four.

In September 1485, officials of the Ministry of Rites complained about poor performance standards and the lack of skilled instrumentalists.[23] To prevent further deterioration of the state sacrificial music, they proposed to organize a special group of musician-dancer-students from the music offices and to train them with regular rehearsals.[24] Ten years later, in May 1495, officials of the Court of Imperial Sacrifices requested replacements for damaged instruments used in five different sacrifices.[25] More calls for rectification and maintenance appeared during Xiaozong's reign (1488–1506). Xiaozong was musically sensitive, and he concerned himself with state sacrifices and music. It was said that he could detect, with his critical ears, mistakes made in performances of state sacrificial music.[26]

Nevertheless, the emperor's concern was not entirely Confucian. In December 1495, he asked the officials of the Grand Secretariat to edit the songs for the sacrifice to the three Daoist deities (*sanqing yuezhang*). Xiaozong' request was flatly rejected by Xu Pu (1428–1499) and other conservative officials who sent in a sharp rebuttal, criticizing the Daoist worship as heretical, its music vulgar, and warning that it might lead to disasters.[27] The Confucian scholar-officials also lectured the emperor that Taizu's system of state sacrifices and music should be faithfully observed. The scholar-officials' rejection of the emperor's request is significant because it demonstrates the power of the conservative scholar-officials and their adherence to orthodox practices. The rejection also reveals the conflicts between the Confucian scholar-officials and their Daoist counterparts, and between Confucian state sacrificial music and Daoist ritual music—the former genre is copiously described in Ming documents, the latter, minimally.

A serious call for music revision came in the summer of 1502, when Ma Wensheng (1426–1510), a minister of personnel, interpreted recent calamities as portents and proposed the rectification of music as one solution.[28] Ma's argument was not only politically powerful but also ideologically persuasive: the notion of portents, which was first formulated by the Han scholar Dong Zhongshu, had become entrenched in the minds of Confucian scholar-officials and rendered connections between human activities and natural phenomenon direct and inseparable. Thus, the court could not ignore Ma's call for rectification. After much discussion, the officials issued a long memorial, criticizing the recent work of the musicians from the Court of Imperial Sacrifices, and proposing a solution to improve the music. This long memorial, which reveals tensions between orthodoxy and creativity, and between theory and practice, reads:

> In the past, Taizu, the founder of the empire, ordered the civil officials to research and rectify music, to repair and make the musical instruments, and to compile the ritual songs. [He also composed texts for the ritual music; in fact] many of the song texts [employed today] are the founder's own compositions. However, since then, more than one hundred and thirty years [have passed] and the music has not been examined again, [so that] there are mistakes in the music which should be corrected.

> Recently, we learned that Your Majesty had ordered the officials of the Court of Imperial Sacrifices, who [are supposed to] know music, to make musical instruments for the great sacrifices. [They] used pure gold to make the bell-chimes and jade to make the stone-chimes. [This is undesirable.] Since [the time when the sage rulers,] Yao and Shun, made music, the bell-chimes have been made of bronze, and the stone-chimes have been made of stones. If pure gold and jade are used to make these instruments, we fear, their sounds may not harmonize with the sound of the other instruments and may not reach and impress the deities.
>
> We request [Your Majesty to stop] those officials of the Court of Imperial Sacrifices, [whose irregular use of raw materials showed that] they are not capable of [properly] carrying out the duty of making the musical instruments and of regulating the pitches. [We ask Your Majesty] to send imperial edicts to the responsible offices throughout the empire, [and order them] to search comprehensively for music masters. [They should search among] the Chinese and foreign officials and workers, and those who live in the mountains and the countryside. If [there are those who] have mastered the musical instruments and [the art of] music, they should be sent to the capital courteously. [In the meantime], our officials will still meet with [those from] the Court of Imperial Sacrifices to further discuss [the issues, and] to find the appropriate [solutions]. [We will] jointly make the musical instruments and correct the musical sounds. In this way, [we hope] the state sacrificial music instituted by the empire's saintly founder can be revived in the present time.[29]

The memorial probably did not lead to extensive revision or drastic actions; if they were realized, they were not described in extant documents of the Ming court, and they did not solve the problems of state sacrificial music. Three years later, in May 1505, new musical instruments were needed for the state sacrifices worshipping the imperial ancestors and the deities of soil and grains. Xiaozong ordered the instruments made and then sent to the Office of Sacrificial Music.[30]

As demonstrated by Xu Pu's rejection of Xiaozong's request for Daoist ritual music, state sacrificial music was by no means the only music practiced in the court. In fact, the genre was constantly challenged by entertainment music, which was needed for various secular functions in the court and which was installed since the beginning of the empire: in December 1367, Taizu established the Office of Entertainment Music, and by October 1370 he had created a system of state banquet music.[31] Being fashionable and enticing, entertainment music flourished in the Ming court, despite unremitting attacks from the Confucian scholar-officials. They could not afford to ease off their attacks because entertainment music was, by their Confucian standards, decadent, something that would not only corrupt people's virtues but would also tarnish state sacrificial music.

Conflicts between state sacrificial music and entertainment music in the Ming court reached a climax during the reign of Wuzong, the tenth Ming emperor. In August 1508, the fun-loving ruler opened the doors for various entertainers to come to the court by construing a clever excuse: to show the greatness of the empire, entertainment music should be performed in celebration banquets that were attended by Chinese and foreign officials; thus, the shortage of musicians for such music had to be remedied.[32] In response, the Ministry of Rites proposed to select young, energetic but unskilled musicians for vigorous training. The proposal was rejected; the emperor was interested only in immediate gratification. Armed with an argument that the officials could not reject, Wuzong ordered the local authorities to recruit and send talented musicians and artists to the palace.

Wuzong's musical frolic made a public mockery of the Confucian notion that music serves as a means of governance and cultivates virtues. However, the emperor died young and childless, and his games soon ended. The swing of the pendulum reverted back to state sacrificial music when Wuzong was succeeded by his cousin, Shizong, who was not born as an heir apparent but was chosen to receive the Ming throne. Unlike previous Ming rulers, who neither wanted to nor dared to change Taizu's system of state sacrifices and music, Shizong carried out drastic revisions in the 1530s and 1540s. He was motivated by a personal agenda—to keep his own genealogical line and consolidate his position in court. His involvement with music was direct and serious.

In July 1524, when the hall of paternal virtue (*Guande dian*), the building for honoring Shizong's biological father, was near completion, he ordered Cui Yuanchu, a music director, to gather more than twenty musicians to begin rehearsing, inside the palace, sacrificial songs that honored the father.[33] Wang Ju (1502 js.), the chief minister of the Court of Imperial Sacrifice, found fault with the music performances and wanted to punish the musicians with the pretext that they entered the palace without formal permission. As a result, the emperor was obliged to ask an official from the Court of Imperial Sacrifices to accompany the musicians whenever they entered the palace, a solution that did not please the officials and elicited further criticism.

Zhu Xizhou, a vice minister of rites, also denounced the rehearsals as an inappropriate use of the musician-dancers of state sacrificial music. His protest was ignored by the emperor. Then Wang Ju forcefully accused the emperor of breaking the rule that state sacrificial music and dance were to be performed only at imperial temples and altar compounds located outside of the palace. Asserting that even the ceremonials held in the hall of ancestral worship (*Fengxian dian*) inside the palace did not employ music and dance, Wang requested that the emperor stop the irregular performances.

The emperor's reply was equally sharp, and he made a valid point. He argued that no music and dance were performed in the hall of ancestral worship because there was no such need: the ancestors worshipped in the hall were formally honored in the imperial ancestral temple, located outside of the palace, where sacrificial ceremonies were performed with music and dance. In contrast, the emperor asserted, ceremonials in the hall of paternal virtue had to employ music and dance because they constituted the only ritual and musical means through which he could honor his biological father, who died as a prince and was not honored in the imperial ancestral temple.

The conflict between Shizong and Wang Ju was a battle between orthodox (general) and personal (specific) understanding and use of state sacrificial music. Wang's criticism represented a conservative scholar-official's efforts to maintain orthodox practices. Shizong's use of the music was a creative solution for an unusual set of problems. First, he wanted to honor his biological father with the most elaborate ceremonials, a desire that could not be realized without the use of state sacrificial music and dance: Music and dance are essential components of ceremonials; the visual and aural expressions of music and dance are explicit and unignorable by all who could hear and see. Second, Shizong was building his imperial power and political base with state sacrifices and music; he could not afford to yield to the official's demands. The emperor had to win, and he did.

By 1530, Shizong had won many battles, and his power in court was solid. Then he began his drastic series of ritual and musical revisions in earnest, launching separate state sacrifices to Heaven and Earth, the sericultural ceremonials, and so forth. Shizong's revisions constituted not only revealing expressions of the emperor's understanding of ritual and music but also his forceful means of governance. Shizong exploited and appropriated state ritual to exercise his imperial authority, a fact that can be illustrated with a brief note on the ways in which the emperor changed the state sacrifice to Confucius.[34]

In December 1530, Shizong stopped the practice of honoring Confucius as a king (*wang*), snatched the philosopher's' title of the Most Accomplished and Virtuous King of Civility, but honored him as the Most Virtuous Progenitor of Teachers (*Zhisheng xianshi*). In other words, Shizong dismantled what Zhou Hongmo had done some fifty years ago. Once again, the dance of the state sacrifice to Confucius was performed in the six-row format; the number of musicians, dancers, and sacrificial food in bamboo baskets and wooden trays was, respectively, reduced to forty-four, thirty-six, and twenty.[35] These changes involved neither new music nor ritual procedures but were still ritually and musically expressive. The changes not only overturned Zhou Hongmo's efforts to elevate the status of Confucius, and by extension, that of Confucian scholar-officials, but also perpetuated Shizong's interpretation of what Confucius was, and how the philosopher should be honored. Furthermore, the changes revealed Shizong's partiality: he honored his biological father as an emperor, even though the father was never one in real life.[36]

Shizong's ritual and musical revisions were extensive. To cope with the musical needs of the new and revised state sacrifices, the Ministry of Rites requested the recruitment of more musician-dancers and the search for a music master to handle the musical matters. The search resulted in Zhang E's appointment, who arrived at court in September 1530, presenting two music treatises and a memorial filled with technical recommendations on the rectification of state sacrificial music. The memorial made such an impact that it was quoted extensively in the *Veritable Records of Shizong* and in the *Ming History*; the rarity of such quotations in official histories of Chinese courts only accentuates Zhang's dramatic but short career in the Ming court.[37] Favorably received by the court, Zhang was named an assistant minister in the Court of State Sacrifices and given the task of rectifying state sacrificial music and dance. However, Zhang was to perform his duties in the hall of perfect harmony, the rehearsal hall in the Office of Sacrificial Music that was controlled by Daoist monk/music masters. Zhang was a Confucian scholar/music master, and thus his assignment to the hall of perfect harmony only aggravated and exposed the rivalry between the Confucian scholar-officials and the Daoist monk/music masters.

One of the two treatises Zhang presented, the *Musical Score and Dance Illustrations for the Sacrifice to Confucius*, is still extant, and it preserves some clues to Zhang's life. Zhang was a native of Linqing, and he had a courtesy name of Yunjian. He once served as a vice minister in the Court of Imperial Stud (*taipusi*)in the Gansu Circuit.[38] Zhang's birth and death dates are unknown, but it is clear that he was active during the Zhengde and Jiajing periods, 1506–1566, and that he was socially connected with contemporary scholar-officials in the capital.

In fact, his summon to court was recommended by Xia Yan, the scholar-official who proposed the sericultural ceremonials to Shizong. Zhang also was highly esteemed by Lü Nan (1479–1542), a famous and prolific Ming scholar-official. Lü's admiration of Zhang's musical knowledge and skills in playing the seven-string zither (*qin*) was clear. In the preface to Zhang's treatise, Lü recounted that he took *qin* lessons from Zhang and how Zhang once played the *qin* piece, the Plum Blossoms, with only six strings when the third string could not be tuned properly due to a damaged peg.

Once commissioned, Zhang was enthusiastic in performing his duties and promptly presented a memorial to report his findings. After listening to the songs of the state sacrifice to the imperial father (*shimiao*), he noticed their erroneous use of the *linzhong* (g) mode, a mode that should not be used in music for ancestors. Upon checking old scores of the music, he confirmed the current use as a mistake—the music was originally and appropriately composed in the mode of *huangzhong*. Zhang, however, did not think the original score was perfect: he noticed that only six out of the seven tones of the *huangzhong* mode was used. To rectify the music so it might properly fulfill its function, Zhang proposed adding the missing seventh tone.

After examining Zhang's memorial, Minister of Rites, Li Shi and other scholar-officials confirmed the music master's findings and made the following recommendations. The tone *bianzhi* (F#, *gou*) would be added, while the tone *biangong* (B, *fan*) would replace the octave *huangzhong* (C'), thus conforming to the orthodox understanding of the seven relative tones of *gong*, *shang*, *jue*, *bianzhi*, *zhi*, *yu*, and *biangong*. Zhang's memorial earned him further recognition: He was then given additional tasks and asked to rectify the music of the state sacrifices offered to the imperial ancestors. In the meantime, the musicians, Shen Jujing, and others who were held responsible for having corrupted the music for the imperial father were judicially investigated; the outcome of the investigation is unreported in historical documents.

Soon, Zhang also gained imperial attention as a facile composer. On April 4, 1531, he presented to the throne his musical settings of the lyrics for the state sacrifice to the deities of imperial soil and grains (*di sheji*). His presentation attracted imperial attention because he was asked to set the lyrics to music only a few days earlier.[39] Zhang's prompt composition of the tunes was thus a sharp contrast to the tardiness of the musicians of the Court of Imperial Sacrifices and the Office of State Sacrificial Music. They once took five months to set the songs for the sacrificial prayer for grain harvest (*qigu*).[40] Zhang's promptness obviously pleased the emperor, as the composer was promoted from assistant to vice minister (*shaoqing*) in no time.

Zhang worked fast because he made use of preexisting musical materials. The set of songs he presented includes one rare and identifiable sample of musical borrowing in Ming state sacrificial songs. As Figure 6.3 shows, the composer took six phrases out of the first song for the state sacrifice to Confucius and used them in the beginning of the second song for the new ceremonial. Such borrowing reveals many things about the composer and about the practice of state sacrificial music. First, Zhang who wrote the *Musical Score and Dance Illustrations for the Sacrifice to Confucius*, was familiar with the music of the ceremonial. Second, when the composer worked under pressure, he relied on preexisting musical materials with which he was familiar. This is not surprising, as the rearranging (recreating) of preexisting musical materials is still a common practice among traditional musicians of Chinese music. Third, even though Ming state sacrificial songs share many musical elements (syllabic text-setting, formulaic motifs, a limited number of pitches, and so on), each individual song is (and has to be) distinctive. Intentionally or intuitively, Zhang knew he had already tested the boundaries marking the identities of two different state sacrificial songs. Thus he refrained from further borrowing: His borrowing was/is however obvious to anyone who was/is familiar with the songs for the Confucian ceremonial.

Zhang's prompt setting and presentation of his songs demonstrate that he was a career official-scholar who knew how to make the best out of his circumstances. On November 6, 1531, Zhang presented an essay, "Discussion of the White Magpie" ("*Baique bian*") to the emperor who had just received some birds that were sent to him as auspicious gifts.[41] Zhang's essay was an obvious effort to curry favor from the emperor, a move that

Figure 6.3.
Zhang E's musical borrowing

The first song of the Ming state sacrifice to Confucius (<u>TCXK</u> 5.33a)

The second song of Zhang E's music for the state sacrifice to the imperial deities of soil and grains (<u>TCXK</u> 8.34a)

was not uncommon among officials in Shizong's court but was still much-despised by the righteous Confucian scholar-officials. Zhang's essay may have pleased the emperor, but it probably did not further Zhang's career much.

In the next four years, Zhang's activities were not recorded in court documents. Then, in July 1535, Zhang appealed to rectify music once again. This time, he proposed to revive the ancient placement of musical instruments in the imperial orchestra and to use the large special-bell (*tezhong*) to mark ritual and musical activities.[42] Zhang also recommended an investigation of accurate pitches for the state sacrificial music with the *houqi* exercise and with the use, as a measuring device, of millet grains from Mountain Yangtou in the Zhangzi District of Shanxi Province. Zhang's appeal turned out to be a swan song. There is no record of what he achieved with his appeal, except that he was indicted, in May 1536, for being disrespectful to the emperor and was banished permanently to the frontier.[43]

Zhang was persecuted for failing to yield to the emperor when they passed each other on the road. Regardless of the truth of the accusation, Zhang was more a casualty in the conflict between the Confucian scholar-officials and the Daoist monk-officials. He became a scapegoat to serve the emperor's need to ease tensions among some court citizens and to divert attack on the Daoists. Zhang was dispensable. He was a Confucian scholar by learning, but his career and behavior was not that of a typical Confucian scholar-official: He was assigned to the hall of perfect harmony controlled by Daoist monk-officials and given rapid promotion, and he curried favor from the emperor. Zhang's persecution occurred in a time when the emperor felt intense animosity toward the Daoist monk-officials, and he had asked the Confucian scholar-officials to discuss the unsuitability of certain people involved in state sacrifices.[44]

Shizong's protection of the Daoist monk-officials reflected not only the emperor's growing interest in Daoist ritual, but also the solidarity the Daoists had built for themselves since the very beginning of the empire.[45] Ming state sacrificial music was ideologically Confucian but it was never without Daoist elements.[46] The first recorded rehearsal of the music in the history of the empire was performed by "Daoist children." The first documented music director, Leng Qian, was always described as a Daoist.[47] The first regulation on the number of musicians and dancers for the state sacrifices specified the use of "Daoist children" as musician-dancers. Daoists were guaranteed a permanent place in Ming state sacrificial music when, in 1379, Taizu instituted the Office of Sacrificial Music, installed Daoist monks as its chief officials, and gave them the privileges of accepting apprentices.[48] As masters and disciples worked together over long periods of time, they developed close relationships, effectively transmitting their musical knowledge as well as political aspirations. Furthermore, many of these music officials originated from a few preferred areas near the capital, their relationships thus further consolidated by a common affinity to local cultures and social networks.[49]

There is little information about how the Daoists practiced and maintained their tradition of Ming state sacrificial music. The ways they thrived, however, suggested the extent of their control of state ritual and music. As early as 1382, a Daoist monk-official, Qiu Xuanqing, was promoted to the rank of a minister in the Court of Imperial Sacrifices. The first person to have risen from the lowest rank of musician-dancer to high positions was Xie Qingzhi, who became an assistant minister in 1400. By the late fifteenth century, Daoist monk-musician-officials had obtained a goodly share of top positions. In May 1495, Cui Zhiduan, a Daoist, was promoted to chief minister of the Court of Imperial Sacrifices. Two years later, in September 1497, two other Daoists, Zhao Jizhong, a former archivist, and Wang Fuguang, a former music director, were promoted to assistant ministers.[50] These were not isolated cases; two other Daoist monk-musicians also were promoted to the position of vice minister in 1539.[51]

In fact, the Daoist monk-musician-officials were so successful that they were under almost constant attack from the Confucian scholar-officials. When Cui Zhiduan was promoted by Xiaozong, Ji Yuan, chief supervising secretary of the ministry of personnel, characterized the appointment as sacrilegious and asked the emperor to rescind it.[52] The emperor refused, replying that Cui had served on the state sacrifices for many years and was for that reason worthy of the promotion.

Among the Daoist monk-musician-officials, Jin Yunren's career was particularly eventful and is illustrative of the ways in which state sacrifice and music became integral parts of court politics and lives. Jin began as a musician-dancer and was promoted to vice minister of the Court of Imperial Sacrifices in 1531. Nine years later, when he presented his treatise on contemporaneous sacrifices, *A Complete Guide for the Court of Imperial Sacrifices* (*Taichang zongji*), which is now lost, he was already a vice minister of rites in charge of the affairs of the Court of Imperial Sacrifices.[53] In the following year, when he earned a merit for completing a term of service as a vice minister, he requested that the merit be awarded to his apprentice, Music Director Chen Zixian. Jin's request was irregular, because Chen was not his direct descendant and should not have been given such transferred merits. Nevertheless, an exception was made, and Chen was promoted one rank.

The good fortune of Jin and Chen ended in June 1543, however, when both men were indicted for embezzlement, the taking of wives, and keeping official land for personal use.[54] As punishment, Jin was deprived of his registration as a Daoist, and Chen, like Zhang E, the Confucian scholar-official-music master, was permanently banished to the frontier. Jin's rise and fall was dramatic but indicative of his power and involvement with state sacrifices and music. In fact, Jin's fame went beyond the physical boundaries of the court. He was so well-known that a late Ming theorist, Wang Sizong, recalled him as being an official who tried to keep his family trade of serving in the state sacrificial music and resisted the radical musical reforms of Li Wencha.[55]

Li Wencha was a music master summoned to the court after Zhang E's downfall in 1536. Coming from Liaozhou in Shanxi Province, where he served as a vice magistrate, Li arrived at the court in June 1538 and presented four musical treatises to the throne. He was assigned as an archivist in the Court of Imperial Sacrifices but was asked to participate in various musical exercises. In 1545, after serving as an archivist for eight years, Li presented two other musical treatises to the throne, a set of pitch pipes, and a long memorial with nine recommendations for the rectification of state sacrificial music. Li Wencha's memorial, which now appears at the end of his *Essential Theories on the Promotion of Proper Music* (*Xingyue yaolun*), tells much about Ming state sacrificial music in the mid-sixteenth century. The recommendations are:

1. To research extensively ancient music (*guyue*) so its desirable features may be emulated and perpetuated
2. To correct the current practice of employing only seven pitches in state sacrificial music; as Li composed music according to the cycle of fifths, he proposed the use of all of the twelve absolute pitches
3. To compose music that would specifically cultivate the crown prince's virtue
4. To string the seven- and twenty-five string zithers more effectively so they would sound properly; and to be more sympathetic

toward the musicians if the strings should break or the frets should collapse during performance; (to avoid undesirable accidents with the musical instruments and consequent punishments, the musicians substituted the required pitches of the music with inaccurate ones; they also lowered the tuning of the musical instruments, so the strings would not break and the frets would not collapse unexpectedly)[56]

5. To regulate the pitches of the bell-chimes and stone-chimes according to the sixteen pitch pipes that Li devised and presented to the throne
6. To revive the use of the panpipes (*paixiao*) in state sacrificial music; the sound of the panpipes would support those of the vertical and transverse flutes (*xiao* and *di*)
7. To pay greater attention to the ocarina (*xun*) and the transverse flute (*chi*), whose soft sounds constitute a crucial part of state sacrificial music; and to ensure correct performance of every individual part by having the instrumentalists rehearse in selected groups before the full orchestral rehearsal
8. To promote the study of proper music throughout the empire by establishing special schools or offices of music
9. To compile an encyclopedia of proper music to spread musical knowledge

Li's nine recommendations sketch a musical scene that was much more complex than what official titles, theoretical prescriptions, and standard histories would reveal. If one compares Li's official title with what he did, it is clear that he did more than what his title would have suggested. Li was nominally an archivist, but his duties, official or not, did not appear to be focused on keeping records of the Court of Imperial Sacrifices. He acted like a music master, theorist, and composer, much like Zhang E, his predecessor who was a vice minister of the Court of Imperial Sacrifices. Li's plea for leniency for the musicians pinpoints that the Confucian scholar-officials' demand for accuracy in ritual/musical performances was serious but it may not have always been realized. To avoid undesirable accidents such as breaking strings, musicians substituted proper notes with more convenient ones that were lower in pitch and did not require that strings be pulled tightly. The quality of musical performances was unstable. Li's attention to individual instrumental parts and pleas for rehearsals for selected groups suggest on one hand the proficiency level a music master could demand, and on the other hand, the extent of coaching the individual musicians would need.

Li's recommendations constitute a vivid reminder of the tensions between orthodoxy and creativity, and theory and practice. Orthodox presumptions propelled Li to present the pitch pipes as the tools to rectify music, to regulate the pitches of the bell-chimes and stone-chimes, and to include all of the twelve absolute pitches in musical composition. Confucian and scholarly concerns dictated Li to call for research on *guyue*, to compile an encyclopedia about the music, and to promote the study of music in schools throughout the empire. On the other hand, the circumstances of Shizong's court—in particular, concern for the education of the heir apparent—and Li's individuality led him to request and compose music to cultivate the virtues of the crown prince. Li's request constituted an unique extension of a familiar notion—music cultivates virtues: there was hardly a more effective use of music if it could be used to cultivate the crown prince, the future emperor; the more cultivated he was, the more benevolent a ruler he would become.

Similarly, Li's proposal to compose songs according to the cycles of fifths was a new twist to an old theory. If music is represented by the twelve absolute pitches, as Li theorized, it should use all of them. (See Figure 7.8 in chapter 7.) Li's proposal is of course more theoretical than practical, and it is not representative of the Ming state sacrificial songs of the mid-sixteenth century. Most of Shizong's musical officials worked with orthodox prescriptions. Even if the state sacrificial songs were newly composed, their basic features followed stylistic norms: syllabic text setting, use of melodic patterns, particular compositional designs, and so forth.

Li's recommendations, theories, and compositions are, however, representative of Ming efforts to pursue the ideal state sacrifices and music. In this sense, Li's discussion of the musical and theoretical particulars reflects Shizong's direct involvement with his ritual and musical revisions. Shizong actually wrote song texts for state sacrifices, such as those for the state sacrifice to the imperial father (1526), the ceremony of reporting to the ancestors (*yugao zaozong*), and the sacrifice to the virtuous kings and emperors of previous dynasties (*xiansheng diwang*) (1552).[57]

Shizong's direct involvement is a crucial factor in the success of his revisions, a fact that is suggested by the increase and decrease in the number of musician-dancers. In 1535, the year before Li Wencha came to court, the number was increased to 2,200 to cope with the newly revised and instituted ceremonials.[58] Three years later, in October 1538, a further increase was again requested. Moreover, as a supplementary solution to ease the shortage of music and dance performers, the Court of Imperial Sacrifices pleaded to relax the rule that each state sacrifice had to have its own group of musician-dancers.[59] Still another 1,229 musician-dancers were recruited in February 1540.[60] This trend of increase sibsided, however, as soon as the emperor's personal interest in the state sacrifices weakened. No request for more musician-dancers was issued after the mid-1540s. Then, cuts in the numbers were made in the last years of Shizong's reign, when he devoted more and more of his energy to Daoist ritual. In 1551, when Shizong was no longer concerned about state sacrificial music, the quota of musician-dancers was set at 1,153.[61]

The monumental scale of Shizong's musical revisions was never repeated again in the Ming dynasty. Subsequent changes were mostly about downsizing the musical personnel; Muzong, Shizong's successor, made substantial cuts. Furthermore, no new sacrificial songs were created after Shizong's reign. Serious interest to revise state sacrificial music did not appear again until the end of the empire. In September 1641, Sizong, the last Ming ruler, wanted a music reform and ordered the Ministry of Works and then the Ministry of Rites to investigate the ideal measurement standards of the pitch pipes.[62] In the following March, the Ministry of Rites proposed a search for a music master to rectify the state sacrificial music. As references for this reform, two important Ming musical treatises were mentioned specifically by the officials: Zhu Zaiyu's *Collected Works on Music Theory* and ex-minister of Rites Huang Yuliang's *Monograph on Music History and Theory.*

Sizong's attempts were, needless to say, too little and too late to save the Ming empire. The unrealized attempts nevertheless spotlighted the sustaining power of the Confucian ideology and the orthodox theories behind state sacrificial music. Even as the Ming empire was collapsing to their faces, the emperor and Confucian scholar-officials still wanted to use state sacrificial music as one of the means to address their problems. Such intended use of the music was dramatic, if not pathetic: their fruitless discussion about music was symptomatic of the ways in which the emperor and his court failed to resolve current conflicts of the people, time, and place. Unlike Taizu or Shizong, who subscribed to the same orthodoxy of state sacrificial music but managed to create unique repertories, Sizong did not have his chance. The Ming empire ended.

CHAPTER SEVEN

Ming State Sacrificial Songs

INTRODUCTION

Ming dynasty state sacrificial songs (hereafter, songs) are created as distinctive statements of proper music and as integral components of specific state sacrifices. To satisfy the first requirement, the songs are orthodoxly shaped according to the stylistic parameters of *guyue*; as a result, the songs are stylistically similar and relate to each other as members of a homogenous repertory. To satisfy the second requirement, the songs are creatively composed as melodies that serve particular state sacrifices and ceremonial stages; as a result, the songs are individualistic in one way or another. Thus, if one broadly surveys the 323 known samples of the songs, she or he will be overwhelmed by a deluge of formulaic phrases, predictable patterns in structural divisions, and other signs of stylistic homogeneity. However, if one takes the time to compare the songs one by one, she or he will be dazzled by the amount and variety of subtle differences found in the songs.

These differences are creative expressions that allow the state sacrifices and music to be identified, appropriated, and interpreted by the concerned participants and critical audiences in the Ming court. When Taizu, Xiaozong, Shizong, Zhang E, Liu Xiang, and other Ming court citizens listened to the songs, they responded as ritual and music masters. They would understand the songs as individual compositions by identifying and interpreting unique features in the music as expressions of particular ideas, people, and events in the Ming court. The expressiveness of the songs depends on their being identified as unique music: music that is not unique in some ways can neither be appropriated nor interpreted for specific purposes.

For the time being, when the ephemeral sounds of the songs have vanished, and when the court citizens can no longer be reached for answers, one can probe into the expressiveness of the songs by studying them as notated music, analyzing their structure, and identifying their distinctive features. Structural analysis, needless to say, cannot reveal how the songs were heard as music performed in temples or altar compounds. Structural analysis, however, would produce data that pinpoints how the songs are structurally distinctive. When one combines such analytical data with contextual and historical information about Ming court citizens and their understanding of state sacrifice and music, one has a factual and theoretical basis to imagine, historically, how the songs touched the hearts and minds of the Ming emperors, scholar-officials, and music masters. It is toward such understanding of the songs that representative samples are analyzed in detail here.

NOTATED SOURCES OF MING DYNASTY STATE SACRIFICIAL MUSIC

Until 1984, the songs were essentially known as a body of texts preserved in the *Ming History* and other standard documents of the Ming. There was no doubt that at one time the texts were sung, but there also was the belief that the melodies were practically all lost—only eight of the songs were preserved and known as notated music. Then, in 1984, I had the fortune to discover four Ming documents that have preserved the notated music of 323 samples of the songs. This notated music is authentic and representative, a fact that can be clearly demonstrated by a brief discussion of the documents. They include:

1. *Collected Ceremonial of the Ming Dynasty* (*Da Ming jili*, hereafter *DMJL*), which preserves, in *lülü* and *gongche* notation, eighty-seven songs for nine state sacrifices
2. *General Record of the Court of Imperial Sacrifices* (*Taichang zonglan*, hereafter *TCZL*), which preserves, in *lülü* and *gongche* notation, fifty-one songs for seven state sacrifices
3. *Monograph on the Court of Imperial Sacrifices* (*Taichang kao*, hereafter *TCK*), which preserves, in *gongche* notation, 177 songs for twenty-four state sacrifices

4. *Expanded Monograph on the Court of Imperial Sacrifices* (*Taichang xukao*, hereafter *TCXK*), which preserves, in *gongche* notation, the same songs notated in the *TCK*

Including the previously known samples (eight) preserved in Zhu Zaiyi's *Essentials of Music Theory* (*Lülü jingyi*), the aforementioned documents have preserved a total of 323 Ming dynasty state sacrificial songs.

The four documents were prepared by scholar-officials who were directly involved with Ming state sacrifices and music. The bibliographic history and physical features of the documents attest to the fact that they have preserved authentic and representative samples of the songs. The *DMJL* is a multivolume document of fifty-three chapters, which was prepared, by and for court officials, as an encyclopedic reference on state ritual and music. Organized according to the five categories of court ceremonials and related matters, the manual includes descriptions and regulations for state sacrifices and other ceremonials, costumes, insignia (*yizhang*), escorts (*lubu*), calligraphy (*zixue*), and music. Music scores, written in *lülü* and *gongche* notation, appear in the chapters devoted to individual state sacrifices and in the last three chapters of the manual, which also include discussions of music theory and instruments.

According to the *Veritable Records of Taizu*, a group of ritual officials and Confucian scholars led by Xu Yikui (1318–ca.1400) received, in September 1369, an imperial command to begin work on the *DMJL*; they presented a completed manual to the throne on October 10, 1370.[1] The manual was not printed, but presumably more than one manuscript copy was prepared. Yang Shiqi reported the survival of two incomplete sets in his *Catalogue of the Wenyuange Library* (*Wenyuange shumu*) of 1441.[2] These sets or other copies must have survived until 1530, when a new edition of the manual was printed as a reference work to help the officials discuss ritual and musical matters. This 1530 edition, which is now the earliest available version, is known to differ from the original manuscript in certain minor aspects. For example, it has fifty-three chapters, while the original manuscript version is known to have only fifty chapters. This 1530 edition, copies of which are still available in major libraries of Ming documents, has been incorporated into the *Siku quanshu* (the *Imperial Library*) of the 1770s, which is now readily available in facsimile editions.

Authenticity of the music notated in the *DMJL* is self-explanatory. The manual was compiled, in an opportune time, by the very scholar-officials who were involved in creating the Ming system of state sacrifices and music. From physical evidence in the 1530 edition, one can conclude that it faithfully transmitted data from its exemplar. In the 1530 edition, the score of the first song for the sacrifice to the earthly deities displays a blank space to mark the lost music (eight notes) for two phrases of the song text.[3] (See Figure 7.1.) The missing music could have been composed anew or replaced with something appropriate, but that was not done, and the relevant space was left blank. This blank space becomes eloquent evidence that the 1530 edition has preserved the songs faithfully.

The authenticity of the preserved music is also confirmed by its style. The tunes preserved in the *DMJL* share a stylistic similarity that is noticeably absent in the songs composed in the 1530s. Unless the *DMJL* tunes are all forgeries made in 1530, which is not possible, they must be authentic music from the beginning of the Ming empire. If there were some musical forgeries in the 1530 edition, they were so cleverly made that they could not be distinguished from what was originally composed in 1370 or earlier years in the beginning of the empire. There is no evidence that Li Shi and other scholar-officials who prepared the 1530 edition were composers and masters of musical forgery. Thus, one has to presume that they did not and could not forge the music and that the 1530 edition has reliably preserved music from the late fourteenth century.

The second notated source of the songs is the *TCZL*, a one-volume manual of six chapters and 115 folios that was prepared for court officials responsible for state sacrifices. The time when the manual was compiled is not recorded, but internal evidence suggests that it falls between 1464 and 1476. An illustration in the manual (see Figure 7.2) mentions five deceased Ming emperors—Taizu, Taizong, Renzong, Xuanzong, and Yingzong.[4] Thus, the manual cannot be compiled before 1464, the year Yingzong died. Similarly, the manual cannot be compiled after 1476, because its description of the state sacrifice to Confucius reflects what was practiced before 1476: The manual prescribes the use of the six-row format for the dances in that ceremonial. In 1476, Xianzong granted the use of dances in the eight-row format, a practice that lasted until 1530.

The *TCZL* is now deposited in the Library of the National Palace Museum in Taipei and is available on microfilm.[5] The authenticity of the manual is suggested by the physical features of its folios of blue-lined paper and by three known bibliographic citations. The first and earliest one is in the 1605 *Catalogue of the Cabinet Library* (*Neige shumu*) of Zhang Xuan, whose description of the contents and number of chapters in the

Figure 7.1.
A blank space in a musical score in the 1530 edition of the *DMJL* (14.32a)

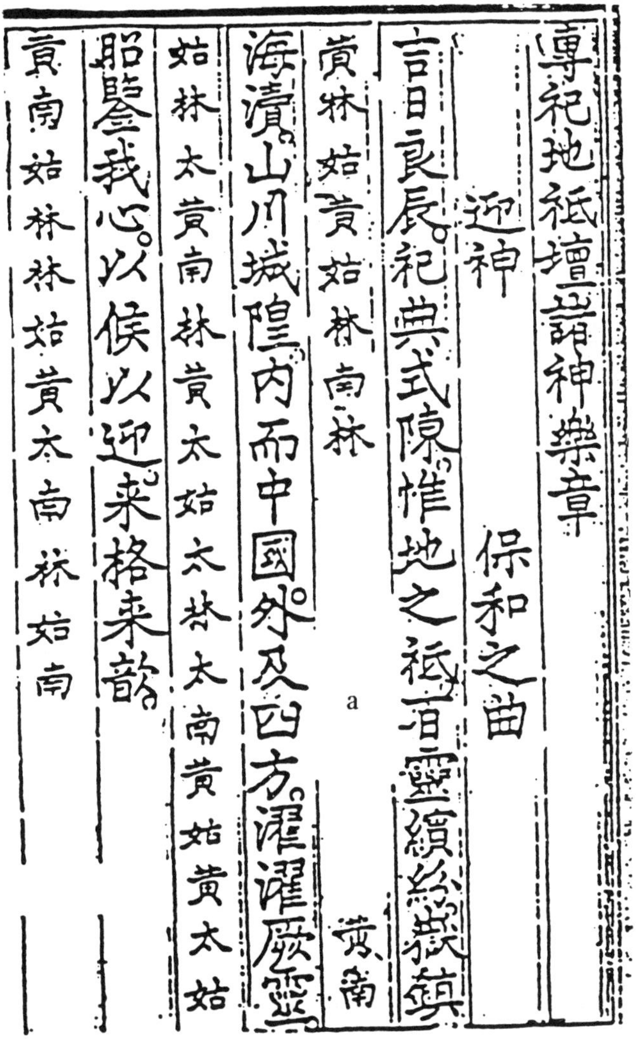

a. The blank space. Columns 3, 5, and 7 give the song text; columns 4, 6, and 8 give the *lülü* notation.

Figure 7.2.
A *TCZL* illustration of a ritual arrangement that names the temple titles of five deceased Ming emperors (2.12a)

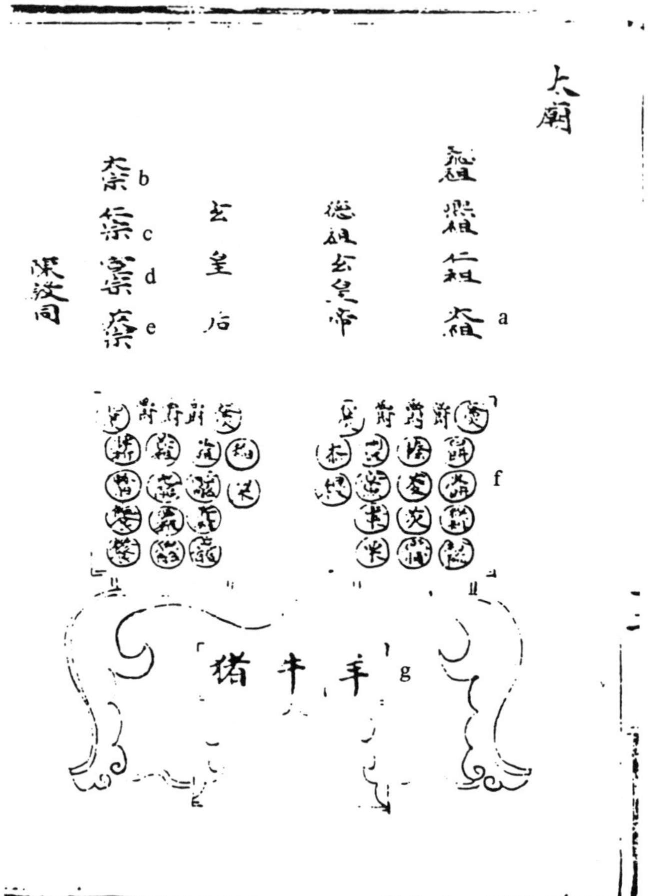

a. Taizu; b. Taizong; c. Renzong; d. Xuanzong;
e. Yingzong; f. sacrificial foods; g. sacrificial victims

TCZL matches its current conditions.[6] The second citation is in the highly reliable *Catalogue of the Qianqing Library* (*Qianqingtang shumu*) from the early seventeenth century, and the third, in Zhu Zaiyu's *Essentials of Music Theory* from the end of the sixteenth century.[7] Distinctive stylistic features and musical concordance between the songs preserved in the *DMJL* and *TCZL* suggest that the latter is a reliable music source.

The third notated source of the songs is the *TCK*, currently housed in the Beijing University Library. A detailed eight-volume manuscript on Ming state sacrifices, this source preserves the earliest available *gongche* notation for 177 songs, most of which were composed after 1530 and thus are not recorded in the *DMJL* and the *TCZL*. Written on blue-lined paper, the *TCK* displays an elegant scribal style and signs of heavy use. (See Figure 7.3.) Most of the lower left corners of the folios in volumes one through three and volume eight are professionally patched with new paper. Such condition shows that the manuscript was once damaged from heavy use.[8]

The reliability of the *TCK* is demonstrated by the corroboration between a bibliographical record and a note in the manuscript. Zhang Xuan's *Catalogue of the Cabinet Library* of 1605 attributes the manuscript to an unknown compiler of the early Wanli (1573–1619) period of the Ming. Indeed, on folio 5a of volume two of the manual, there is a note that refers to the Jiajing period (1522–1565) as a time two generations ago; the *Wanli* period is two generations after the Jiajing period. If Zhang Xuan, a contemporary and respected bibliographer, did not challenge the reliability of the *TCK* when it appeared between the years of 1573 and 1605, there is no reason to doubt its authenticity and the music it has preserved.

The historical significance of the *TCK* has been recognized, as it has been copied twice in the early decades of the twentieth century. One of these modern copies is the "Ming Dynasty Ritual and Music" (*Mingdai liyue*), which is now deposited in the library of the Research Institute of Music in Beijing. Despite the change in title, the "Ming Dynasty Ritual and Music" is an exact copy of the *TCK*. The second modern copy of the *TCK*, which is bound into twelve volumes, is deposited in the National Beijing Library.

The fourth notated source of the songs is the *TCXK*, a large and detailed monograph that is closely related to the *TCK*. The *TCXK* was probably completed soon after 1643, the last date entered in its text, and the last but one year in the Ming empire. The original copy (or copies) of the *TCXK* is no longer available, but an edition of the monograph has been incorporated into the *Siku quanshu* and is now readily accessible through facsimile reprints.

The close relationship between the *TCXK* and the *TCK* is clear. The two share the same texts in the same order and are identical except for

Figure 7.3.
A musical score from the *TCK* (4.14b-15a)

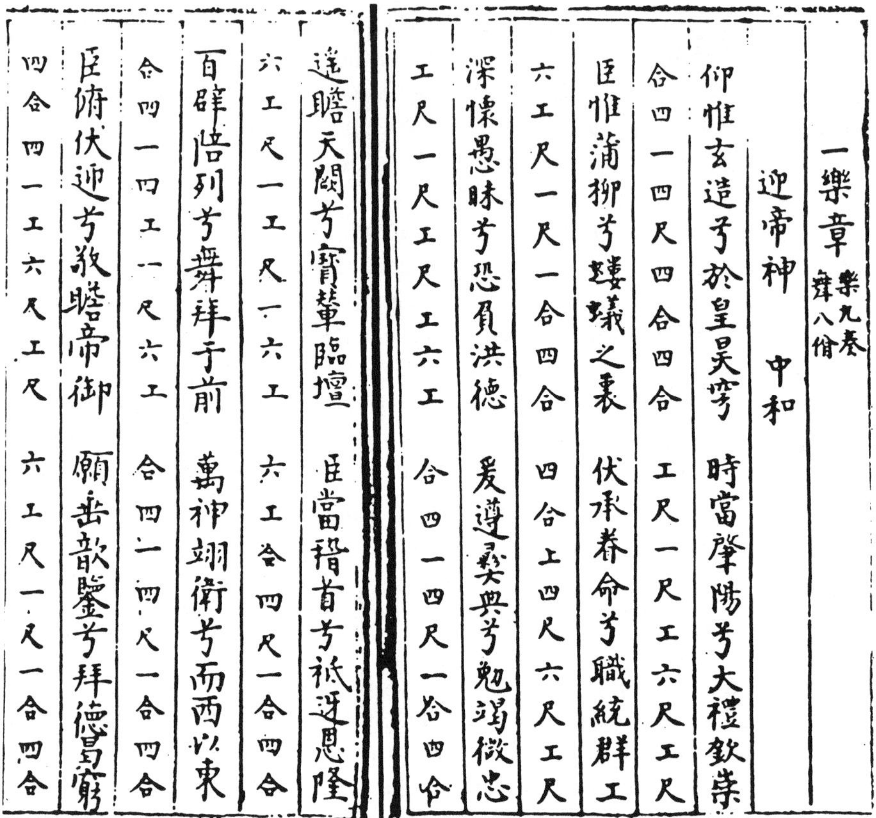

This score, which shows the music of TCYQ1, should be read from top to bottom and from right to left. Except for the first two columns, which give the titles and performance instructions, the odd numbered ones show the song text, the even numbered ones the *gongche* notation.

additional materials included in the *TCXK*: an extended historical description of Ming state sacrifices, lists of the five highest-ranking officials in the Court of Imperial Sacrifices, and records of ritual events that happened after 1580. As it is not likely for two unrelated works to have such similar contents and organization, the *TCXK* must be related to the *TCK*. In fact, the Chinese titles of the two documents differ from each other by only one character: the Chinese title of the *TCXK* includes the character "*xu*," which means, literally, "to continue." Thus, even the title of the *TCXK* reveals that it is developed from a preexistent source, which is most likely the *TCK*.

THE REPERTORY OF MING DYNASTY STATE SACRIFICIAL MUSIC

As it now exists, the repertory of the songs includes 323 items. This number counts each song, as represented in notation, as an individual piece, and ignores the fact that some of the songs are musical counterparts (songs that are musically identical but textually different) and versions (versions of a same song that differ from one another by pitch variants). When counterparts and versions are excluded in the counting of the songs, the repertory becomes smaller and includes only 283 pieces.

Counterparts can be grouped into two types, according to where they appear. The first type includes songs shared among related ceremonials and contained in the same source; examples are the songs for the sacrifices to the sun and moon in the *DMJL*. The second type includes songs in two or more of the four sources; examples are the three identical songs for the sacrifice to the meritorious sovereigns of past dynasties, which are preserved, respectively, in the *TCZL*, *TCK*, and *TCXK*.

Versions of a same song are scattered among the four notated sources. Most versions differ from one another in fewer than ten variant notes. Variants are "musical" when their changes are derived from melodic considerations. A typical "musical" variant, as found in two versions of a song performed in the state sacrifice to the imperial ancestors, is the use of C' as a substitute of C to avoid a large melodic skip in the melody. Variants are "nonmusical" when they cannot be explained musically, and they are possible scribal errors or changes caused by nonmusical reasons. For example, the cursive forms of the notational signs for the *gong* () and *shang* () tones can easily be confused with one another. (See Figure 7.8.)

ANALYSES OF MING DYNASTY STATE SACRIFICIAL MUSIC

As a repertory, the 323 songs constitute a stylistically homogenous body of music that was created and maintained as an imperial privilege. The songs were not produced as independent and free expressions of sounds, but as a reconstruction or an emulation of the idealized ancient music, and as a musical component of particular state sacrifices. Texts and tunes of the songs were composed in response to imperial commands. Except for rehearsals, the songs were only performed inside temple and altar complexes during performances of sacrificial ceremonies. Only authorized musicians, namely those affiliated with the Office of State Sacrificial Music and Office of Imperial Sacrifices, would learn and perform the music.

Subjected to strict theoretical prescriptions, contextual (ritual and court) and performance requirements, the songs demonstrate a distinctive style, the fundamental features of which can be summarized as follows.

1. The songs are set, syllabically, to lyrics written for specific state sacrifices; thus, the songs will only have as many notes as the number of words in their lyrics; similarly, a set of songs for a particular state sacrifice will only have as many pieces as the state sacrifice needs
2. The songs are composed with nine or less pitches that fall within the range of a ninth
3. The songs demonstrate modal identities through the use of particular sets of pitches and through strategic use of some of those pitches as initials, finals, and internal cadences; a set of songs for a particular state sacrifice will employ more than one mode; the first and last songs of the set will be modally identical; the rest of the songs in the set will include at least one change of modes
4. The songs are phrased according to the structure of the lyrics; thus, the melodies are divided into phrases, couplets, and even stanzas like those of the text
5. The songs reveal structural designs that relate melodic phrases through repetition and referential patterns of pitches; the musical relationships demonstrated may or may not match the semantic relationships of the textual phrases
6. The songs include melodic phrases of diverse shapes (contour), many of which involve at least one intervalic skip equal to or larger than a third
7. The songs rarely include repeated notes in their melodic phrases
8. The songs include many melodic phrases that appear to be formulaic (shared by many state sacrificial songs); some of these melodic phrases occur much more frequently than others

9. The songs show stylistic changes during the course of their existence; songs from three different periods of the Ming dynasty—the late fourteenth century, mid-fifteenth century, and mid-sixteenth century—exhibit subtle but discernible stylistic differences

Despite their stylistic homogeneity as a distinctive body of music, the songs are, individually, distinctive compositions. Ritual, musical, and practical considerations require that individual songs be distinctive. State sacrifices serve particular deities and purposes so that their components, including music, must be proper for the occasion and designed accordingly. Indistinctive musical pieces annihilate the purposes of individual state sacrifices, undermining their propriety and efficacy and creating confusion among unrelated ceremonials. Indistinctive songs cannot be identified, appropriated, and interpreted for specific purposes.

The possibilities and the extent for the songs to become distinctive is, however, very limited; the creativity involved must function within established boundaries of the musical language of the genre. For this reason, the songs can only be analyzed in their own terms and compared with other members of the repertory: comparison with different genres of Chinese and non-Chinese music would only highlight the stylistic limitations of the songs and would not reveal differences among individual pieces composed in different periods of the Ming dynasty. The following analysis will examine four sets of songs that reveal unique features in individual pieces and stylistic changes in the repertory.[9]

The first three sets of songs are music for the state sacrifice to Heaven or to Heaven and Earth, the most important Ming ceremonials. The set of DMYQ 1-9 songs includes nine songs from the early Ming, which were composed some time before 1370, the year when the *DMJL* was presented to the throne.[10] The second set of ZLTD 1-8 songs includes eight songs that were originally composed before 1375. As preserved in the *TCZL*, which was compiled between 1464 and 1476, and as the occurrence of variants warranted, the ZLTD 1-8 songs represent mid-fifteen century samples of the repertory. The set of TCYQ 1-9 songs includes nine songs for the state sacrifice to Heaven, which were composed in 1530, the year the ceremonial was restored by Shizong. The songs represent mid-sixteenth century samples of the repertory.

The fourth set is the TCZM 1-6 songs for the state sacrifice to the imperial ancestors, which were first composed between 1367 and 1370.

The set was practiced and maintained throughout the Ming empire. Versions of individual songs in this set vividly demonstrate the subtle and creative changes in a music that is not supposed to change at all.

The nine DMYQ songs are set syllablically to lyrics that mark the ritual stages in the sacrificial ceremony honoring Heaven: the welcoming of the deities, the offering of silk and jade, the offering of food, the three offerings of wine, the clearing of sacrificial food, the farewell to the deities, and the burning of ritual paraphernalia. As marked in Figure 7.4, the couplet structure of the songs and the relationship among the phrases are explicit. The songs use nine or less pitches that do not, however, make regular pentatonic or heptatonic scales. DMYQ 1,2,3 use the pitches of CDE^{b}GA; DMYQ 5, CD^{b}FGA^{b}; DMYQ 6, CDFGA^{b}; DMYQ 7, DEGAB^{b}; DMYQ 8 and 9, CDEGA. These irregular scales as well as the use of the individual notes as cadences, initials, and finals give the songs distinctive modal characters. The repeated appearances of melodic phases, such as CGAG and GDAC, reveal formulaic use of the pitches. Melodic movements in the songs are essentially disjunct; the frequent occurrences of large interval skips divide the melodies into distinct melodic-textual units.

Each of the DMYQ songs exists as a distinctive tune set to a particular text, revealing individualistic features. DMYQ 1 has four distinctive features. Its tune is uncommonly long because it is set to a text of ten couplets, which explains the purpose of the ceremony and depicts the richly attired deities coming to the round-mound-altar in chariots of dragons and phoenixes. The tune projects a strong melodic unity through repeated use of the pitch sequences (motive) of CDE^{b} and GAG. It reveals two remarkable structural designs. The second couplet is almost a palindrome: CDE^{b} . . . GAG, GAG . . . E^{b}DC. The two phrases in the third couplet correspond to each other with the pitch sequence of DAC.

DMYQ 2 displays a binary structure through a distinctive correspondence among the phrases. Phrases 1 and 5 share the pitch sequence of GAG. Phrases 2 and 6 use the same four notes. Phrases 3 and 7 share an identical pitch sequence of two notes (DG).

DMYQ 3 distinguishes itself with the notes of D,G, and A. Except for phrase 8, all phrases in the song include a completed or suggested pitch sequence of the three notes. Furthermore, the pitch sequence of AG appears in four of the eight phrases of the song, giving it a strong pitch focus.

DMYQ 4 includes twelve phrases that are divided into five unequal couplets: phrases 1–3, 4–5, 6–7, 8–10, and 11–12. The piece is dominated

Figure 7.4.
Nine songs for the early Ming state sacrifice to Heaven
(*DMJL* 2.9a–12a)

DMYQ 1. Welcoming the deities

DMYQ 2. Offering of jade and silk

Figure 7.4. (continued).

DMYQ3. Offering of sacrificial food

DMYQ4. First offering of wine

DMYQ 5. Second offering of wine

Figure 7.4. (continued).

DMYQ 6. Last offering of wine

DMYQ 7. Removal of the sacrificial food

by two related pitch sequences. The pitch sequence of ADE^{b}D appears in phrases 4, 6, and 9. The sequence of AGDE^{b}D appears, in complete and incomplete forms, in phrases 1, 3, 5, 7, 8, 10, and 11.

DMYQ 5 has two identifying features. Phrases 2 and 5 are identical. Phrases 3, 7 and 8 are marked by the pitch sequence of D^{b}C.

DMYQ 6 is the only song with eleven phrases, and it is marked by various disguises of A^{b}CDC and A^{b}FGF. The former sequence appears in phrases 3, 4, 6, and 7. The latter sequence appears in phrases 2, 5, and 10.

Figure 7.4 (continued).

DMYQ 8. Farewell to the deities

DMYQ 9. Burning of the sacrificial articles

DMYQ 7 has unmistakable repetitions. It has three pairs of repeated phrases: phrases 1 and 2; 3 and 6; and 4 and 8.

DMYQ 8 has six phrases and three couplets. However, its musical structure is more binary than tripartite. The correspondence between phrases 1 and 4, 2 and 5, and 3 and 6 gives the piece a binary structure.

DMYQ 9 has an extremely disjunct melodic movement and an inconspicuous repetition of two pitch sequences. The pitch sequence of AC occurs in phrases 1, 3, 5, and 8. The sequence of EG occurs in phrases 2, 4, and 5.

Compared to the songs of DMYQ 1-9, the set of ZLTD 1-8 songs are distinguished by the pitch C', the dominance of a particular scale and

Figure 7.5.
Eight songs for the middle Ming state sacrifice to Heaven and Earth
(*TCZL* 2.15a–17a)

ZLTD 1. Welcoming the deities

ZLTD 2. Offering of jade and silk

mode, longer phrases, smoother melodic contours, and a freer structure. The set includes eight pieces in which the match between music and text is close. Even the two semantic units in the textual phrases, which are separated by the auxillary word *xi*, are reflected by the fact that all of the musical phrases can be divided into two formulaic units. Seven of the eight songs use a pentatonic mode (CDEGAC') and employ C as initials and

Figure 7.5. (continued).

ZLTD 3. First offering of wine

ZLTD 4. Second offering of wine

ZLTD 5. Last offering of wine

finals. Only ZLTD 6 appears in a different mode by employing a scale of CDFGA^{b}C' and using D as initial and final notes. Melodic movement in the songs is mostly conjunct, projecting smooth and rippled contour. The appearance of similar melodic motives in all of the songs except no. 6 renders them a particularly unified set.

Figure 7.5. (continued).

ZLTD 6. Removal of the sacrificial food

ZLTD 7. Farewell to the deities

ZLTD 8. Burning of the sacrificial articles

ZLTD 1 employs its motives in such a way that they constitute a unified but free-floating structure. The pitch sequence of CDEG appears in phrases 1, 3 and 8, all with some disguise. The pitch sequence of GAG and its transposition, CDC, appears in phrases 1, 3, 4, 7 and 8. The pitch sequence of EGDC occurs in phrases 2 and 4. The structure of ZLTD 1 depends on the repetition of pitch sequences, but the tune does not sound repetitious.

ZLTD 2 has parallel phrases. Phrases 1 and 3 end with the same pitch sequence, while phrases 2 and 4 show another sequence and its transposition. Phrases 3 and 4 are related by the common melodic formula of C'AGE.

ZLTD 3 is short and includes phrases of differing lengths. Its first couplet includes phrases of five notes, while the second one includes phrases of seven notes. Besides a general similarity in the use of pitches belonging to the same mode, this song does not reveal any particular pitch sequence or structural features.

ZLTD 4 has irregular phrase lengths. Phrase 1 has five notes; phrase 3 has six notes; phrase 2 and 4 have seven notes. This song is divided into two parallel couplets. Phrases 1 and 3 are almost identical, while phrases 2 and 4 share a similar melodic contour.

ZLTD 5 also has phrases of varying lengths. Phrases 1 and 4 have six notes; phrase 2 has nine; and phrase 3 has eight. The pitch sequence of AGEC appears in phrases 2 and 4; a transposition of the sequence appears in phrase 3. Phrases 2 and 3 share the pitch sequence of GDC. Phrase 2 is marked by two large skips, a fifth, and a sixth.

ZLTD 6 employs an unusual scale of CDFGA^{b}C'. The change of mode and the relative disjunct melodies of the song render it different from other songs of the set.

ZLTD 7 is a through-composed song. The only direct reference among its four phrases is the pitch sequence of AGEC and its transposition, C'AGE, in phrases 2 and 3.

ZLTD 8 is another through-composed song, and includes no obvious use of pitch sequence or repeated materials. The song has two kinds of phrase lengths. Phrases 1 and 3 include seven notes each; phrases 2 and 4 include six notes each.

The TCYQ set of songs for the state sacrifice to Heaven is stylistically closer to the ZLTD set than to the DMYQ set. Prominent similarities include, for example, the binary structure of the phrases, the use of the pitch C', and the dominance of a particular type of pentatonic scale. Never-

Figure 7.6.
Nine songs for the late Ming state sacrifice to Heaven

TCYQ 1. Welcoming the deities

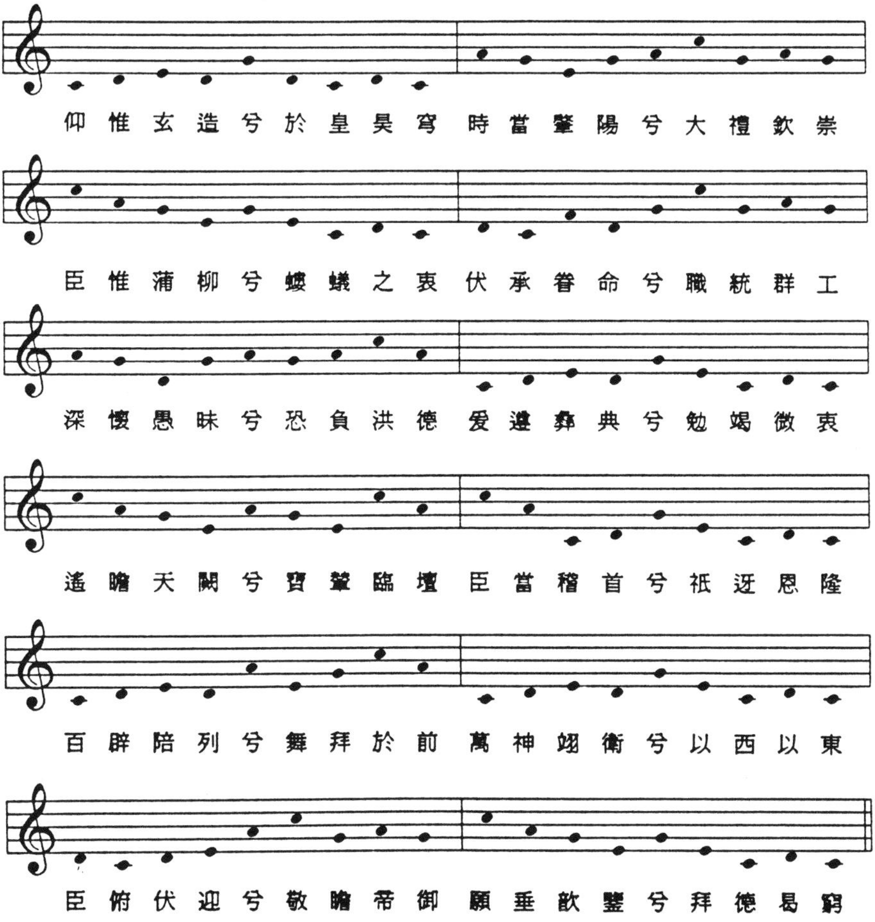

theless, the TCYQ songs are distinguished by a scale of CDEFGAC', a relatively standardized use of pitch sequences and/or formulaic materials. Only one song, TCYQ 2, is modally different from the others. It begins and ends with the pitch E, and it does not use the pitch F. The unusual lengths of the first and eighth pieces in the set are distinctive, demonstrating a deliberate emphasis on the ritual stages—welcome and farewell—the music accompanied.

Figure 7.6. (continued).

TCYQ 2. Offering of jade and silk

TCYQ 3. Offering of sacrificial food

TCYQ 4. First offering of wine

TCYQ 1 includes twelve phrases, each of which includes nine notes that can be divided into two units of melodic formula. The third phrase, for example, includes the formulas of C' AGE and ECDC. While the musical structure corresponds to that of the text, musical unity of the tune is achieved by an identical formula appearing at corresponding locations. The

Figure 7.6. (continued).

TCYQ 5. Second offering of wine

TCYQ 6. Last offering of wine

TCYQ 7. Removal of the sacrificial food

Figure 7.6. (continued).

TCYQ 8. Farewell to the deities

formula of CDED, for example, appears in the beginnings of phrases 1, 6, 9, and 10. Similarly, phrases 2 and 4 end with GAG, while the other even-numbered phrases close with ECDC.

TCYQ 2 is through-composed and there is no explicit relationship among its phrases. It uses a mode different from the rest of the songs in the set.

Figure 7.6. (continued).

TCYQ 9. Burning of the sacrificial articles

TCYQ 3 is also through-composed, but phrasal relationships are clear. The CDFD in phrase 1 is changed to CDED in phrase 4. The pitch sequence of AGEC in phrase 2 is transposed in phrase 3. The EGDC that closes phrase 2 is transformed as GEDC in phrase 4.

TCYQ 4 includes two parallel couplets, the second of which can be considered a variation of the first. The first three notes in phrase 3 are substitutes for those in phrase 1. Phrases 2 and 4 are identical, except for the order of two notes—GE and EG.

TCYQ 5 is distinguished by the appearance of C'AGE in three of its four phrases. Its binary structure is apparent. Phrases 1 and 3 are related: the latter is developed from the former. Phrases 2 and 4 are identical, except for the substitution of an E with a C.

TCYQ 6 is a through-composed song. There is no clear references among the phrases, except that the pitch sequences of C'GAG and ECDA are obviously not unrelated.

TCYQ 7 has two parallel couplets in which the respective beginnings of phrases 1 and 2 are identical to those in phrases 3 and 4.

TCYQ 8 is as long as TCYQ 1, and its use of formulaic pitch sequences is equally predictable. The sequence of CDED begins phrases 1, 4, 7, and 10. The sequence of GCDC ends phrases 2, 8 and 10. The sequence of ECDC concludes phrases 4, 6, and 12. The sequence of C'AGE appears in the beginning of phrases 6, 9 and 11.

TCYQ 9 is through-composed. Its pitch sequences form no exact repetitions, but they are still clearly identifiable.

The above analysis demonstrates that the songs are on one hand stylistically similar and on the other hand structurally distinctive. They also are simultaneously orthodox and creative. Despite conservative scholar-officials' best intentions and efforts to fend off any possible deviations, the songs changed to cope with the practical needs and creative urges of the emperors, scholar-officials, music masters, and performers. The changes may be very subtle, but they are nevertheless expressive changes. The versions of the songs offered to the imperial ancestors, which are respectively preserved in the *DMJL*, *TCZL* and *TCK*, are illustrative. When the DMZM 1-11 songs were first composed in the beginning of the empire, they were supposed to serve the empire forever. However, a simplification of the state sacrifice, which occurred in 1388, rendered five of the eleven songs unnecessary. Since then, the music honoring the imperial ancestors included only six songs. They were faithfully transmitted and carefully maintained throughout the Ming empire, but they also incurred detail changes along the way.

As demonstrated in the comparative score of Figure 7.7, there are quite a number of pitch variants among the three versions of the songs. As the DMZM version preserves the original tunes, it stands apart from the TCZM and TCZM versions, which are temporally closer and exhibit fewer pitch variants. Many of the pitch variants are creative changes introduced for clearly identifiable musical reasons. For example, the substitution of E^b with E in the third song of the set (DMZM 8, ZLZM 3, and TCZM 3) reflects a change in the understanding of modes. With the E^b, the song uses a hemitonic mode that evokes historical Chinese music; with the E, the song uses an anhemitonic mode that is found in many types of traditional Chinese music performed today. The replacement of C with C' in many phrases of the six songs reveals a concern for smooth melodic contour. The use of C' in the first two phrases of ZLZM 1 and TCZM 1, for example, would give them a smooth melody of eight notes. The use of C in DMZM generates a disjunct contour. Some pitch variants have less identifiable reasons. The penultimate notes in the last song of the set (DMZM11, ZLZM 6, and TCZM 6) reveal a fascinating case. It is clear that the use of either C' or A would smooth the contour, but there is no demonstrable reason why one of the two notes should be preferred over the other. The choice appears to be personal.

Figure 7.7.
Versions of six songs for the Ming state sacrifice to the imperial ancestors
(*DMJL* 4.9a-11a; *TCZL* 2.17a-18b; *TCXK* 2.38b-40a)

DMZM 1. Welcoming the deities

ZLZM 1. Welcoming the deities

TCZM 1. Welcoming the deities

Figure 7.7. (continued).

DMZM 4. First offering of wine

ZLZM 2. First offering of wine

TCZM 2. First offering of wine

Figure 7.7. (continued).

Figure 7.7. (continued).

DMZM 9. Last offering of wine

ZLZM 4. Last offering of wine

TCZM 4. Last offering of wine

Figure 7.7. (continued).

DMZM 10. Removal of the sacrificial food

ZLZM 5. Removal of the sacrificial food

TCZM 5. Removal of the sacrificial food

Figure 7.7. (continued).

DMZM 11. Farewell to the deities

ZLZM 6. Farewell to the deities

TCZM 6. Farewell to the deities

Figure 7.8.
Three pseudo-ritual songs by Ming music theorists

Admonitory song from the Xia Dynasty
(Zhu, *Lülü jingyi waibian*, 8.44)

PSEUDO-RITUAL MUSIC BY MING THEORISTS

The changing of E^b to E or the substitution of C with C' are subtle musical changes, and they beg the questions of whether they play any significant roles in rendering the songs distinctive and identifiable. They do; they are obvious signs of musical creativity to anyone who was or is familiar with the style and who knew or knows the boundaries where creativity should stop. A comparison between TCZM 1 and three compositional exercises by Li Wencha, Liu Lian, and Zhu Zaiyu's would illustrate the argument. As Figure 7.8 shows, the pseudo-ritual songs by the three Ming music theorists are similar to the songs in their syllabic setting and use of limited pitches. However, the theorists' exercises are, stylistically, totally different from authentic samples of the songs in at least the

Figure 7.8. (continued).

"Luming" from the *Classic of Odes*
(Liu, *Yuejing yuanyi* 5.14a)

Song no. 1 of music for the crown prince
(Li Wencha, *Qing gong yuediao*, in *Lishi yueshu*, 1.17a)

following crucial aspects: contours of the melodic phrases, interrelationship among the phrases, and structural design of individual songs. Zhu Zaiyu's song, for example, shows neither structural repetition of phrases nor judicious use of identical pitch sequences. Liu Lian's song is marked by repeated notes and the narrow range of his melody. Li Wencha's song is essentially composed according to his cycles of fifths; the modal character of his theoretical exercise is unique.

That the three theorists cannot compose their music exactly like authentic samples of the songs is eloquent evidence that individualistic melodies of the songs are distinctive. Created for particular ritual stages in specific ceremonials, and set to unique texts, the songs are unique expressions of emperors, scholar-officials, and music masters in the Ming court.

CHAPTER EIGHT

Orthodoxy, Creativity, Expressiveness, and Critical Audiences of Ming State Sacrifices and Music

The previous chapters have discussed Ming state sacrifices and music as large-scale and presentational ritual and music, described their orthodox and creative features, and analyzed complex processes of instituting, maintaining, revising, and interpreting the ceremonials. By highlighting the words and deeds of emperors and scholar-officials directly involved with the ceremonials, the chapters have emphasized the concerned participants' understandings. To balance these understandings with different views, and to further illustrate the roles subtle but distinctive features played in rendering the state sacrifices and music expressive over a long period of time, several views from the critical audiences will be presented here.

Wang Tingxiang (1474–1544), a noted Ming scholar-official, poet, philosopher, and music theorist known for his integrity, wrote a series of five short poems describing Shizong's 1534 performance of the state sacrifice to Heaven.[1] The poems constitute one critical audience's report because they are descriptive in tone and because Wang, who was one of Shizong's favored officials, did not appear to have played an active role in the ritual and musical revisions of the time. Compared to other laudatory writings, the poems are relatively neutral and personal: they describe only a sympathetic official's positive account of the ceremony, revealing his intellectual and emotional reactions, support for the emperor's actions, and concern for the sovereign's well-being.[2] Wang's poems read as follows.[3]

The green altar compound is far away by the blue sky;
The spirit-thrones on the altar proper are so high that they reach
the imperial palace of the northern star.
Were it not for the shuttling of the celestial beings;
The deity of Heaven would still be far away in the Five Clouds.

In the southern and northern skies, the stars twinkle brilliantly;
Above and beneath the altar proper, fragrant incense permeates
the air.
Were it not for the Jade Emperor's coming down through the
clouds;
Why would the sacred wind flutter the banners of feathers and
bells?

On the auspicious day of the sacrificial ceremony in the southern
suburb, warm air returns;
Here and there, the deities' chariots draw up into the human world.
When the pearl curtain [of the emperor's chariot] is rolled up,
one can see the emperor's robe;
It is because of these annual performances that people in the
capital have learned to recognize the emperor's face.

Wearing an imperial crown of gems and a robe with heavenly
designs;
The emperor ascends to the top of the altar proper, and offers
jade to Heaven.
Even though it is a clear night that is perfect for worshipping;
The many ceremonial gestures would, I fear, exhaust the emperor.

The sacrificial ceremony at the round-mound-altar is completed
and the celebration banquet toasted;
In the palaces and halls, the bells and the drums make music all
through the night.
Even when the Zhou court celebrated their state sacrifices with
poems like those of "Fuyi" and "Yuzao";
That is no match for the success enjoyed by our emperor.

Wang's poems comprehensively depict a sympathetic witness's reaction to the sacrificial ceremony, pinpointing what he found stimulating.

The poems leave no doubts that Wang understood the ceremony well. Succinctly, he pointed out all of the key ritual ideas and features: the altar compound in the southern suburb of the capital, the deity of Heaven, the sacrificial jade, the emperor's ritual regalia, the fragrant incense, the classic poems of "Fuyi" and "Yuzao," and so forth. Wang's familiarity with the state sacrifice and its ritual and musical features was no accident: he was a scholar-official who studied classical documents and authored many poems, essays, and discussions about his experiences with state sacrifices and music.[4]

Yet in his efforts to describe the ceremony and his responses to its expressiveness, Wang focused on distinctive particulars that had apparently made an impression on him. Wang did not discuss the state ritual and music as a means of governance and self-cultivation. Such functions were well-known and were not something that would distinguish the performance Wang attended from others. Thus, Wang talked about the towering height of the spirit-thrones, the sacred wind that fluttered the banners and the bells, the auspicious return of warm air for the occasion. These were things Wang found distinctive, appealing, and suggestive of the efficacy and success of Shizong's performance of the sacrificial ceremony.

In particular, Wang highlighted three features and explained why they were uniquely expressive to him: the rolling up of the pearl curtain that allowed visual contact between emperor and commoners; the many ceremonial gestures of the emperor that made Wang worry if the emperor would be exhausted; and the celebration banquet that led Wang to compare Shizong's state sacrifice to Heaven favorably with those of antiquity. Wang concluded his poems by stating that Shizong's ceremonial was so successful that it brought peace and prosperity to the empire, the ultimate goal and confirmation of an efficacious state sacrifice. Wang's interpretation of the performance was emotional and subjective. His assessment of the ceremonial efficacy was more wishful thinking than realistic description of the social-political realities of the time.[5] However, Wang's poems demonstrate the ways in which a sympathetic and critical court citizen would respond to the expressiveness of a sacrificial ceremony. He identified and interpreted distinctive features in the ceremony to formulate his own interpretations. He accepted orthodox meanings of the ceremony but embedded them in the contexts of a particular time, people, and thoughts.

Another noted Ming author, Wang Shenzhong (1509–1559), also left "Odes on the State Sacrifice to Heaven" ("*Yinsi song*"), a series of seven poems describing the main events in the 1530 performance of the ceremonial.[6] The fifth poem, entitled "Music Rehearsal," is a unique literary work that describes state sacrificial music and dance. It also is a personal report by a young, learned, and politically insignificant official in Shizong's court. At the time of the music rehearsal, Wang was a twenty-one-year-old official in the Ministry of Rites who passed the national examinations and became a scholar-official in 1526 at the young age of seventeen. The introduction and text of Wang's poem read as follows.[7]

> The court had scheduled a performance of the sacrificial ceremony to honor Heaven, and officials in the Ministry of Rites had reported to the emperor that the proper music for the ceremony was not yet "harmonious." Thus, the emperor summoned Zhang E to court and ordered him to make the sacrificial songs "musical." Shortly after, the emperor asked palace officials to transport gold bell-chimes and jade stone-chimes from the inner court to the altar-compound, and asked Zhang to test the musical instruments there. Then, officials from the Ministry of Rites and the Court of Imperial Sacrifices visited the Office of State Sacrificial Music located inside the altar-compound in the southern suburb of the capital. There they attended a rehearsal of the music. I was in the company of these officials.

> Proper music comes from the yang element;
> Primordial sounds begin with the trigram of *yu*.
> [Now, as state sacrificial music of the Ming,] they match the perfect Shao of the Yu court,
> Reviving ancient music for the present and the future.
> The musical instruments are ready for the elaborate rehearsal;
> The dancers' feather banners are lined up along the four sides of the altar proper.
> The officers holding the banners look splendid and cultivated;
> The musicians and dancers appear young and rustic.
> The harmonious mouth-organs blow their bamboo pipes;
> The red strings reverberate the solitary notes of state sacrificial music.
> The music begins like a flash;
> The interludes are like strings of pearls.
> The songs expound the teachings of the six classics;

The pitches activate the eight winds.
The drum beats echo through the sky;
The zithers project their plucked tones.
The rows of graceful dancers are arranged like the abundant stars;
The elaborate choreography is programmed like the paired clouds.
Expanding and contracting, the five musical tones converge [into melodies];
From beginning to end, the music and dances develop into nine pieces.
As a lowly scholar-official, I am lucky to have this chance;
To respond to the imperial command with the other officials;
They listen to the music and discuss its manifestation of virtues;
They observe the dances and proclaim their merits.
I am ashamed that I do not have the listening [skills] of Yanzhou;
Undeservedly, I have come to this Daoist shrine of state sacrificial music.

Wang's poem is not only a report of what he found distinctive in the rehearsal but also a bravura of orthodox understanding of state sacrificial music. Wang's erudition is clear from his cadenza of technical terms and concepts of Ming music theory: the yin and yang elements, the trigram of *yu*, the pitch pipes, the syllabic style, the musical manifestations of the six classics, and so forth. Nevertheless, Wang reacted to the performance and noticed many things that only an actual audience would observe: the visual contrast between the handsome officers holding the banners and the young and rustic musician-dancers; the solitary sounds of state sacrificial music, the stylistic contrast between the beginnings and the interludes of the music; the echoing drum beats; the grandeur of the sixty-four dancers arranged in eight-rows and their elaborate choreography. Wang probably noticed many more distinctive features in the music, but he could not express them in a poetic language that was loaded with orthodox terms and concepts.[8] Thus he gracefully admitted his lack of analytical skills of listening and described his attendance of the rehearsal as undeserving. After all, Wang was only a young but critical audience, not a music master like Zhang E who could detect mistakes in the musical modes by listening and who had access to notated scores of state sacrificial music.

Wang Tingxiang and Wang Shenzhong were only two of many critical audiences who were sympathetic to Shizong's ritual and music revisions. There were, of course, many others who opposed and challenged the emperor's revision. Because these challengers were often punished and suppressed, their comments have not been abundantly preserved. Nevertheless, summaries of court debates preserved in the *Veritable Record of Shizong* and other standard documents of the time clearly demonstrate the ways in which the challengers reacted and argued about distinctive and creative ritual and musical features.

Censor Li Guan's disapproval of Shizong's revising of the state sacrifice to Confucius is illustrative.[9] Adamantly, Li wanted to keep the imperial status for Confucius, arguing that it was customary to give persons being worshipped ranks higher than what they actually achieved. To make his point, Li cited Taizu's bestowal of imperial status on four generations of ancestors who were never emperors and highlighted the traditional practice of honoring meritorious generals and officials with regal titles. Furthermore, Li struck Shizong where he was vulnerable: Li asked how the emperor could honor his biological father, with all ritual means that were possible, but question whether the regal status for Confucius was an excessive honor. Li's criticism of Shizong was loud and clear, and Shizong wanted to punish the official severely. Only when it was clear that the court could not survive another battle over ritual matters did the emperor ease off, banishing Li from the court.[10]

Shizong was, however, not so lenient with challengers from outside the court. Qin Tang and other scholars from Puzhou in the Shanxi province, who charged Shizong for violating Taizu's legacy of state sacrifices and music, were sent to the local authorities and persecuted.[11] As much as he tried, nevertheless, Shizong could not suppress all critical audiences; negative criticism continued even after the emperor's death. In 1575, Zhang Juzheng (1525–1582), the most powerful official of the time, presented to the throne his analysis of the suburban sacrifices instituted by Taizu and Shizong and suggested a revision. However, out of theoretical and practical concerns, Zhang did not push his proposal forcefully. Still, he made it perfectly clear why he found Shizong's state sacrifices faulty.

First, unlike Taizu's combined state sacrifice to Heaven and Earth, which was performed indoors and during spring, Shizong's outdoor ceremonials were physically taxing; the ceremony honoring Heaven was performed in the coldness of winter, and the one honoring Earth performed in the heat of summer. Second, unlike Taizu's efforts to simplify the ritual system, Shizong expanded it so much that it became exhausting, thus impractical. Third, Shizong honored only Taizu as a companion in the state sacrifice to Heaven. Shizong terminated the century-old practice of including Chengzu, the third Ming emperor, as a companion of Heaven's; thus Shizong glossed over the fact that Chengzu was the imperial ancestor who "reconstituted" the empire—Chengzu took, by force, the Ming throne from his nephew, the second Ming ruler. To illustrate his arguments, Zhang contrasted the fact that Taizu's system operated effectively for one and one-half centuries, while Shizong's revised state sacrifices and music were soon paralyzed by practical difficulties. Zhang pointed out that, by the 1540s, Shizong's revised ceremonials were either curtailed or performed by delegates. Unequivocally, Zhang concluded that Shizong's ceremonials were faulty in theory and in practice, and they ruffled people's emotions.[12]

The critical comments by Wang Tingxiang, Wang Shenzhong, Li Guan, and Zhang Juzheng are similar in their focus on Shizong and on specific ritual features. This focus underscores three reasons why Ming state sacrifices and music were continuously expressive. First, the concerned participants and critical audiences in the Ming court neither questioned the Confucian ideology of employing state sacrifices and music as a means of governance and self-cultivation nor challenged the structure of the state ritual and music. There were few debates on schedules of abstention, inspection of the sacrificial animals, the nine coordinated stages in the sacrificial ceremony, the syllabic setting and modes of the music, and other ritual and musical elements. This was so because the structure and various elements were orthodox: they were copiously described in classical documents, vividly illustrated by historical models from the Tang, Song, and earlier dynasties, and painstakingly mastered by the court citizens through many years of studies, discussions, and practice. Thus, when the court citizens describe their reaction to the state sacrifices and music, they do not need to reiterate the orthodox ideology and familiar musical and ritual features in their critical comments. They need only to take the orthodox elements as a basis to identify and interpret distinctive and creative features in individual performances of the state ritual and music.

Second, subtly distinctive and creative features in what are otherwise orthodox state ritual and music elicit the strongest intellectual and emotional reactions from concerned participants and critical audiences. The features appear in visual, aural, and other media, challenging the concerned participants and critical audiences to engage. Being ritual and musical masters, they would promptly notice the features as something different from the orthodox norm, asking what and why the features express.

Third, the expressiveness of the state sacrifices and music is inseparable from the concerned participants and critical audiences. For example, Shizong's state ritual and music cannot be understood without references to the emperor's ritual-political agenda, and the conflicts between his supporters and opponents and between the Confucian scholar-officials and Daoist monk-official-musicians. By the same token, Zhang Juzheng's criticism of Shizong's state ritual and music is acute and tragic, only because Zhang was the most powerful official of his time who refrained from pushing a ritual reform. Zhang wanted to reintroduce Taizu's combined state sacrifice to Heaven and Earth, but he was awed by Shizong's status as the grandfather of the emperor he was serving. He also was concerned about the Herculean scale of the task and its numerous ramifications: every detail of the large-scale and presentational state sacrifices and music had to be properly coordinated; every performance had to be tailored to specific contextual needs; intense debates and ferocious criticism would arise. State sacrifices and music were not only orthodox formalities but creative expressions of the concerned participants and critical audiences.

Like Zhang, these concerned participants and critical audiences were court citizens who acquired masterly knowledge about the state ritual and music and who witnessed many performances of them. Given their knowledge and abilities to critically assess performances of the ceremonials, they had to be heartless and mindless if they could refrain from intellectual and emotional reactions. Given their familiarity with the ritual and music, they had to be blind and deaf if they failed to notice features that were creative and yet posed no challenge to orthodox theories and practices. Given the social-political dynamics of the court, they had no choice but to engage and react. They had to negotiate and appropriate the state sacrifices and music as personal expressions that were constantly orthodox and creative.

Notes

This Notes section uses a short form and the abbreviations listed. For complete names of authors, titles, and other publication data, see the Works Cited, section of this book.

Abbreviations:

DMJL	*Da Ming jili* (Collected Ceremonial of the Ming Dynasty)
GQ	*Guoque* (An Evaluation of the Events of Our Dynasty)
MHD	*Ming huidian* (Collected Statues of the Ming)
MS	*Mingshi* (Ming History)
SFL	*Huang Ming shifalu* (A Collection of Ming Documents and Personal Records)
SHSL	*Shenzong xianhuangdi shilu* (The Veritable Records of Shenzong)
SZSL	*Shizong suhuangdi shilu* (The Veritable Records of Shizong)
TCK	*Taichang kao* (Monograph on the Court of Imperial Sacrifices)
TCXK	*Taichang xukao* (Expanded Monograph on the Court of Imperial Sacrifices)
TCZL	*Taichang zonglan* (General Record of the Court of Imperial Sacrifices)
TZSL	*Taizu gaohuangdi shilu* (The Veritable Records of Taizu)
WLTK	*Wuli tongkao* (Comprehensive Study of the Five Categories of Rites)

WZSL	*Wuzong yihuangdi shilu* (The Veritable Records of Wuzong)
XANSL	*Xianzong chunhuangdi shilu* (The Veritable Records of Xianzong)
XAOSL	*Xiaozong jinghuangdi shilu* (The Veritable Records of Xiaozong)

CHAPTER 1

1. See, for example, Ahern, *Chinese Ritual and Politics*; Bell, *Ritual Theory, Ritual Practice*; Bloch, *Ritual, History and Power*; David Cannadine and Simon Price, eds., *Rituals of Royalty*; Robert Grimes, "Bibliography on Chinese Music and Ritual"; Ronald L. Grimes, *Ritual Criticism*; Tambiah, "A Performative Approach to Ritual"; James Watson and Evelyn S. Rawski, eds., *Death Ritual in Late Imperial and Modern China*, Bell Yung, Evelyn S. Rawski and Rubie Watson, eds., *Harmony and Counterpoint.*

2. For a recent summary of the various attributes of ritual, see Evan M. Zuesse, "Ritual."

3. One of such discussions is Rawski's description of Qing Shizong's performance of additional "three kneelings and nine prostrations" in the death ritual of his father, Qing Shengzu. See Rawski, "The Imperial Way of Death," p. 248.

4. *TCXK* 1.20a.

5. An American example is the "draft-card rites" in demonstrations against the Vietnam war. See Kertzer, *Ritual, Politics and Power*, pp. 121–22. See also Turner, *The Ritual Process*, pp. 44–93.

6. See Wakeman, "Mao's Remains."

7. Geertz, *The Interpretation of Cultures*, 93–95.

8. See Schechner et al., *By Means of Performance*; Schieffeln, "Performance and the Cultural Construction of Reality."

9. See Hansen, *Changing Gods*; Lam, "The Yin and Yang of Chinese Music Historiography."

10. *Ming wenheng* 19.10.

11. *Dictionary of Ming Biographies*, s.v. "Chu Hou-Ts'ung."

12. Long, *Ming huiyao*, 3.89. See Ray Huang's discussion on the importance of court ritual and Shenzong's negligence of it (*1587 A Year of No Significance*, pp. 46–47). For a court official's criticism on Shenzong's negligence, see *SHSL* 262.2.

13. Wuzong delegated many performances of the state sacrifices to imperial clansmen and court officials. For a sample of court criticisms on such delegations, see *WZSL*, 169. For a chronological list of performances of state sacrifices by Wuzong's delegates, see Li Guoxiang and Yang Chang, *Mingshilu leizuan*, pp. 1202–17.

14. There is no denial that there were insincere responses. However, based on data preserved in Ming documents, I argue that most Ming court citizens' responses were sincere.

15. *SZSL* 119.3b.

16. MacKinnon, "Creative Talent", p. 485. See also Gardner, *A Cognitive Approach to Creativity*; Runco et. al., *Theories of Creativity*; Sternberg, *The Nature of Creativity*; Weisberg, *Creativity*.

CHAPTER 2

1. *TZSL*, 26.1a.

2. See K. C. Chang, *Art, Myth, and Ritual*, pp. 45, 101, and 107. See also McMullen, "Bureaucrats and cosmology"; Wechsler, *Offerings of Jade and Silk*; and Smith, "Ritual in Ch'ing Culture."

3. Zhang Hequan, *Zhoudai jisi yanjiu.*

4. Wechsler, *Offerings of Jade and Silk*, especially, pp. 123–60; Rawski, "The Imperial Way of Death."

5. Ching K'un Yang, *Religion in Chinese Society*, p. 199.

6. Traditional Chinese believed that, after death, people exist as spirits (*ling*) and have supernatural powers; the spirits of the deceased rulers of an empire were considered deities who protected the regime. Among such deities, the founder of the empire was supposed to be particularly powerful, as he had direct access to Heaven.

7. *Xunzi xinzhu*, p. 330.

8. Ching K'un Yang, *Religion in Chinese Society*, p. 49. For a current introduction to the issues about whether or not Confucianism is a religion, see Tu Weiming, Milan Hejtmanek, and Alan Wachman, eds., *The Confucian World Observed*, especially, pp. 91–106.

9. It is obvious that scholar-officials could easily manipulate the avenue for personal and political gains. See Pye, *The Spirit of Chinese Politics*.

10. See Lam, "Ritual and Musical Politics in the Court of Ming Shizong."

11. For a concise biography of Taizu, see *Dictionary of Ming Biography*, s.v. "Chu Yuan-chang. See also Wu, *Zhu Yuanzhang zhuan*.

12. See *TCXK* (7.18b–45b) for a list of annual supplies for the state sacrifices and salaries for the ritual and musical staffs.

13. *MS* 47.1225. The figure is a generalization. As Ming state sacrifices witnessed numerous changes—additions, suspensions, and revisions—the actual number of state sacrifices fluctuated during different periods of the dynasty.

14. Although the ritual places where Ming state sacrifices were performed are always referred to as altars (*tan*) or temples (*miao*), each is actually a compound of buildings—the altar (or temple) proper and a series of other structures, such as the abstention hall (*zhaigong*), the houses for the breeding of the sacrificial animals, and so on. The more important the alter (or temple) is, the bigger its compound. To facilitate discussion in this chapter, I will use the term "altar proper" to refer to the ritual place where the sacrificial ceremonies were actually performed. I will use the term "altar compound" (or "temple compound") to refer to the whole or part of the series of buildings forming the compound.

15. For further details about the Ming temple of imperial ancestors, especially the changes introduced by Shizong, see *MS* 58.1313–28 and *MHD* 86.497–505.

16. *MS* 47.1225.

17. *TCXK* 3.43b and 8.48b.

18. *TCXK* 3.75a–76a.

19. This account of the Ming state sacrifice to Heaven is based on the description in the *TCXK* (1.18b–43b). It is not identical with those described in *MS* (48.1252–53) or *MHD* (82.467–8). The discrepancies among the three descriptions attest to my arguments that Ming state sacrifices always include individualistic and creative elements in their realizations.

20. Unless specified, the term "ritual staffs" will be used to refer to the officials and workers who performed a variety of tasks on and off the altar proper. It should be noted that many of these officials and workers have specific titles, such as the official who reads the prayer (*duzhu guan*), which reflect the nature of their tasks and the complexity of the ceremonial.

21. It is not clear how the performance of the music was suspended. The musical compositions for this stage are not particularly longer than the music for the other stages.

22. The problems are exacerbated by the fact that the verbal descriptions were written with different perspectives and understandings of the ceremonials, and that words cannot comprehensively describe performative features in detail. In this discussion, I am presenting the features as they are described and relevant to the discussion.

23. *WLTK*, 10.635–37.

24. See *Da Tang Kaiyuan li* 4; McMullen, "Bureaucrats and cosmology".

25. *DMJL* 2.12a–24a.

26. *SS* 99.2442–43.

27. *WLTK* 9.1a.

28. *SS* 99.2433–34.

29. *DMJL* 1.4a.

30. *MS* 50.1297–99.

CHAPTER 3

1. *TZSL* 22.4a.

2. See Wu, *Zhu Yuanzhang zhuan*, especially pp. 286–89, and Farmer, " Social Regulations of the First Ming Emperor." See also Dardess, *Confucianism and Autocracy*.

3. This discussion is based on materials preserved in the *TZSL*. Many of Taizu's edicts and writings discussed here are also available in other Ming documents. See, for example, Qian Bocheng, Wei Tongxian, and Ma Zhanggen eds., *Quan Mingwen*, and Hu Shi'e, ed., *Ming Taizuji*. See also Taylor, *Basic Annals of Ming T'ai-tsu*.

4. Here I use the three classical works to demonstrate how well Taizu learned from the Confucian canon. Needless to say, Taizu may have learned the ideas from other classical works that discuss the same ideas.

5. *Yueji pizhu*, 33.

6. *Yueji pizhu*, 1.

7. *Yueji pizhu*, 46.

8. *Yueji pizhu*, 1.

9. *Yueji pizhu*, 51.

10. *Yueji pizhu*, 20.

11. Wang Mengou, 292.

12. Wang Mengou, 1, 322.

13. Wang Mengou, 349.

14. Wang Mengou, 308.
15. *Lunyu yizhu*, "Bayi."
16. *Lunyu yizhu*, "Bayi."
17. *Lunyu yizhu*, "Xianwen."
18. *TZSL* 14.13a, 37.1b. The historical issues about whether Han Wendi actually failed are beyond the scope of this discussion.
19. *MS* 136.3926.
20. *TZSL* 162.4b.
21. *TZSL* 24.la–b.
22. Obviously, Taizu had good information about the weather. Nevertheless, the stakes were still very high.
23. *TZSL* 41.3a.
24. *TZSL* 69.1a.
25. *TZSL* 78.3b.
26. *TZSL* 53.3b.
27. For an evocative description of Zhu's early years, see Wu Han, pp. 1–10.
28. *TZSL* 16.21a–b.
29. The battles in 1366 were decisive. See Sun Zhengrong, p. 112, and Dreyer, pp. 58–59.
30. *TZSL* 25.4b.
31. *TZSL* 18.3b.
32. *TZSL* 257.3b.
33. It should be noted that Taizu is famous as a brutal despot and not as the benevolent emperor suggested in the quotations presented here. His ruthlessness does not, however, render his words about ritual and music invalid. He simply practiced state sacrifices and music for idealistic aspirations and mercilessly crushed offenders for practical realities.

However, it would be fitting to cite one of Taizu's comments to show his use of strong measures to control his people as well. In April 1364, he said:

> Being wicked, fierce, proud, violent are not the natural characters of the people, but their habits. If there are rituals and laws (*lifa*) to regulate them, then the wicked and the fierce will become good and gentle; the proud and the violent can be made obedient like a reined horse, which becomes tamed after a period of good training. Now, at the initial stage of building

the empire, there must be *lifa*, otherwise, people have nothing to follow. Thus, [we] must use such measures to erase their acquired [bad] habits (*TZSL* 14.5a).

34. *TZSL* 257.3b.
35. *TZSL* 25.1a.
36. *TZSL* 79.1a.
37. *TZSL* 25.5b.
38. *TZSL* 25.5b.
39. As described in *DMJL* (4.13b), the utensils are orthodox. As described in *TZSL* (25.5b), the ritual utensils appeared to be different from orthodox practices. As described in *MS* (47.1237), the utensils, except for the bamboo baskets, were made of porcelain, instead of the prescribed wood, jade, and earth. The discrepancies among the descriptions suggest that a considerable amount of flexibility and change existed in the actual details of the utensils.
40. See *WLTK* 1.255–87.
41. *MS* 25.1269; *TZSL* 48.3b–5a.
42. *TCXK* 1.9b; Hu, *Ming Taizu ji*, pp. 405–6.
43. *TCXK* 1.12b.
44. *TCXK* 1.12b.
45. *MHD* 226.5a.
46. *TCXK* 1.2b–3b.
47. A most famous case is the presence of Wei Hanjin in Huizong's (reigned 1100–1125) court. See *Songshi* 128.2997–98.
48. The deity of Tianshou Shan was installed in the spirit-throne of the northern mountains. See *TCXK* 1.13b.
49. *YLSL* 236.1a–b.

CHAPTER 4

1. For a description of Shizong's sericultural ceremonials as a case study of ritual and musical politics, see my "Ritual and Musical Politics in the Court of Ming Shizong."
2. The *SZSL* is a comprehensive chronicle of court events, and each entry is marked by a date. However, entries may include descriptions of events that happened earlier (and sometimes much earlier) than the dates indicated. For convenience of discussion, I will take the entry dates as the

time when the main events described in the entry actually happened. For further details about the *SZSL* or the *Veritable Records of the Ming*, see Franke, *An Introduction to the Sources of Ming History*, especially pp. 8–23, 30–33 and Mano Senryu, *Mindai Bunkashi Kenkyu.*

3. See Fisher, *The Chosen One*. For general information about Shjizong's reign, see the *Dictionary of Ming Biography* s.v. "Chu Hou-ts'ung"; and Huai, *Jiajing zhuanzhi zhengzhi yu fazhi*.

4. *SZSL* 76.2b–4a.

5. *MS* 48.1258–59.

6. Official titles are given here to demonstrate that state ritual and music was a concern for all court citizens.

7. *SZSL* 109.2b–3a.

8. *SZSL* 109.3b–3b.

9. *SZSL* 109.3b.

10. *SZSL* 109.3b–4a.

11. *SZSL* 109.4a–4b.

12. *SZSL* 109.4b–5a.

13. *SZSL* 109.5a–5b.

14. *SZSL* 109.10a–b.

15. *SZSL* 110.1a.

16. The figure is based on the approximation that 1 *zhang* equals 141 inches.

17. *SZSL* 110.1a.

18. *SZSL* 110.1b–4a.

19. *SZSL* 110.11b.

20. The last sentence is not a literal translation, but a summary of a long passage providing detailed descriptions of the costumes.

21. *SZSL* 110.12a–13a.

22. *SZSL* 111.5a.

23. *SZSL* 111.14a.

24. *SZSL* 112.1a–1b.

25. *SZSL* 112.16b.

26. *SZSL* 112.15b–16a.

Huo's first objection to the institution of the sericultural ceremonials brought him a rebuke from the emperor only. However, his subsequent attacks on the ceremonials, the introduction of independent state sacrifices to honor Heaven and Earth, and his libel on Xia Yan finally led to his punishment. At this point, the political friction between Xia Yan and his rivals had become serious. Natural disasters were interpreted as portents that the emperor's actions had not been accurate, or at least that he had been misled by treacherous officials. Two entries in the *SZSL* discuss the portents specifically. In the entry date May 7, 1530 (*SZSL* 112.6a–7a), the emperor admitted some faults but also attributed some to the officials. He proposed, in great detail, ways to solve the problems and to eradicate undesirable conduct of some of the officials. In the entry dated May 23, 1530 (*SZSL* 112.16a), the Censor Xiong Jue asked the emperor to examine his acts and his use of people because there had been many disasters since he ascended to the throne nine years earlier. The sericultural ceremonials are not solely responsible for these political repercussions, but they are among the factors.

27. *SZSL* 119.1b.

28. *SZSL* 122.1a.

29. *SZSL* 122.1a.

30. *SZSL* 123.3b–4b.

31. Compare the descriptions of the sericultural ceremonials in *TCXK* (8.49–50a), *MHD* (92.526), *Da Tang Kaiyuan li* (48.1–13), and *Xing Tang shu* (15.367–371).

CHAPTER 5

1. For general surveys of Han theories about music, see DeWoskin, *A Song for One or Two*, and Nakasone, "Symbolism in Ancient Chinese Music Theory," *Journal of Music Theory* 1 (1957), 147–80.

2. An example of recent debates is *Yueji lunbian* (1983), a collection of studies on authorship, theories, and other related issues of the document.

3. See Pian, *Song Dynasty Musical Sources and Their Interpretation*.

4. In the *Guoxue jiben congshu* edition (Taipei, 1968) of Zhu's *Yuelü quanshu*, the bibliography is inserted before the first chapter of *Lülü jingyi neipian*.

5. See Needham, *Science and Civilization in China*, IV/1, pp. 126–228.

6. Zhu Zaiyu, Bibliography for *Yuelü quanshu*.

7. See Franke, *An Introduction*, p. 6.

8. *MHD* 91.18b.

9. Except for court documents and the *Lülü jingyi* of Zhu Zaiyu, no Ming music treatises include notated examples of Ming state sacrificial music.

10. In this discussion, Chinese philosophical terms are interpreted and translated according to general practices and contexts of music theories. For a standard reference on the terms, see Fung, *A History of Chinese Philosophy.*

11. *Lunyu yizhu*, "Shuer"; *Yueji pizhu*, "Weiwen hou."

12. *Lunyu yizhu*, "Bayi."

13. The heart and the mind are not antithetical in Chinese culture.

14. Henderson, *The Development & Decline of Chinese Cosmology*, pp. 22–24.

15. Xu Zhen, *Lülü xinshu fenzhu tusuan*, Ye Liangpei preface, la.

16. Zhang Yu, *Yayue yanyue* f.1a.

17. Huang Jiqing, *Yuelü guanjian*, preface.

18. See *MDH* 81.464–467 for Ming illustrations of some of the instruments.

19. Ji Ben, *Yuelü zuanyao*, f.la.

20. Yang pitches and pipes are always referred to as *lü*, while those of the yin are always referred to as *lü*. When they are discussing function of the pitches as standards, theorists always refer to only the yang pitches.

21. Derek Bodde. "The Chinese Cosmic Magic Known as 'Watching for the Ethers'."

22. *DMJL* 48.10a–10b.

23. Traditional studies on the measurement of the pitch pipes and the resulting pitches occupied such a central position in technical discussions of music that the studies engendered a specialized branch of Chinese knowledge called *lüxue*, the study of pitch measurements. See Wu Nanxun, *Lüxue huitong.*

24. Deng Wenxian, *Congke lülü jiezhu*, Cao Kui preface, la.

25. Wan Gong, *Wenmiao liyueshu* 5.4b.

26. For a chronological survey of pitch standards and other technical aspects of Chinese music theory, see Wu Nanxun, *Lüxue huitong.*

27. For example, a pipe with two-thirds the length of the pipe producing the pitch "C" will give the pitch "G", which is a fifth higher than "C"; similarly, a pipe that is four-thirds the length of the pipe producing the pitch "C'" will give a "G", that is a fourth lower than "C'".

28. Ji Ben, *Lülü bieshu*, preface and fol. 3a.

29. Cai Yuanding proposed to obtain six more pitches by continuing the cycles of fifths and to use them, when needed, as substitutes for some of the twelve absolute pitches. For further information, see Yang, *Zhongguo yinyue shigang*, pp. 291–96.

30. See Needham, *Science and Civilization in China*, Vol. IV, no. 1, p. 223. See also, Kuttner, "Prince Chu Tsai-yu's Life and Work."

31. See *Zhongguo yinyue cidian*, s.v. "*yun*," "*gongdiao*," "*lülü*". See also Pian, *Song Dynasty Musical Sources and Their Interpretation*, 43–58, and Pian, "Modes, Transposed Scales, Melody Types, and Tune Types."

32. See Chao, "Tone, Intonation, Singsong, Chanting, Recitative, Tonal Composition, and Atonal Composition," and Yung, *Cantonese Opera*, pp. 82–91.

33. Wang Sizong, *Huangzhong yuantong* 2.4b.

34. Wang Sizong, *Huangzhong yuantong* 2.6a–b.

35. *Yueji pizhu*, p. 80.

36. Wan Gong, *Wenmiao liyueshu* 5.61a–b.

37. Zhu, *Lülü jingyi waipian* 3.21a–25a.

38. Zhu, *Lülü jingyi waipian* 2.28–35.

39. Jiao Hong ed., *Guochao xianchenglu* 89.27a–31a.

40. *Qishi* refers to *huangzhong*/Heaven, *dalü*/men, *gusien*/spring, *ruibin*/summer, *linzhong*/earth, *nanlü*/autumn, *yingzhong*/winter.

41. Ji Ben, *Yuelü zuanyao* f.22a.

42. ji Ben, *Lülü bieshu* f.6b.

43. Henderson, *The Development & Decline of Chinese Cosmology*.

CHAPTER 6

1. *SFL* 22.661.

2. *GQ* 1.297.

3. *TZSL* 19.5a–5b. There is no information about who and what the "Daoist children" were—young Daoist apprentices or children of Daoist monks?

4. This chapter will include translated titles of court officials to demonstrate that state sacrificial music was a concern for all court citizens, even when their primary duties were unrelated to music. Except for those for the music officials, all translations of titles conform to

Charles Hucker's *A Dictionary of Official Titles in Imperial China*, which also includes an excellent introduction to the organization of the Ming government.

5. *TZSL* 19.8b.
6. *TZSL* 19.10b–11a.
7. *TZSL* 20.1b.
8. *TZSL* 21.7a.
9. There is no clear record about when the songs for the state sacrifice to Heaven were composed, but they had to be completed before November 1368, when the ceremonial was first performed. There also is no clear record about when the songs for the state sacrifices to the imperial ancestors were composed, but they had to be around September 1367, when the imperial ancestral temple was first completed. Thus, the composition dates of the two sets of songs could not be more than two years apart.
10. *TZSL* 21.8b.
11. *TZSL* 45.17a.
12. *TZSL* 93.3b–4a.
13. The reasons for Taizu's dissatisfaction were complex. In addition to the military and political problems of the time, bad weather during ritual performances appeared to have been a significant factor.
14. *TZSL* 99.1b–2a.
15. *TZSL* 122.5a.
16. A famous case is Wei Hanjin's (?–1105) involvement with state sacrificial music in Song Huizong's court. See *Songshi* 128.2997–98.
17. Most of the complaints originated from ritual and other non-musical reasons, but the consequences affected state sacrificial music.
18. *SFL* 22.667.
19. See Lü Nan, *Shiyue tupu*.
20. *SFL* 22.667.
21. *XANSL* 155.9b–11b.
22. *XANSL* 157.6b–7a.
23. *SFL* 22.667.
24. The complaint primarily targeted musicians of the Office of Entertainment Music (*jiaofang*), but state sacrificial music also was involved. Among the types of musicians found lacking were those playing the twenty-five-stringed zither (*se*), bell-chimes, and stone-chimes, which were essentially musical instruments for state sacrificial music.

25. *XAOSL* 99.8b.
26. *SFL* 22.669.
27. *XAOZL* 107.1b–3a.
28. *SFL* 22.669.
29. *XAOSL* 188.11a.
30. *SFL* 22.669.
31. *TZSL* 57.3b.
32. *WZSL* 40.4b.
33. Xia Xie, *Ming tongjian*, 1909.
34. Huai, *Jiajing zhuanzhi zhengzhi yu fazhi*.
35. *SZSL* 119.11b.
36. Fisher, *The Chosen One*.
37. *SZSL* 117.9b–13a.
38. See also *SZSL* 117.9b–13a.
39. *SZSL* 123.15a.
40. *SZSL* 115.4a.; *SFL* 22.671.
41. *SZSL* 130.8a.
42. *SZSL* 176.2b.
43. *SZSL* 186.9a–10b.
44. *SZSL* 186.9b–10b.
45. For a brief survey of materials on Daoists in the Ming court, see *Daojiaoshi ziliao*, pp. 352–83.
46. A comprehensive analysis of the Daoist elements in Ming state sacrifices and music is beyond the scope of the present discussion. Many questions about source materials and Ming religious-musical culture are yet to be asked and answered, for example, how the Daoist-musician-officials were trained as monks and/or musicians.

The discussion here simply illustrates the complexity of the ritual-musical culture in the Ming court, in which literal application of Confucian and orthodox prescriptions was impossible and creative solutions were needed. As Romeyn Taylor demonstrated in his article, "Official and Popular Religion and the Political Organization of Chinese Society in the Ming," the official religion, which was embodied in the state ritual and music, was "a complex, internally contradictory, and unstable collection of cults of various sorts: classical, pseudoclassical, popular, and Toaist" (p. 156).

The discussion here also highlights the fact that Ming state sacrificial music was never merely a Confucian and theoretical product. Even though it was essentially promoted and described by Confucianists

—scholar-officials, ritual experts, music theorists, and composers—who relied on classical models and knowledge, Ming state sacrificial music was very much a product of its time and was not unrelated to other contemporaneous music. For a discussion on the ways in which court musicians appropriated the commoners' music, see Yang Yinliu, *Zhongguo gudai yinyue shigao*, 1005–9.

47. See the *Dictionary of Ming Biography*, s.v. "Leng Ch'ien."

48. *MHD* 226.1110–13.

49. *TCXK* 7.51b–97a.

50. *GQ* 43.2708

51. *GQ* 57.3579.

52. *XAOSL* 99.7b–8b.

53. *GQ* 57.3597.

54. *GQ* 58.3643.

55. Wang Sizong, *Huangzhong yuantong*, preface.

56. Traditionally, the breaking of a string or fret in the middle of a performance is very inauspicious.

57. *SFL* 22.671; 22.675; *GQ* 60.3793.

58. *SFL* 22.674.

59. *SZSL* 217.1a.

60. *GQ* 57.3588.

61. *SFL* 22.675.

62. Sun Chengze, *Siling dianliji* 3.16a–20b.

CHAPTER 7

1. Wang Yunmei believes that the compilation of the *DMJL* began as early as July 1367; see his *Mingshi kaozheng*, p. 382.

2. Yang Shiqi, *Wenyuange shumu*, 1.7.

3. *DMJL*, 14.30a.

4. The five emperors were the first, third, fourth, fifth, and seventh rulers of the empire; the second and sixth emperors are not mentioned because they were considered "illegitimate," and were not worshipped.

5. National Library of Peiping Rare Books Collection, microfilm no. 964.

6. Zhang Xuan, *Neige shumu* 1.13a.

7. Zhu Zaiyu, *Lülü jingyi* I,7.6.

8. The folios of traditional Chinese books are flipped from the left to the right.

9. For further analysis of the songs, see Lam, "Creativity within Bounds," pp. 355–462.

10. The labels of the songs refer to the notated sources, the state sacrifices, and the order in which the songs appear. Thus, DMYQ 1 refers to the first song in the state sacrifice to Heaven, which is notated in the *DMJL*; ZLTD 1–8 refers to the songs for the state sacrifice to Heaven and Earth, which are preserved in the *TCZL*; TCYQ 1–9 refers to the songs for the state sacrifice to Heaven, which are preserved in the *TCK* (*TCXK*); the DMZM, ZLZM, and TCZM are songs for the state sacrifice to the imperial ancestors, which can be found in all of the aforementioned notated sources.

CHAPTER 8

1. For Wang's biography, see *Dictionary of Ming Biography*, s.v. "Wang T'ing-hsiang."

2. For samples of laudatory writings, see the praises by Gui E and Qu Luan, which are cited in *SZSL* (119.17b–18b).

3. Wang Xiaoyu, ed, *Wang Tingxiang ji*, pp. 903–04. To render the particulars and images described by the poet intelligible to general readers, I have translated some words interpretively. For example, a literal translation of the second line of the third poem should be "the deities' chariots illusively come out to the human world." Similarly, the last line of the fifth poem would be translated as "That is not like the peace enjoyed by the emperor."

4. See Wang Xiaoyu, ed., *Wang Tingxiang ji*.

5. The 1530s had its share of political, military, and social turmoil. There was a mutiny in Datong earlier in the year 1534.

6. For a biography of Wang Shenzhong, see the *Dictionary of Ming Biography*, s.v. "Wang Shen-chung."

7. This translation is based on a version of Wang's text, preserved in Sun Chengze's *Tianfu guangji*, p. 698. Wang's text is very difficult to translate because its poetic but academic language depends on many direct and indirect references and symbolism to classical terms and things: In the early years of his career as a man of letters, Wang was

famous for his devotion to classical literature from the Qin and Han dynasties. My translation here only attempts to present, in simple English, Wang's observations of the music and dance and his response to their expressiveness.

8. It should be stressed that verbalization of distinctive musical features is extremely difficult; music and language are different medias of expression.

9. *SZSL* 119.6b–7a.

10. *SZSL* 119.8b–9a.

11. *GQ* 55.3478.

12. *GQ* 96.4279; Sun, *Tianfu guangji*, 6.62–63.

Glossary

bai	拜
baiwei	拜位
banwei	版位
bayi	八佾
biandou	籩豆
biangong	變宮
biansheng	變聲
bianzhi	變徵
binli	賓禮
Cai Yuanding	蔡元定
cangong lingchu	蠶宮令署
Cao Kui	曹逵
changzan	唱贊
Chen Yang	陳暘
Chen Zixian	陳自暹
chenghuang	城隍
chezhuan	徹饌
chi	篪
chuxian	初獻
congsi	從祀
Cui Zhiduan	崔志端
cun	寸
Dacheng zhishen wenxuan wang	大成至聖文宣王

dadi	大禘
dalü	大呂
Dasidian	大祀殿
daxia	大祫
daxiang	大享
daxueshi	大學士
dayu	大雩
Deng Wenxian	鄧文憲
Deng Xian	鄧憲
di	笛
di shezhi	帝社稷
dian yubo	奠玉帛
dianyue guan	典樂官
diao	調
Dong Zhongshu	董仲舒
duan ru guanzhu	端如貫珠
duzhu guan	讀祝官
fan	凡
fanchai	燔柴
fengtiao	奉祧
Fengxian dian	奉先殿
fengyun leiyu	風雲雷雨
fenxian guan	分獻官
"Fuyi"	鳧鷖
fufu	伏服
Gansu taipusi	甘肅太僕寺
gaoji	告祭
gaoru kang	高如抗
gong	宮
Gong Yao	拱榣
gongche	工尺
gongchen	功臣
gongxuan	宮懸
gou	勾

gua	卦
guan	觀
Guande dian	觀德殿
guansheng	官生
Guan Zhong	管仲
Guanzi	管子
gui	跪
Guoyu	國語
guozi jian	國子監
guozi jijiu	國子祭酒
guxian	姑洗
guyue	古樂
Han Bangqi	韓邦奇
he	和
hesheng	和聲
houqi	候氣
huang taizi	皇太子
huangzhong	黃鐘
huiluan ge	回鑾歌
Huo Tao	霍韜
ji Kong	祭孔
Ji Yuan	季源
Jiajing	嘉靖
jiali	嘉禮
jian shihao	薦謚號
jiaofang	教坊
jiaoji	郊祭
jiazhong	夾鐘
jigao	祭告
jijiu	祭酒
jili	吉禮
Jin Yunren	金贇仁
jingshi jiumiao	京師九廟
jinzu	進饌

jue	角
juge	句格
junli	軍禮
junzi	君子
juzhong gou	句中勾
juzhong ju	句中矩
Kong Keren	孔克仁
Kui	夔
Leng Qian	冷謙
li	禮
Li Chengxun	李承勛
Li Shi	李時
Liao Daonan	廖道南
liaotan	燎壇
Liaozhou	遼州
lidai diwang	歷代帝王
lifa	禮法
like du jishizhong	禮課都給事中
ling	靈
Ling Lun	伶倫
linzhong	林鐘
litan	厲壇
Liu Ji	劉基
Liu Lian	劉廉
Liu Minyue	劉民悦
Liu Xiang	劉翔
liuyi	六佾
Lu	魯
Lü Nan	呂柟
lubu	鹵簿
lülü	律呂
Ma Wensheng	馬文昇
mashen	馬神
miao	廟

Ming Yuzhen	明玉珍
Mingdai liyue	明代禮樂
Mingde	明德
mingtang	明堂
Nanjing Jiangxi daoshi yushi	南京江西道試御史
Nanjing shenmiao	南京神廟
nanlü	南呂
paixiao	排簫
peiwei	配位
qi	氣
qidu	旗毒
qigu	祈穀
qiji	祈祭
qijuzhu	起居注
qin	琴
qindian	寢殿
qing	清
qing	卿
qingcheng	青城
qisheng	七聲
qishi	七始
qitong	七通
Qiu Xuanqing	丘玄清
qu ru zhe	曲如折
ren	仁
ruibin	蕤賓
Ruichang wangfu	瑞昌王府
sanfen sunyi	三分損益
sangong	三公
sanhuang	三皇
sanpen shou	三盆手
sanqing yuezhang	三清樂章
se	瑟
shang	商

shang ru kang	上如抗
Shao	韶
Shaoqing	少卿
sheji	社稷
shenfu	昇祔
sheng	笙
shengshi	聖師
shengyue guan	神樂觀
shenzuo	神座
shi'erlü	十二律
shimiao	世廟
shixia	時祫
shiyue	詩樂
shizi	世子
shouzuo	受胙
Shujing	書經
Shun	舜
si	巳
sibai	四拜
sicheng	寺丞
siqing	四清
Sizhouling	泗州靈
song dishen	送帝神
Song Lian	宋濂
taichang boshi	太常博士
taichang qing	太常卿
Taichang zongji	太常總記
taichangsi	太常寺
taicou	太簇
Taihe dian	太和殿
taimiao	太廟
taipusi	太僕寺
taisui	太歲
taitan	泰壇

Taiyi qiongdao	太液瓊島
taiyue ling	太樂令
tan	壇
Tang liudian	唐六典
Tao An	陶安
texiang	特享
tezhong	特鐘
tianshen dizhi	天神地祇
Tianshoushan	天壽山
tiaomiao	祧廟
Tongdian	通典
wang	王
wang erbu fan	往而不返
Wang Fuguang	王福廣
Wang Ju	汪舉
Wang Shenzhong	王慎中
Wang Sizong	王思宗
Wang Tingxiang	王廷相
wangliao	望燎
Wei Hanjin	魏漢津
wu bujing	勿不敬
Wu Yinglung	吳應隆
Wudi	五帝
wuli	五禮
wusheng	五聲
wusi	五祀
wuyi	無射
wuyin	五音
xia ru zhui	下如墜
Xia Yan	夏言
xian	仙
xiancan	先蠶
xiang'an	香案
xiangli	享禮

xiannong	先農
Xiansheng diwang	先聖帝王
xianshi	先師
xiao	簫
Xie Qingzhi	謝靖直
xielü lang	協律郎
xin	心
Xiong Ding	熊鼎
xiongli	凶禮
xiyue	夕月
xu	續
Xu Pu	徐溥
xun	塤
Xunan Sichuan jiancha yushi	巡案四川監察御史
Yang Lian	楊廉
yanyue	燕樂
Yao	堯
yapai	牙牌
yaxian	亞獻
Ye Liangpei	葉良佩
yimou wucheng	疑謀勿成
yin	音
yin fujiu	飲福酒
ying dishen	迎帝神
yingzhong	應鐘
yize	夷則
yizhang	儀仗
yizhu	儀注
yu	敔
yu	羽
yuanqiu	圜丘
yuansheng	元聲
yue	樂
Yue Hesheng	岳和聲

yuejiang	月將
Yueshu	樂書
yuewu sheng	樂舞生
yuexuan	樂懸
Yuezheng haidu	岳鎮海瀆
yugao zaozong	預告祖宗
yun	均
"Yuzao"	漁藻
Zan Tong	詹同
Zanshifu zanshi	詹事府詹事
zhaigong	齋宮
zhang	丈
Zhang Cong	張璁
Zhang E	張鶚
Zhang Juzheng	張居正
Zhang Mao	章懋
Zhang Shicheng	張士誠
Zhangli fang	掌禮房
Zhao Jizhong	趙繼宗
zhaori	朝日
Zhejiang buzhengsi	浙江佈政司
zhengdian	正殿
zhengsheng	鄭聲
zhengwei	正位
zhenren	真人
zhi	徵
zhi ru gaomu	止如槁木
Zhisheng xianshi	至聖先師
zhizhai	致齋
zhonglü	仲呂
zhongxian	終獻
Zhou Guanzheng	周觀政
Zhou Hongmo	周洪謨
zhu	柷

Zhu Sheng	朱昇
Zhu Xizhou	朱希周
Zhu Zaiyu	朱載堉
zhujiao	助教
zhushen	諸神
zhushi	祝史
zixue	字學

Works Cited

I. PRIMARY SOURCES

Chen, Renxi 陳仁錫. [1630] 1965. *Huang Ming shifalu* 皇明世法錄 (A Collection of Ming Documents and Personal Records). Reprint, Taipei: Xuesheng shuju.

Da Ming jili 大明集禮. (Collected Ceremonial of the Ming Dynasty). [1370; 1530] 1972. Reprint, *SKQS* edition, Taipei: Commercial Press.

Da Tang Kaiyuanli 大唐開元禮. (Ritual of the Tang Kaiyuan Period). [732] 1972. Reprint, *SKQS* edition, Taipei: Commercial Press.

Deng, Wenxian 鄧文憲. *Congke lülü jiezhu* 重刻律呂解注. (A new edition of Exegesis on Cai Yuanding's "A New Treatise on Regulating the Pitch Pipes"). Preface dated 1539. Library of the Research Institute of Music, Beijing.

Hu, Shie 胡士萼, ed. 1991. *Ming Taizu ji* 明太祖集. (An Anthology of Ming Taizu's Writings). Hefei: Huangshan shushe.

Huang, Jiqing 黃積慶. *Yuelü guanjian* 樂律管見 (Some Limited Views of Music Theory). Preface dated 1551. Library of Research Institute of Music, Beijing.

Huang Ming taixue ji 皇明太學記. Preface dated 1557. National Central Library, Taipei.

Huang, Yuji 黃虞稷. [1853] 1916. *Qianqingtang shumu* 千頃堂書目 (Catalogue of the Qianqing Library). Reprint, Shiyuan congshu edition.

Huang, Yuliang 黃汝良. *Yuelü zhi* 樂律志 (Monograph on Music History and Theory). Preface dated 1633. Naikaku Bunko, Tokyo.

Ji, Ben 季本. "Yuelü zuanyao" 樂律纂要 (A Treatise on the Essentials of Music Theory). Preface dated 1539. Manuscript. Beijing University Library, Beijing.

———. "Lülü bieshu" 律呂別書 (A Supplementary Treatise on Music Theory). Preface dated 1554. Manuscript. Beijing University Library, Beijing.

Jiao, Hong 焦紘, ed. [1616] 1965. *Guochao xianchenglu* 國朝獻徵錄 (Biographies of Eminent Ming Personages). Reprint, Taipei: Xuesheng.

Li, Wencha 李文察. *Lishi yueshu* 李氏樂書 (Collection of Li Wencha's Musical Treatises). Preface dated 1545. National Library of Peiping Rare Books Collection Microfilm, no. 250.

Li, Zhizao 李之藻. [1618] 1970. *Panguan li yueshu* 頖宮禮樂疏 (A Proposal for the Performance of the Confucian Ceremonial in Schools). 2 vols. Reprint, Taipei: National Central Library.

Liu, Ji 劉基. [1370] 1967. "Si Fangqiu song 祀方丘頌. " In *Ming wen heng* 明文衡 (A Critical Collection of Ming Writings), 19.10. Reprint, Taipei: Shijie shuju.

Liu, Lian 劉廉. *Yuejing yuanyi* 樂經元義 (Original Meaning of the Classic of Music). Preface dated 1550. National Library of Peiping Rare Books Collection Microfilm, no. 239.

Lü, Huai 呂懷, *Lülü guyi* 律呂古義 (Ancient Meanings of Music). Preface dated 1549. Library of Research Institute of Music, Beijing.

Lü, Nan 呂柟, et al., eds. *Shiyue tupu* 詩樂圖譜 (Illustrated Scores of Poetic Music). Preface dated 1536. National Library of Peiping Rare Books Collection Microfilm, no. 456.

Ming huidian 明會典. [1587] 1963. [Collected Statutes of the Ming]. Reprint, Taipei: Dongnan shubaoshe.

Mingdai liyue 明代禮樂 (Ming Dynasty Rituals and Music). n.d. Manuscript. Library of the Research Institute of Music, Beijing.

Mingshi 明史 [Ming History]. [1739] 1974. Beijing: Zhonghua shuju.

Qin, Huitian 秦蕙田. [1753] 1985. *Wuli tongkao* 五禮通考 (Comprehensive Study of the Five Categories of Rites). Reprint, Taipei: Commercial Press.

Shenzong xianhuangdi shilu 神宗顯皇帝實錄 (The Veritable Records of Shenzong). [1630] 1962–67. Taipei: Academica Sinica.

Shizong suhuangdi shilu 世宗肅皇帝實錄 (The Veritable Records of Shizong). [1577] 1962–67. Taipei: Academica Sinica.

Songshi 宋史 (Song History). [1345] 1977. Beijing: Zhonghua shuju.

Sun, Chengze 孫承澤. [1640s] 1937. *Siling dianliji* 思陵典禮記 (Ritual of Emperor Sizong). Jieyue shanfang huichao edition. Changsha: Commercial Press.

———. [1671] 1983. *Tianfu guangji* 天府廣記 (History of Beijing). Beijing: Guji chubanshe.

Taichang kao 太常考 (Monograph on the Court of Imperial Sacrifices). 1580s. Manuscript. Beijing University Library, Beijing.

Taichang Xukao 太常續考 (Expanded Monograph on the Court of Imperial Sacrifices). [1640s] 1970s. Reprint, *SKQS edition*, Taipei: Commercial Press.

Taichang zonglan 太常總覽 (General Record of the Court of Imperial Sacrifices). 1470s. Manuscript. National Library of Peiping Rare Books Collection Microfilm, no. 964.

Taizong wenhuangdi shilu 太宗文皇帝實錄 (Veritable Records of Taizong). [1430] 1962–67. Taipei: Academica Sinica.

Taizu gaohuangdi shilu 太祖高皇帝實錄 (Veritable Records of Taizu). [1418] 1940. Jiangsu guoxue tushuguang chuanchao ben.

Tan, Qian 談遷. [1653] 1958. *Guo Que* 國榷 [An Evaluation of the Events of Our Dynasty]. Beijing: Guji chubanshe.

Wan, Gong 萬恭. *Wenmiao liyueshu* 文廟禮樂書 (A Manual of Ceremonies and Music for the Temple of Confucius). Preface dated 1583. Library of Research Institute of Music, Beijing.

Wang, Sizong 王思宗. *Huangzhong yuantong* 黃鐘元統 (Huangzhong as thc Originating Tone). Preface dated 1566. Library of Research Institute of Music, Beijing.

Wang, Tingxiang 王廷相. [1636–1637] 1976. "Miscellaneous Writings: 雜論 Discussion on Music Theory." In *Wangshi jiacangji* 王氏家藏集. Reprint, Taipei: Weiwen.

Wuzong yihuangdi shilu 武宗毅皇帝實錄 (The Veritable Records of Wuzong). [1525] 1962–67. Taipei: Academica Sinica.

Xianzong chunhuangdi shilu 憲宗純皇帝實錄 (The Veritable Records of Xianzong). [1491] 1962–67. Taipei: Academica Sinica.

Xiaozong jing huangdi shilu 孝宗敬皇帝實錄 (The Veritable Records of Xiaozong). [1509] 1962–67. Taipei: Academica Sinica.

Xin Tangshu 新唐書 (New Tang History). [1601] 1975. Beijing: Xinhua shuju.

Xu, Zhen 許珍. *Lülü xinshu fenzhu tusuan* 律呂新書分注圖算 (An Illustrated Commentary to Cai Yuan-ding's New Treatise on the

Regulation of the Pitch Pipes). Preface dated 1541. Library of Research Institute of Music, Beijing.
Xunzi xinzhu 荀子新注 (Xunzi, with new annotation). 1979. Beijing: Zhonghua shuju.
Yang, Shiqi 楊士奇, et al., eds. [1441] 1967. *Wenyuange shumu* 文淵閣書目 [Catalogue of Wen-yuan Library]. Reprint, Taipei: Commercial Press.
Zhang, E 張鶚. *Dacheng yuewu tupu* 大成樂舞圖譜 (Musical Score and Dance Illustrations for the Sacrifice to Confucius). Preface dated 1520. Manuscript. Naikaku Bunko, Tokyo.
Zhang, Xuan 張萱, et al., eds, [1605] 1916. *Neige shumu* 內閣書目 [Catalogue of the Cabinet Library]. Shiyuan congshu edition.
Zhang, Yu 張敔. *Yayue yenyue* 雅樂燕樂 (Proper Music and Entertainment Music). Preface dated 1530. Manuscript. Beijing University Library, Beijing.
Zhu, Zaiyu 朱載堉. [1590s] 1970s. *Lülü jingyi*. In *Yuelü quanshu* 樂律全書 (Collected Works on Music Theory). Reprint, Taipei: Commercial Press.

II. SECONDARY CHINESE AND JAPANESE SOURCES

Cui, Fuzhang 崔富章. 1983. "Yuelü quanshu kao" 樂律全書考 (Editions of Zhu Zaiyu's 'Collection of Musical Treatises'). In *Guji luncong* 古籍論叢, edited by Xie Guozhen et al. Fuzhou: Fujian renmin chubanshe, pp. 48–60.
Daojiaoshi zhiliu 道教史資料 (Sources of History of Daoism). 1991. Shanghai: Shanghai guji chubanshe.
He, Baoshan 何寶善. 1987. *Jiajing huangdi Zhu Houcong* 嘉靖皇帝朱厚熜 (Zhu Houcong, the Jiajing Emperor). Beijing: Beijing yanshan chubanshe.
Huai, Xiaofeng 怀效峰. 1989. *Jiajing zhuanzhi zhengzhi yu fazhi* 嘉靖專制政治與法治 (Dictatorial politics and legal government in the Jiajing period). Changsha: Hunan jiaoyu chubanshe.
Li, Guoxiang and Yang, Chang 李國祥, 楊昶. 1992. *Ming shilu leizuan gongting shiliao juan* 明實錄類纂宮廷史料卷 (An Anthology of Historical Materials from the *Veritable Records of the Ming*: Ming Court). Wuhan: Wuhan chubanshe.

Lunyu yizhu 論語譯注 (The *Analects of Confucius*, translated and annotated). 1962. Beijing: Zhonghua shuju.

Mano, Senryu 間野潛龍. 1979. *Mindai Bunkashi Kenkyu* 明代文化史研究 (A Study on Ming Cultural History). Tōyōshi Kenkyū Shokan. Kyoto: Doosha.

Wang, Meng'ou 王夢鷗. 1988. *Liji jinzhu jinyi* 禮記今註今譯 (A Modern Translation and Annotation of the *Book of Ceremonial*). Tianjin: Tianjin guji chubanshe.

Wang, Xiaoyu 王孝魚, ed. 1989. *Wang Tingxiang ji* 王廷相集 (Collected Writings of Wang Tingxiang). Beijing: Zhonghua shuju.

Wang, Yunmei 王雲眉. 1980. *Mingshi kaozheng* 明史考證 (Textual Criticism of Ming History). Beijing: Zhonghua.

Wu, Han 吳晗. 1965. *Zhu Yuanzhang zhuan* 朱元璋傳 [Biography of Zhu Yuanzhang]. Beijing: Sanlian Shudian.

Wu, Nanxun 吳南薰. 1964. *Lüxue huitong* 律學會通 (Comprehensive Study of Pitch Temperaments). Beijing: Kexue chubenshe.

Yang, Yinliu· 楊蔭瀏. 1981. *Zhongguo gudai yinyue shigao* 中國古代音樂史稿 [Draft History of Ancient Chinese Music]. Beijing: Renmin yinyue chubanshe.

———. *Zhongguo yinyue shigang* 中國音樂史綱 [Outline History of Ancient Chinese Music]. 1953. Shanghai: Wanye.

Yueji lunbian 樂記論辯 (Studies on the *Record of Music*). 1983. Beijing: Renmin yinyue chubanshe.

Yueji pizhu 樂記批注 (Critical Comments on *The Record of Music*). 1976. Beijing: Renmin yinyue chubanshe.

Zhang, Hequan 張鶴泉. 1993. *Zhoudai jisi yanjiu* 周代祭祀研究 (A Study on State Sacrifices of the Zhou Dynasty). Taipei: Wenjin chubanshe.

Zhongguo yishu yanjiuyuan yinyue yanjiusuo 中國藝術研究院音樂研究所. 1984. *Zhongguo yinyue cidian* 中國音樂詞典 (Dictionary of Chinese Musical Terms). Beijing: Renmin Yinyue chubanshe.

III. SECONDARY WESTERN SOURCES

Ahern, Emily M. 1981. *Chinese Ritual and Politics*. Cambridge: Cambridge University Press.

Bell, Catherine. 1992. *Ritual Theory, Ritual Practice*. New York: Oxford University Press.

Bloch, Maurice. 1989. *Ritual, History and Power: Selected Papers in Anthropology*. London: The Athlone Press.

Bodde, Derek. 1959. "The Chinese Cosmic Magic Known as 'Watching for the Ethers"', in *Studia Serica Bernhard Karlgren Dedicata*, edited by E. Glahn, 14–35. Copenhagen: Munksgarrd.

Cannadine, David and Simon Price, eds. 1987. *Rituals of Royalty: Power and Ceremonial In Traditional Societies*. Cambridge: Cambridge University Press.

Chang, K.C. 1983. *Art, Myth, and Ritual: the Path to Political Authority in Ancient China*. Cambridge: Harvard University Press.

Chao, Yuen-ren. 1956. "Tone, Intonation, Singsong, Chanting, Recitative, Tonal Composition and Atonal Composition." In *For Roman Jakobson: Essays on the Occasion of His Sixtieth Birthday, 11 October, 1956*, compiled and edited by Morris Halle, et al. The Hague: Mouton and Co.

Dardess, John. 1983. *Confucianism and Autocracy: Professional Elites in the Founding of the Ming Dynasty*. Berkeley: University of California Press.

DeWoskin, Kenneth. 1982. *A Song for One or Two: Music and the Concept of Art in Early China*. Michigan Papers in Chinese Studies, no. 42. Ann Arbor: Center for Chinese Studies, University of Michigan.

Dictionary of Ming Biography, edited by Carrington L. Goodrich and Chaoying Fang. 1976. New York: Columbia University Press.

Dreyer, Edward L. 1982. *Early Ming China: A Political History, 1355–1435*. Stanford: Stanford University Press.

Farmer, Edward L. 1990. "Social Regulations of the First Ming Emperor: Orthodoxy as a Function of Authority." In *Orthodoxy in Late Imperial China*, edited by Kwang-Ching Liu. Berkeley: University of California Press.

Fisher, Carney T. 1990. *The Chosen One: Succession and Adoption in the Court of Ming Shizong*. Sydney: Allen & Unwin.

Franke, Wolfgang. 1968. *An Introduction to the Sources of Ming History*. Kuala Lumpur: University of Malaya Press.

Fung Yu-lan. 1952. *A History of Chinese Philosophy*. 2 vols. Translated by Derk Bodde. 2d ed. Princeton: Princeton University Press.

Gardner, Howard. 1982. *Art, Mind, and Brain: A Cognitive Approach to Creativity*. New York: Basic Books.

Geertz, Clifford. 1973. *The Interpretation of Cultures*. New York: Basic Books.

Grimes, Robert. 1991. "Bibliography on Chinese Music and Ritual." *Association for Chinese Music Research Newsletter* 4/2: 13–21.

Grimes, Ronald L. 1990. *Ritual Criticism: Case Studies in Its Practice, Essays on Its Theory*. Columbia: University of South Carolina Press.

Hansen, Valerie. 1990. *Changing Gods in Medieval China, 1127–1276*. Princeton: Princeton University Press.

Henderson, John B. 1984. *The Development & Decline of Chinese Cosmology*. New York: Columbia University Press.

Huang, Ray. 1981. *1587, A Year of No Significance*. New Haven: Yale University Press.

Hucker, Charles. 1985. *A Dictionary of Official Titles in Imperial China*. Stanford: Stanford University Press.

Kertzer, David I. 1988. *Ritual, Politics and Power*. New Haven: Yale University Press.

Kuttner, Fritz A. 1975. "Prince Chu Tsai-yu's Life and Work: A Re-evaluation of His Contribution to Equal Temperament Theory." *Journal of Ethnomusicology* 19: 163–204.

Lam, Joseph S. C. 1988. "Creativity within Bounds: State Sacrificial Songs from the Ming Dynasty (A.D. 1368–1644)." Ph.D. Dissertation, Harvard University.

———. "Ritual and Musical Politics in the Court of Ming Shizong." 1996. In *Harmony and Counterpoint: Ritual Music in Chinese Context*, edited by Bell Yung, Evelyn Rawski, Rubie Watson, 35–53. Stanford, Calif.: Stanford University Press.

———. 1995. "The Yin and Yang of Chinese Music Historiography: The Case of Confucian Ceremonial Music." *Yearbook for Traditional Music* 27: 34–51.

MacKinnon, Donald W. 1962. "The Nature and Nurture of Creative Talent." *American Psychologist* 17: 484–95.

McMullen, David. 1987. "Bureaucrats and Cosmology: The Ritual Code of T'ang China." In *Rituals of Royalty: Power and Cermeonial in Tradtional Societies*, edited by David Cannadine and Simon Price, 181–236. Cambridge: Cambridge University Press.

Mote, Frederick W. and Denis Twitchett, eds. 1988. *The Cambridge History of China, vol. 7, The Ming Dynasty, 1368–1644, Part I*. Cambridge: Cambridge University Press.

Nakasone, Kazu. 1957. "Symbolism in Ancient Chinese Music Theory." *Journal of Music Theory 1*: 147–80.

Needham, Joseph. 1962. *Science and Civilization in China*. Volume IV, no. 1. London: Cambridge University Press.

Pian, Rulan Chao. 1967. *Song Dynasty Musical Sources and Their Interpretation*. Cambridge: Harvard University Press.

———. "Modes, Transposed Scales, Melody Types and Tune Types." 1981. In *Report of the Twelfth Congress, Berkeley 1977*, edited by Daniel Heartz and Bonnie Wade, 536–49. Barenreiter Kassel: Barenreiter-Verlag Kassel.

Pye, Lucian W. 1992. *The Spirit of Chinese Politics*. New ed. Cambridge: Harvard University Press.

Rawski, Evelyn S. 1988. "The Imperial Way of Death: Ming and Ch'ing Emperors and Death Ritual." In *Death Ritual in Late Imperial and Modern China*, edited by James L., Waton, and Evelyn S. Rawski, 228–53. Berkeley: University of California Press.

Runco, Mark A. and Robert S. Albert. 1990. *Theories of Creativity*. Newbury Park, Calif.: SAGE Publications.

Schechner, Richard, and Appel, Willa, eds. 1990. *By Means of Performance: Intercultural Studies of Theatre and Ritual*. Cam-bridge: Cambridge University Press.

Schieffelin, Edward L. 1993. "Performance and the Cultural Construction of Reality: A New Guinea Example." In *Creativity/Anthropology*, edited by Smadar Lavie, Kirin Narayan, and Renato Rosaldo, 270–95. Ithaca: Cornell University Press.

Simth, Richard J. 1990. "Ritual in Ch'ing Culture." In *Orthodoxy in Late Imperial China*, edited by Kwang-Ching Liu, 281–310. Berkeley: University of California Press.

Sternberg, R. J, ed. 1988. *The Nature of Creativity: Contemporary Psychological Perspectives*. Cambridge: Cambridge University Press.

Tambiah, Stanley J. 1979. "A Performative Approach to Ritual." *Proceedings of the British Academy* 65: 113–69.

Taylor, Romeyn. 1990. "Official and Popular Religion and the Political Organization of Chinese Society in the Ming." In *Orthodoxy in Late Imperial China*, edited by Kwang-Ching Liu, 126–57. Berkeley: University of California Press.

Taylor, Romeyn, trans. 1975. *Basic Annals of Ming T'ai-tsu*. San Francisco: Chinese Materials Center.

Tu Weiming, Milan Hejtmanek, and Alan Wachman, eds. 1992. *The Confucian World Observed: A Contemporary Discussion of Confucian Humanism in East Asia*. Honolulu: The East-West Center.

Turner, Victor W. 1966. *The Ritual Process: Structure and Anti-Structure*. Chicago: Aldine.

Wakeman Jr., Frederic 1988. "Mao's Remains." In *Death Ritual in Late Imperial and Modern China*, edited by James L., Watson, and Evelyn S. Rawski, 254–88. Berkeley: University of California Press.

Watson, James L. 1985. "Standardizing the Gods: The Promotion of T'ien Hou ('Empress of Heaven') Along the South China Coast, 960–1960." In *Popular Culture in Late Imperial China*, edited by David Johnson, Andrew J. Nathan, and Evelyn S. Rawski, 292–324. Berkeley: University of California Press.

Wechsler, Howard J. 1985. *Offerings of Jade and Silk: Ritual and Symbol in the Legitimation of the T'ang Dynasty*. New Haven: Yale University Press.

Weisberg, Robert W. 1992. *Creativity: Beyond the Myth of Genius*. New York: W. H. Freeman.

Yang, Ching K'un. 1961. *Religion in Chinese Society*. Berkeley: University of California Press.

Yung, Bell. 1989. *Cantonese Opera: Performance as Creative Process*. Cambridge: Cambridge University Press.

Zuesse, Evan M. 1987. "Ritual." In *The Encyclopedia of Religion*, edited by Mircea Eliade. New York: Macmillan.

Index